VOCATION

VOCATION

Discerning Our Callings in Life

Douglas J. Schuurman

WILLIAM B. EERDMANS PUBLISHING COMPANY

GRAND RAPIDS, MICHIGAN / CAMBRIDGE, U.K.

© 2004 Wm. B. Eerdmans Publishing Co.
All rights reserved

Wm. B. Eerdmans Publishing Co.
255 Jefferson Ave. S.E., Grand Rapids, Michigan 49503 /
P.O. Box 163, Cambridge CB3 9PU U.K.
www.eerdmans.com

Printed in the United States of America

09 08 07 06 05 04   7 6 5 4 3 2 1

ISBN 0-8028-0137-4

In honor of my father,
Henry Jacob Schuurman
February 6, 1922–August 27, 1996
and my mother,
Hester Schuurman
June 2, 1923–December 19, 2000

Contents

Acknowledgments

I would never have finished this book were it not for the encouragement and support of numerous persons and institutions. I gratefully acknowledge here at least some of these sources of support. Students in several seminars on the topic of vocation, at St. Olaf College and at Calvin College and Seminary, helped clarify and deepen my view of vocation. Former students Haakon Nelson, Beth VandeVoort, and Christopher Wells were especially helpful. The following friends and colleagues read and provided helpful comments on earlier drafts of parts of this book: Douglas Ottati, Harlan Beckley, Dirk Smit, Johan Botha, Russel Botman, Nico Koopman, Jo Beld, James Gustafson, Max Stackhouse, Richard Mouw, Gilbert Meilaender, Paul Pribbenow, Virgil Lew, Gordon Preece, Robert Banks, Gary DeKrey, Stanley Hauerwas, Bonnie Miller-McLemore, Anne Carr, John Bolt, and John Burgess. Ed Visser, Randy Wilburn, John Stumme, Steven Pope, Cornelius Plantinga Jr., and John Barbour provided written comments on the complete penultimate draft. Special thanks to Eerdmans editor David Bratt, who made this book much better than it would have otherwise been, and to Jon Pott, Eerdmans Editor in Chief, whose patience with me in this project knew no bounds.

Several invitations to deliver lectures to church, college, and university groups were seminal in the development of this book. Two were especially important for the early stages of this project: the lecture for the spring 1992 *Vrieze Philosophy Conference* at Trinity College in Palos Heights, Illinois, and the series of five lectures for an *Interpreting the*

Acknowledgments

Faith conference at Union Theological Seminary (Virginia) in the summer of 1992. When I was about to give up on the idea of completing a book on vocation, my resolve was renewed by the enthusiastic encouragement of South African theologian Dirk J. Smit, and his invitation — with support from the South African government's *Centre for Science Development* — to deliver a keynote address for a conference on "Vocation and Industrial Work" in Paarl, and to give other lectures on vocation at the universities of the Western Cape, Stellenbosch, Port Elizabeth, and Pretoria, in the summer of 1998. I thank Johan Botha, P. J. Naude, Etienne De Villiers, Dirk and Ria Smit, and Elna Mouton for their hospitality and interest in my work.

The Lilly-funded Louisville Institute for the Study of Protestantism and American Culture provided crucial financial support for this project by giving me a summer stipend in 1993 and a grant in 2001, enabling me to take a full year's sabbatical to complete this manuscript. Special thanks to the Board of the Louisville Institute, and to its Executive Director, James W. Lewis. Thanks also to St. Olaf College for awarding me a released-time grant and sabbatical support for this project, and for bringing together students, faculty, and staff in a context where fruitful reflection on vocation is possible.

My Religion Department colleagues provided personal and professional support for my work on this project. Second only to the personal support of my wife, Edmund N. Santurri's friendship helped get me through the trials of losing both parents and getting three daughters through the teen years during the decade or so that I worked on this project. Richard B. Schuurman, my late uncle, commented insightfully on early drafts of this material. He and Ann, his wife, were constant sources of encouragement for me in my work on vocation.

Words cannot express my thanks to my wife, Kathy, for her friendship, wisdom, and tolerance for my shortcomings. I also thank Sarah, Krista, and Laura — three daughters who have taught me a great deal about the topic of this book, and whose love and affection I cherish beyond measure.

Introduction

College students often become increasingly anxious about major life decisions as they come nearer to graduation. Seniors who have not yet made plans dread the question "What are you doing after this?" Those who have made important decisions about career plans often wonder whether they have made good decisions. And the challenges of integrating career paths with hopes for marriage and family life are daunting, whether or not a student has a ready answer to the dreaded question. Graduation seemed so far away when they first moved their belongings into their dorm room, but its complications become more and more unavoidable as the day approaches. Throughout adult life we all struggle with similar anxieties, though perhaps not as intensely as college students. Have I made wise choices in my line of work? Should I accept this transfer? Should I change jobs, or even careers? How can I reconcile the demands of my job with obligations to my spouse, children, parents, friends, and community groups? What am I worth if I'm unemployed or underemployed? Did I make a huge mistake when I entered this profession? Anxiety, regret, guilt, and other demons can haunt our lives over the deceptively simple question of what to do for a living.

Christians seek forgiveness, assurance, and guidance in these important matters through their faith. Students expect some help, if help is to be found, in the doctrine of vocation. They expect it particularly to help guide career choices. In its classic Protestant form, the doctrine of vocation is not concerned with how to make choices between this and that career path, though it does have deep concerns that may have implications for such choices. But it is more about how to relate Christian faith to the totality of one's life than it is about "vocational" guidance counseling. It is a lens through which to see the obligations of our specific and varied social locations as avenues of God's Call.

Until they read and reflect on the doctrine of vocation, very few of my students feel that they have a calling. Many of them have never thought about their lives in light of vocation. Those who have thought about it usually see being called as a rare, extraordinary, miraculous event in which God tells a person to enter a specific career path. The career path they envision usually is a church-related one: God calls a few exceptional individuals to become pastors, missionaries, priests, monks, or nuns. When they do not have a church-related career path in mind, they usually associate having a calling with an especially fulfilling, often service-oriented career. Those who think of vocation in this way typically fear they will miss their one chance to "discover" their calling.

Students are surprised when they learn that, in their classic Protestant form, vocation and calling do not begin their relevance when it's time to select a career. Rather, God calls each student to be in school to contribute to the life of its community and to make use of opportunities it supplies for building lives of worth and service. God not only calls a person to this or that career; God calls students to study and learn here and now. God not only calls people into a given form of paid work; family relations, friendships, extracurricular commitments — indeed, all significant social relations are places into which God calls us to serve God and neighbor. God's call is not normally experienced as an audible, miraculous voice or visible sign in the heavens; rather, the lens of faith discerns God's call in and through the duties and opportunities of our varied social locations. As students begin to understand the doctrine of vocation, they are challenged to see the totality of their lives in relation to God, and to wrestle with what that means for how they live their lives.

My primary aim in this book is to develop a contemporary articulation of the classic Protestant doctrine of vocation. This doctrine and the religious impulses it reflects have had a profound influence upon the way many Christians understand and integrate their faith and life, but in recent years core aspects of Protestant vocation have come under assault by our culture and by non-Christian and Christian thinkers alike.

xi

The social and cultural milieu of America today is opposed to constitutive themes of Protestant vocation, making it exceedingly difficult to sustain a sense of life as vocation. Vocation infuses mundane secular life with religious meaning, but secularism and capitalism strip mundane life of its religious meaning. Vocation sets the obligations of one's social locations within larger ethical frames, such as God's revealed law, natural law, and the common good; but individualistic and expressivist utilitarianism constrict normative fields and relativize normative principles. Vocation acknowledges a special providential role for persons and positions of social power, subjects them to the King of kings and Lord of lords, and transforms their positions into places of service; egalitarianism rebels against the very idea of authority, both denying the reality of social power and failing to bring appropriate ethical/religious norms to bear upon its exercise.

Many Christian theologians and ethicists reject or radically revise vocation in light of these and other concerns. Gary Badcock, Jacques Ellul, and Stanley Hauerwas, for example, argue that Protestant vocation is unbiblical and that it wrongly confers religious meaning upon secular life. They say that the biblical idea of calling confers religious meaning on church-related roles and activities alone. Ellul also argues that, under modern conditions of technology and industrial capitalism, paid work is at best a necessity of survival and not a calling. He asserts that even if such work were a calling at the time of the Reformation, it surely cannot be so today. Miroslav Volf criticizes the way Luther and other reformers ground vocation in creation and providence, arguing that this makes vocation too static, conservative, and conformist; he instead turns to eschatology for theological bearings relating to vocation.

For these and other reasons, many Christians in America, like my students, find it difficult and strange to interpret their social, economic, political, and cultural life as responses to God's callings. In spite of the challenges, and also because of them, Robert Bellah and other noteworthy social theorists reaffirm Protestant vocation to combat the bureaucratic, individualist tenor of so much American cultural and institutional life. I think Bellah and others are right: Christians must recover anew the language, meaning, and reality of life as vocation.

A central task of pastoral ministry is evoking a sense of God's call and reminding Christians that God calls them into their homes, neighborhoods, workplaces, and civic and political communities to serve God and neighbor. This task is neglected or endangered in many American churches by a resurgent church-centeredness that ascribes religious meaning exclusively or primarily to church-related roles and activities. Though renewed focus upon the church in our secular and fragmenting culture is needed, it must not come at the expense of the religious meaning vocation confers on "secular" life. Churches and church-related colleges should lead the way in a recovery of life as vocation. Pastoral care, teaching, liturgy, hymnody, preaching, and sacrament must all be reexamined in light of the church's task to evoke and sustain a sense for all of life as an integrated response to God's callings. Church-related college curricula and community can become crucial avenues for expanding and deepening a sense of calling in students, faculty, administration, and staff.

Many pastors and leaders of religious institutions already discern the importance of this task. The Religion and American Life wing of the Lilly Endowment recently awarded over 88 church-related colleges and universities substantial grants to develop proposals for "Programs for the Theological Exploration of Vocation." College leaders are reexamining everything from general education curricula to employee development policy with a view to vocation. It is my hope that what I have written will contribute to this effort, helping literate laypersons, college students, pastors, professors, and administrators recover a sense of life as vocation.

Constructive treatments of vocation for the past few decades constrict the idea to paid work, neglecting the potential of vocation to integrate paid and unpaid work, domestic and "public" life, church and world, personal identity and varied roles, faith and life. The way vocation has become synonymous with paid work — even within theological treatments — expresses the sad state of affairs in which an originally expansive concept has become tidily constricted (and conscripted) in modern life.

Although my primary dialogue partners have been students at St. Olaf College, I have also spoken and written about vocation in other contexts. The notion of writing a book on vocation began when I was invited to deliver a series of five lectures on vocation to pastors and church leaders at Union Theological Seminary's "Interpreting the Faith" conference. Since then I have given workshops, seminars, and public lectures on vocation for church adult education groups, college faculty, and administrators. South African friends invited me to speak on vocation at four universities (Western Cape, Stellenbosch, Port Elizabeth, and Pretoria) with graduate students, faculty, staff, and administrators. They also asked me to give a keynote address at a conference on "Vocation and Industrial Work" in Paarl, attended by industrial workers, business leaders, graduate students, and church leaders. I hope that the genesis of this book in materials prepared for these audiences help make it accessible and interesting for readers outside as well as inside the guild of professional theologians and ethicists.

I have drawn primarily from the Lutheran and Calvinist traditions of the Protestant Reformation, though I try to do so in a way that is irenic and respectful of other Christian traditions. This book is primarily for Christians who want to think about what vocation means and how it may be significant for their lives, though I hope non-Christians who are curious about Christian notions of vocation will also find something of worth and interest in this book. Christians, like so many modern people in our fragmented culture, are searching for ways to integrate their lives — public and private, religious and secular, home and office. The doctrine of vocation can provide invaluable help in contributing to such integration.

CHAPTER ONE

Vocation under Assault:
Can It Be Salvaged?

The most common understanding of vocation today is the secular-ized one where vocation refers to one's paid work. Sometimes voca-tion refers to any form of paid work; sometimes it refers to particular forms of paid work, those forms that involve public service or higher pay or status. We speak of vocational training, vocational schools, vo-cational counseling, choosing a vocation. Here "vocation" and "voca-tional" are synonymous with "career" and "technical." The secular use also rarely, if ever, includes the spheres of family, citizenship, and friendship. Identifying activities outside of paid work as "avocations" only illustrates the more restrictive modern usage. Both the religious aspects of vocation and its reference to relational spheres in addition to paid work, central to classic Protestant vocation, have been largely lost.

When "vocation" does have religious connotations it usually refers to church-related occupations and activities. In a Catholic context, vo-cation means becoming a priest. When I told a young monk at St. John's Abbey that I was working on the Protestant idea of vocation, he replied that he knew a group of Protestants who had formed an inten-tional Christian community in the Twin Cities, imitating to a degree the monastic vocation. Since Vatican II Roman Catholicism has taught that marriage and family, labor, culture, and temporal affairs have dignity and participate in God's unfolding work of creation and redemption — a theme central to Protestant vocation. But in much of-ficial and most popular Catholic usage, the terms "vocation" and "calling" designate church-related activities or heroic, extraordinary forms of service.[1]

Many Protestants use "vocation" and "calling" in a similar way. When they teach Sunday school, lead prayer and Bible study meetings, evangelize, and serve on church committees, they are fulfilling their callings. Many evangelicals speak of "full-time" and "part-time" service. Those who have a full-time church-related paid job are in full-time service to the Lord; those who work a "regular" job and volunteer much of their time to church activities are serving the Lord part time — that is, in their church activities.

Interestingly, the term "calling," synonymous with "vocation" for much of the Protestant tradition, today seems less secularized and restricted to paid work than the term "vocation."[2] There is no parallel,

---

1. The entry for "vocation" in the *Catholic Encyclopedia*, for example, includes only "Ecclesiastical and Religious Vocation," omitting non-ecclesial forms of vocation altogether (www.newadvent.org/cathen/15498a.htm). However, the *Catechism of the Catholic Church* (Second Edition) describes the "vocation of lay people" in a way that resonates with the best of the Protestant tradition: "By reason of their special vocation it belongs to the laity to seek the kingdom of God by engaging in temporal affairs and directing them according to God's will. . . . It pertains to them in a special way so to illuminate and order all temporal things with which they are closely associated that these may always be effected and grow according to Christ and may be to the glory of the Creator and Redeemer" (par. 898). And "Hence the laity, dedicated as they are to Christ and anointed by the Holy Spirit, are marvelously called and prepared so that even the richer fruits of the Spirit may be produced in them. For all their works, prayers, and apostolic undertakings, family and married life, daily work, relaxation of mind and body, if they are accomplished in the Spirit — indeed even the hardships of life if patiently borne — all these become spiritual sacrifices acceptable to God through Jesus Christ. In the celebration of the Eucharist these may most fittingly be offered to the Father along with the body of the Lord. And so, worshipping everywhere by their holy actions, the laity consecrate the world itself to God. . . ." par. 901 (www.scborromeo.org/ccc/p123a9p4.htm#ll). Calvin or Luther would respond to these words with a hearty "Amen!"

2. *The Compact Oxford English Dictionary*, 2d Edition (Oxford: Oxford University Press, 1991) defines "vocation" and "calling" with nearly identical entries. The entry for "calling" includes "The summons, invitation, or impulse of God to salvation or to his service. . ." (definition 9a); "Position, estate, or station in life. . ." (10); and "Ordinary occupation, means by which livelihood is earned, business, trade . . ." (11a), (p. 202). The entry for "vocation" includes "The action on the part of God calling a person to exercise some special function, especially of spiritual nature, or to fill a certain position; divine influence or guidance towards a definite (esp. religious) career; the fact of being so called or directed to a special work in life. . ." (1a); "The action on the part of God (or

for example, where the term "calling" functions as an equivalent to "vocation" in vocational schools, vocational counseling, etc. President George W. Bush recently said that the campaign of eradicating terrorism around the globe is "our calling."[3] The title of a recent *Newsweek* article asks, "Washington is Calling. Will Anyone Answer?"[4] Here "calling" is secularized, but is more expansive than paid work and refers to a special task assigned by "destiny" or "Washington." Within the realm of paid work, "vocation" functions as a secular term for paid work in the broader society, but "calling" typically refers only to church-related occupations. Since, within this more restricted usage, "calling" retains religious meaning, it is less often used in a thoroughly secularized way. In its secularized form, "calling" often refers to what one loves to do, whether for pay or not. If a person loves her or his job, it is said that this job is a calling. It refers to a person's passion. "Her job may be mechanical engineering, but golf is her calling." Or, "His job may be social work, but cooking is his calling." Because one's core passions and loves are central to religion, this usage has religious connotations even when applied to secular domains of life. Thus "vocation," more so than "calling," is restricted to paid work and secularized in popular usage (outside the Catholic church).

These popular uses of "vocation" and "calling" both reflect and contribute to the fact that many Christians fail to see most of their lives in terms of vocation. Many also assume that "hearing" God's call is an extraordinary, miraculous event, and so fail to discern God's callings in their lives. The vast majority of my Christian students are perplexed when I suggest that their work as students, relationships with friends and family, and extracurricular activities are among their callings. They never heard God speaking from a burning bush, or from the heavenly courtroom, resonant with echoes of cherubim. God does sometimes call in such extraordinary ways, but for the vast majority of

---

Christ) of calling persons or mankind to a state of salvation or union with Himself; the fact or condition of being so called" (1b); "The particular function or station to which a person is called by God; a mode of life or sphere of action regarded as so determined" (2a); "One's ordinary occupation, business, or profession" (2b); and "A call to a public position" (3a), (p. 2,246)

3. "NATO Offers Larger Anti-Terror Role," Associated Press, October 10, 2001.

4. Dan Sullivan, "Washington is Calling. Will Anyone Answer?" *Newsweek* (October 22, 2001): 12.

Christians God's callings are discerned quietly, when the heart of faith joins opportunities and gifts with the needs of others.

Emil Brunner observes that there is no more in common between the original meaning of vocation and contemporary usage than the term itself. Calling has been degraded into "something quite trivial" having been stripped of "its daring and liberating religious meaning." He asks whether Christians should renounce the term altogether. He responds,

> [I]t is a conception which in its Scriptural sense is so full of force and so pregnant in meaning, it gathers up so clearly the final meaning of God's acts of grace — the Calling — and the concrete character of the Divine Command in view of the world in which man has to act, that to renounce this expression would mean losing a central part of the Christian message. We must not throw it away, but we must regain its original meaning.[5]

If we are to recover the power of vocation to infuse all of life with religious meaning, and extend its range into all relational fields, then we must return to the expansive, religiously rich understanding of vocation in the Bible and the Reformation.

The development of the doctrine of vocation was a distinctive and influential feature of the Lutheran and Reformed wings of the Protestant Reformation.[6] According to this doctrine all relational spheres — domestic, economic, political, cultural — are religiously and morally meaningful as divinely given avenues through which persons respond obediently to the call of God to serve their neighbor in love. Human beings participate in God's provident care for creation through their activities as parents, artisans, farmers, princes, and preachers. Trust in Christ issues forth in gratitude that motivates Christians to

---

5. Emil Brunner, *The Divine Imperative,* trans. Olive Wyon (Philadelphia: Westminster, 1937), 205-6.

6. When I use the word "Protestant" without qualification I mean the Lutheran and Reformed branches of the Reformation. For especially helpful treatments of Protestant vocation, see Ernst Troeltsch, *The Social Teaching of the Christian Churches,* trans. O. Wyon, intro. H. Richard Niebuhr, 2 vols. (New York: Harper Torchbooks, 1960), especially 2:461-625; Gustaf Wingren, *Luther on Vocation,* trans. C. C. Rasmussen (Philadelphia: Muhlenberg Press, 1957); and Fred W. Graham, *The Constructive Revolutionary* (Atlanta: John Knox Press, 1971).

see themselves as participants in God's providence through their callings. The particular shape action was to take within the "offices" of parent, spouse, judge, lawyer, or farmer was to a significant degree determined by intelligent discernment of obligations germane to the relevant context. "Faith active in love through one's callings" became the benchmark of Reformation ethics. This vision of life as vocation, and the tensions embedded within it, has deep roots in the Judeo-Christian heritage, and has had a profound influence upon the modern West.[7]

Vocation in Three Themes

1. All Aspects of Life Are Holy

Vocation infuses all mundane activities — domestic, economic, political, educational, and cultural — with a *religious significance* the Catholic Church of Luther's day restricted to monastic or ecclesial activities. As Luther saw it, the labors of the cobbler and the preacher are equally holy and equally valued by God if undertaken in faith. Luther was more inclined to equalize all occupations than was Calvin, but both reformers insisted that all legitimate social roles were holy if undertaken in faith.[8] The term "vocation" derives from the Latin *vocare* (and its Greek

---

7. See Michael Walzer, *The Revolution of the Saints: A Study in the Origins of Radical Politics* (Cambridge: Harvard University Press, 1965), and Max Weber, *The Protestant Ethic and the Spirit of Capitalism,* trans. T. Parsons, foreword by R. H. Tawney (New York: Charles Scribner's Sons, 1958), for two provocative accounts of this impact upon political and economic life in the modern West.

8. Their position was developed in relation to two alternative views: the late medieval Catholic view, which restricted "vocations" to ecclesial occupations (such as priest, monk, or nun), and the Anabaptist view, which affirmed the vocational status of many mundane roles but condemned occupations involving retributive justice and coercion (such as prince, soldier, judge, or executioner). Luther and Calvin emphasized the importance of rightly distinguishing the "two kingdoms" in order to affirm the vocational status of occupations rejected or subordinated by these two schools. See, for example, Luther, "Temporal Authority: To What Extent It Should be Obeyed" in *Luther's Works: Volume 45: The Christian In Society II,* eds. W. I. Brandt and H. T. Lehmann (Philadelphia: Fortress Press, 1962), 75-129, and Calvin's "Against the Anabaptists" in *John Calvin: Treatises Against the Anabaptists and Against the Libertines,* ed. and trans. B. W. Farley (Grand Rapids: Baker Books, 1988).

equivalent *kalein*) meaning "to call." This call sanctifies *all* of life, inviting Christians to offer every aspect of life as their divine worship. By identifying mundane roles as vocations or callings, the reformers rejected the church/world dichotomy prevalent in their day; indeed, they saw an inherent dignity in everyday activities. For Calvin and Luther, vital service to God takes place not just in church or religious orders, but in more mundane callings as well.

2. Duties Are to Be Governed by God's Will

The duties of one's station in life are "expressions" or "specifications" of the will of God.[9] As Luther put it,

> Picture before you the humblest state. Are you a husband, and you think you have not enough to do in that sphere. . . ? Again: Are you a son or daughter, and do you think you have not enough work with yourself, to continue chaste, pure, and temperate during your youth, obey your parents, and offend no one by word or deed? . . . See, as no one is without some commission and calling, so no one is without some kind of work. . . . [S]erve God and keep his commandments; then . . . all time will be too short, all places too cramped, all resources of help too weak.[10]

9. Wingren sums up Luther on this point: "Vocation is law and commandment, a synthesis of God's commands to the person who occupies the particular place on earth that his offices indicate. . . . Both law and gospel press themselves home upon man in tangible earthly form, the law through vocation . . . and the gospel through the church . . ." (*Luther on Vocation,* 28). Robert M. Adams's understanding of the "narrow" sense of vocations as situationally determined tasks is very much in keeping with classic Protestantism. He writes, "Clearly there are cases in which it is situationally determined that something is morally my task or your task or some other individual's task. And such situationally determined tasks are often called 'vocations,' with the thought that the general ethical principles involved are backed by God's commands." Adams, "Vocation," *Faith and Philosophy* 4/4 (October 1987): 450. Adams denies that vocation entails a comprehensive divine command ethics, and seeks to supplement vocation so that it "can take the form of an *invitation* that offers a possibility to a particular individual, rather than of a command that strictly obliges" (p. 451).

10. Luther, *Church Postils,* Gospel for the Day of St. John the Evangelist (*Luther's Works,* vol. 22) as cited in Constance Gengenbach, "The Secularization of Vocation and the Worship of Work," *The Cresset* 51/2 (December 1987): 8.

Theologically, the doctrines of providence and incarnation come into play here. Fulfilling a station's lawful duties is a participation in God's provident ways, and recipients of services are Christ incarnate within human need. Thus Luther says that God milks the cows through the milkmaids, and he encourages fathers to imagine they are holding the baby Jesus in their hands when they change their infant's dirty diapers.

Though for the most part Luther and Calvin stress *concord* between God's will and a station's duties, they also recognize *conflict* between them. They condemn thievery and pimping, for example, on the ground that they are contrary to the law of God.[11] Even within occupations deemed legitimate, some practices are prohibited as violations of God's law or the common good. Luther does not condemn being a merchant, but he does condemn monopolies, taking advantage of another's vulnerability, and excessive profiteering.[12] Though Luther and Calvin are hardly blind optimists about corruption in society, they also recognize God's provident, ordering care in social institutions.

3. Officials Are God's Representatives

The doctrine of vocation confers theological legitimacy upon the authority of persons occupying positions of power within the social order. Parents, princes, employers, teachers, pastors, and judges represent in their offices not themselves, but God. For Luther, God speaks through ministers, parents, and other superiors, "lest we be carried about by every wind of doctrine":

> Let children listen to their parents, let the citizens listen to the magistrate, let the Christian listen to the elder and the ministers of the Word, let the pupil listen to the teacher. . . . [I]f the Word is present, I have sure consolation: whether I am a father, mother, or son, I hear

---

11. They condemned the papal priesthood of their day because of their view of its pervasive corruption. They would likely have a very different assessment of contemporary Roman Catholic teaching and clergy.

12. Luther, "On Trade and Usury," *Luther's Works* 45:251. Luther often counters contemporary practices by appealing to principles of justice, the law of God, the common good, and specific biblical texts. Those who see Luther as recommending only or mainly conformity to the status quo often overlook this reformist strand of Luther's ethics.

the word and I know what I ought to believe and do, for God speaks to me in that very station of life in which I happen to live.[13]

Though Luther stresses it more than Calvin does, both reformers emphasize that God ordains offices and appoints individuals to exercise divine governance through them. Persons subject to authority are to see God's will in the expectations of authorities, and so obey God by obeying them.[14] Though relativized by the supreme authority of the Word of God, this structuring of obligations and freedoms in terms of one's place amid varied authorities is deeply bound up with the early reformers' idea of calling.

Modern Challenges to Vocation

These themes are central to Protestant vocation. With modifications, they persist into mid-twentieth century ethics of Bonhoeffer, Brunner, and Barth. But in modern times all three themes have come under attack.

One source of the attack is the forces of secularism and capitalism, which assault the religious significance vocation confers upon everyday life. Can a vital sense of God's call amid mundane activities be sustained in a society that systematically privatizes religion in splendid isolation from the secular social orders? Can life be experienced as a response to divine calling when our economic system stresses the exchange value of work and seems to dominate other contexts such as family, politics, and education? Is it yet possible to perceive God's call in and through labor made repetitive, boring, competitive, and inhuman by the demands of technology or industry, or when that labor serves (often without or against our wills) to exacerbate the poverty of others?

Some sociologists fear that even the family, once thought to be a

13. *Luther's Works* 43:8-15, as cited by Gengenbach, "Secularization of Vocation," 9.

14. Luther was less inclined than was Calvin to challenge the divine authority of persons holding "offices" in the Temporal Kingdom, and of the social structures themselves. For explanations of this difference that are especially attentive to the interaction of theology and socioeconomic change, see Troeltsch, *The Social Teaching* 2:515-660, and R. H. Tawney, *Religion and the Rise of Capitalism* (New York: Mentor Books, 1926), 72-115.

haven for religious meaning and value in the heartless world of industrial production and economic competition, may be an endangered species. Sociologist Arlie Hocschild warns of the way families are threatened in today's society: "For all the talk about the importance of children, the cultural climate has become subtly less hospitable to parents who put children first. This is not because parents love children less, but because a 'job culture' has expanded at the expense of a 'family culture.' . . . Corporations have done little to accommodate the needs of working parents, and the government has done little to prod them."[15] According to sociologist Robert Bellah, we are shifting more and more from a "child-centered" to an "adult-centered" family; an individual does not "belong" to a family, an individual "uses" the family.[16] The pull of the market draws people away from their communities and extended families. As Saul Bellow put it, "Nobody truly occupies a station in life any more. There are displaced persons everywhere."[17] The habit of perceiving everything in terms of economic advance and personal well-being has likewise displaced the religious centers of valuation and perception.

Part of the difficulty is that there are few, if any, institutional reminders of the sacred character of mundane life. As sociologist Robert Wuthnow notes, before World War II, Methodists operated 77 colleges and universities; Presbyterians, 71 colleges; Southern Baptists 53 colleges. Religious organizations controlled one-third of all endowments for higher education. In 1929, Protestant churches operated 15 percent of our nation's hospitals and 42 percent of its homes for the aged.[18] The clear and obvious religious motivation for these endeavors helped people who worked within these church-related institutions to experience a meaningful sense of vocation. It also helped, symbolically, to sustain a general sense of the religious meaning of other worldly affairs for those who worked elsewhere.

Today a great many of these educational and welfare institutions have been taken over by the state or by private enterprise. The newer governing norms of making a profit, gaining prestige — and sometimes

15. As cited in Robert N. Bellah et al., *The Good Society* (New York: Knopf, 1991), 48.

16. Bellah, *The Good Society,* 46.

17. As cited by Bellah in *The Good Society,* 57.

18. See Wuthnow, *The Struggle for America's Soul: Evangelicals, Liberals, and Secularism* (Grand Rapids: Eerdmans, 1989), 108.

a vague sense of the "public good" — have usurped the explicitly religious tone of earlier times. Often all that remains of the earlier Christian structure is the name — St. Mary's Hospital — or the mottoes of places like Princeton, Yale, and Harvard. My point is not that the church must return to running hospitals, educational institutions, and homes for the aged; it is rather that the institutional support our society once provided for a vital sense of the vocational significance of mundane life is no longer there. For those who remain committed to Christ and the church, vocation has more and more come to refer to church-related professions, or to extraordinary, heroic forms of Christian service. This is the view of vocation Luther and Calvin thundered against, because in it vocation applies less and less to the day-to-day activities that constitute the lion's portion of most people's lives.

Whereas at one time business, media, and government had to yield to a significant degree to Christian values and concerns, today it seems that the church dances to the tunes of these and other drummers. In 1796, the first effort to put out a Sunday paper folded after one issue because, as one commentator put it, "the religious tradition against selling papers on Sunday proved too strong."[19] Today it is the market that often seems to have taken over religion. Robert Bellah, in *The Good Society*, puts it this way: "In the twentieth century, and especially since World War II, religion has been invaded by the market mentality, so that it has become in many instances another consumer good. 'Consumer Christians' shop for the church that is most convenient for their needs and switch, as casually as they change brands of dishwasher detergent, if they think they can get a better package deal elsewhere."[20] The deep liturgical and theological foundations for the church's social mission have been concealed, and sometimes cut off, by the church's piecemeal participation in "interest group" political lobbying.

When I selected a college some 30 years ago, I did not sift through a barrage of material from solicitous college admissions officers; I chose the college founded by my church, the one my elder siblings had attended. I wanted to go to college because I hoped to enter the occupations my family and community told me — directly and indirectly — were among the most worthy and noble occupations: pastoral ministry,

---

19. Witold Rybczynski, *Waiting for the Weekend* (New York: Viking, 1991), 14.
20. Bellah, *The Good Society*, 183.

world missions, or teaching. Today students and their parents face a mountain of unsolicited information sent to them by numerous colleges, and they apply "cost-benefit" analyses in hopes of choosing a college most likely to gain them the social status and economic success their parents now enjoy. Liberal arts, once distinguished by its pursuit of knowledge as an end in itself, today is all too often "servile arts" education, merely a means to the end of economic advancement for students.[21]The late Harold Ditmanson, theologian of the former American Lutheran Church and long-time professor of theology at St. Olaf College, once lamented the shift in priorities seen in St. Olaf students. He recalled that earlier in his career between 50 and 75 percent of the students graduating "Cum Laude," "Magna Cum Laude," and "Summa Cum Laude" were bound for Lutheran seminaries. In recent years it is rare to find students with such outstanding academic gifts headed for seminary. They are headed to the top-ranked law schools, to this or that medical school, to Ph.D. programs in economics, biology, or chemistry, to engineering schools — to the highly paid, prestigious professions. They are not attending seminary.[22]

Add to these already powerful economic and social influences the cultural forces involving systematic exclusion of Christianity from public education, a pervasive moral individualism in the service of self-expression, the dominance of a "scientific" view of nature and a managerial view of social relations — and the religious value of life as vocation becomes exceedingly difficult to sustain. Is it any wonder why so many people find it difficult to see their lives as permeated with a sense of God and religious significance?

Vocation's tendency to insist upon larger moral contexts, long-range consequences, and fundamental moral norms also faces profound challenges. Bureaucratic, managerial emphases upon short-term ends, limited objectives, and efficiency have eclipsed the broader moral frameworks of the common good, the law of God, and of reason, classically understood. Can it be a divine calling to work for an enterprise

---

21. See Joseph Pieper, *Leisure: The Basis of Culture,* intro T. S. Eliot (New York: Random House, 1963), 34.

22. A high grade point average is not a sufficient condition for being a good pastor, but it certainly helps. The point here is that the values many American Christian communities are conveying to their children have shifted away from the church and toward worldly success.

that appears to have either no connection to the common good or a deleterious effect upon it? What degree of complicity in the exploitive procedures and consequences of a given corporation should be tolerated if work is to serve the neighbor? Do norms of love and justice find any place in the hearts and minds of people as they live and work?

Whereas vocation encourages deep, covenantal understandings of important relationships, contemporary society often encourages a moral minimalism where obligations are seen as short-term, legal, and contractual. James M. Gustafson cites a story from the *John Deere Magazine* in 1920 that highlights the contrast between this minimalism and the sense of obligation generated by vocation:

> During a protracted hot spell along about 1906, there were few men on the job in the blacksmith shop any day. On the hottest day of the period the men began dropping out at nine in the morning. At three in the afternoon the shop was practically deserted. At three-thirty the foreman walked through the shop to see that everything was all right before he shut down the plant for the day. He heard a noise emanating from the vicinity of Nels Moody's forge. He strolled over there and found Nels, unmindful of the heat, turning out work in the accustomed manner. The foreman was perplexed, for it was not cost effective to keep the shop running with only one man on the job. He inquired from the superintendent what he should do. "Keep the plant running as long as Moody wants to work," were the instructions from the superintendent. Nels finished out the day and then walked home.

Gustafson comments, "It is not hard to see why Nels Moody was a 'model employee'! He had a profound sense of calling, which in his case included a deep sense of duty or obligation to his employer. It also included a sense of self-reliance that would make Ronald Reagan happy. Regarding the employee's pension plan, the report states, 'Inasmuch as the pension is a gift of the company, [Moody] feels that he is not entitled to it.' 'He deems it a privilege to work.'" He adds, "He was as vulnerable to exploitation as a blacksmith as many a social worker has been simply because of a profound sense of calling."[23]

23. James M. Gustafson, "Professions as 'Callings,'" *The Social Service Review* 56/4 (December 1982): 505.

One of the clearest examples of how concerns for efficiency and profit determine corporate decision-making at the expense of deeper obligations to employees and their communities is the film *Roger and Me*. It tells the story of the devastating effects of the closing of the General Motors plant in Flint, Michigan. The toll upon the cultural, familial, educational, social, and political life of that city cannot be calculated. In the documentary, repeated efforts were made to contact the head of General Motors to ask why this plant was closed, but all invitations to discuss the decision were refused. The movie suggested that corporations operate on the basis of a Darwinian economic morality in which decisions that ensure efficiency, profits, and more profits, are valued and rewarded. A dynamic market requires an oxymoronic "creative destruction," which in turn conflicts with vocational understandings of economic life.[24]

Economic forces have eclipsed the role vocation used to play in shaping relations between employer and employee, between business and community. Vocation generates loyalty, mutual trust, and concern for the larger, long-term ends of an occupation. These qualities are exceedingly difficult to sustain in today's bureaucratic context.

Vocation has been blamed for encouraging tolerance of dehumanizing work by glossing it over with a veneer of religious dignity. The tendency for work to become more and more specialized, controlled, and efficient has increased this danger. The most minimal standards for humane work and working conditions are regularly and systematically violated in many parts of the world. Even in more prosperous societies, people have difficulty finding satisfaction in their work. According to Witold Rybczynski, in his book, *Waiting for the Weekend,* the modern penchant for improving one's skill at tennis, golf, skiing, and other leisure activities derives in part from a loss of meaning at work.

---

24. Bellah tells the story of Marian Metzger, whose innovative marketing work contributed to a paint company's success, making it the target of a corporate takeover by a larger paint producer. The new management terminated Marian's position. "'The whole thing — the takeover, the sudden change of management, all that — made my work seem basically futile,' she said when she reflected on her experience. 'I mean, I'd done a lot, without much initial support from my boss, to get the marketing operations going successfully in a new direction.' Despite her sense of futility, she proceeded energetically with her final management task. 'I've always taken pride,' she explained, 'in doing the job well, whatever it is." *The Good Society,* 21.

He writes, "The desire to do something well, whether it is sailing a boat — or building a boat — reflects a need that was previously met in the workplace. Competence was shown on the job — holidays were for messing around." Today the situation is reversed:

> Technology has removed craft from most occupations. This is true in assembly line jobs . . . [and] in most service positions (store clerks, fast-food attendants). . . . But it's also increasingly true in such skill-dependent work as house construction, where the majority of parts come ready-made from the factory and the carpenter merely assembles them, or automobile repair, which consists largely in replacing one throwaway part with another. Nor is the reduction of skills limited to manual work. Memory, once the prerequisite skill of the white-collar worker, has been rendered superfluous by computers; teachers, who once needed dramatic skills, now depend on mechanical aids such as slide projectors and video machines; in politics, oratory has been killed by the thirty-second sound bite. . . . For many, weekend free time has become not a chance to escape work but a chance to create work that is more meaningful . . . in order to realize the personal satisfactions that the workplace no longer offers.[25]

The moral dimensions to vocation are also challenged by the ways our work implicates us in unjust practices that harm others. Can it be a vocation, for example, to produce pornographic materials intended to inflame the sexual passions of others? Can it be a vocation to work for an advertising agency that aims not to inform, but to generate desires for luxuries by means of deceptive techniques? Can it be a calling to devote one's creative energies to devising computer-generated composites of pencil-thin female body profiles? Working for the Mafia can't be a vocation. But how about working to develop strategic nuclear weapons for the government? For a chemical company whose research and production endanger the environment? In this day of global economic interdependence, to participate in the economic order at all is to get your hands dirty. But are there degrees of guilt and complicity? Luther and Calvin assume that the basic institutions of the social and political orders were ordained by God and serving the common good. Ought we to still have that confidence?

25. Rybczynski, *Waiting for the Weekend,* 223-24.

Vocation's third tenet, which provides theological legitimization for hierarchical social structures and the authority of persons in positions of power, is in conflict with the democratic, egalitarian tenor of the modern West. Americans like to pretend there are no differences of status and authority, and they tend to emphasize equality to the point of utter disregard for differences in knowledge, power, and status. But those differences do in fact exist, and we neglect our responsibilities when we pretend otherwise. For as liberation theologians have stressed, God identifies not with the powerful, but with the weak, the poor, and the crushed members of our society.

The doctrine of vocation is blamed for engendering and sustaining oppression. Marxists have long condemned the ways in which the rich and powerful use the idea of vocation to keep economically oppressed people from challenging those who oppress them. Liberals suggest that the concept of vocation has perpetuated inequalities in economic opportunity and remuneration by encouraging ascription (by arguing, for example, that women's vocation is domestic) and by justifying lower-than-normal wages (since it is a vocation to teach at a religious institution, one should not press authorities for higher wages). More recently, feminists perceive in the idea of vocation an affirmation of a hierarchical understanding of human nature, society, and God. The effect of vocation is thought to inhibit moral agency and autonomy by encouraging "obedience" to the "summons" of the Divine Commander.[26] In the minds of many, vocation smacks of a conservative quietism in its religious interpretation of authority and, insofar as the reformist or revolutionary spirit of the modern West is at odds with conservatism, this spirit condemns conservatism's alleged ally, vocation.

Clearly, the doctrine of vocation faces many pitfalls, and it can be and has been misused to exploitative and oppressive ends. But it remains a vital source of wisdom about faithful Christian living in the modern world. To recover that wisdom, we need to think again about vocation in the tradition of Luther and Calvin. For I believe it is imperative for Christians to regain key elements of their view. Those elements have deep roots in the Bible, as we will see in Chapter Two. They

---

26. For an illuminating analysis of Calvinist divine command theory that is attentive to these concerns, see Richard J. Mouw, *The God Who Commands* (Notre Dame: University of Notre Dame Press, 1990), esp. 6-21, 159-175.

are not exclusively Protestant, but have many resonances with the Roman Catholic and Orthodox traditions. My approach is not to take on the modern challenge point by point, but rather to trace central aspects of vocation anew in light of the modern milieu to see if there are ways we can review and reexperience life as vocation.

CHAPTER TWO

The Bible on Vocation

It has become almost commonplace among Bible scholars and theologians to argue that the Protestant doctrine of vocation lacks adequate biblical foundations. The criticism is not only that the distance between the world of the Reformation and that of modern Christians makes the doctrine of vocation seem untenable today, but also that the early reformers were wrong in the first place. The Protestant doctrine of vocation, critics allege, finds no support in the Bible. This is a serious charge that must be taken seriously, but a careful review of the evidence will show that it does not hold up. Because of the wide range of biblical meanings, such a review requires distinguishing several biblical ideas of vocation, drawing together various strands, and showing how vocation is related to similar concepts, such as divine command and permission.

In the Bible, vocation has two primary meanings. The first, and by far more prevalent, meaning is the call to become a member of the people of God and to take up the duties that pertain to that membership. The Puritans referred to this as God's "general calling"; Luther referred to it as God's "spiritual calling." The second meaning is God's diverse and particular callings — special tasks, offices, or places of responsibility within the covenant community and in the broader society. Luther referred to this as God's "external calling"; the Puritans referred to it as God's "particular calling." It is this second sense of vocation that many Bible scholars and theologians in recent years have disdained.

Biblical Idea of Vocation

Terms for vocation and calling permeate the Old and New Testaments. *Kalein* and its variants mean either "to name," on the one hand, or "to invite" or "to summon," on the other. The two meanings are not entirely separate, because in the Bible one's name frequently sums up the divinely given purpose or identity to which God calls that person. The Hebrew term *qahal* refers to the people God has called together for service. The Septuagint (the Greek translation of the Hebrew Bible, ca. 200 B.C.E.) translates this term into the Greek *ekklesia,* which in the New Testament means "church." *Ek* (from, out of) and *klesia,* (*klēsis,* calling) together define the church as the assembly of "called out ones." Israel and the church are a people called out of the world by God to serve God in the world. Calling and election are closely associated in the Bible: "And those whom he predestined he also called . . ." (Rom. 8:30; see also 2 Pet. 1:10). The Hebrew verb "to call" *(qara')* is closely connected with "election" *(bahar),* as for example in Isaiah 41:8-9:

> But you, Israel, my servant, Jacob, whom I have chosen,
> The offspring of Abraham, my friend;
> You whom I took from the ends of the earth,
> And called from its farthest corners,
> Saying to you, "You are my servant,
> I have chosen you and not cast you off."

The ones God chooses, God calls or summons or invites for a particular purpose. God calls people to salvation, hope, repentance, feasting, performing a task, undertaking a labor, fellowship, and more. God calls first of all a people, Israel and the church; individuals have their callings within the corporate calling. Put in general terms, the purpose of God's call is for the people of God to worship God, and to participate in God's creative and redemptive purposes for the world, to enjoy, hope for, pray for, and work toward God's shalom. This is what it means for Christians to be in Christ and to follow Christ.

The Call to Become a Member of God's People

God Is the One Who Calls

God, as caller, takes the initiative. God's initiative is seen in the close relation between election and calling noted above. God initiates the covenant with a call to Abram, Isaac, Jacob, and Israel. Two of the three unsuccessful call stories in Luke 9:57-62 involve "volunteers" whom Jesus rejects because they lack both the divine initiative and a willingness to forsake all immediately.[1] Jesus said, "You did not choose me but I chose you" (John 15:16). The king "sent his slaves to call [*kalesai*] those who had been invited to the wedding banquet, but they would not come" (Matt. 22:3). Or again, "For I have come to call [*kalesai*] not the righteous but sinners" (Matt. 9:13). In the book of Proverbs, God is personified Wisdom calling all and from many places:

> Does not wisdom call,
> and does not understanding raise her voice?
> On the heights, beside the way,
> at the crossroads she takes her stand;
> beside the gates in front of the town,
> at the entrance of the portals she cries out:
> "To you, O people, I call,
> and my cry is to all that live. . . ."
>
> (Prov. 8:1-4)

Though it is God who calls, God uses mediators to communicate that call to its recipients. God sends prophets to call an unfaithful Israel back to fidelity to God. In the parable noted above, the king sends his slaves (the prophets) to call those invited to the banquet. In language remarkably similar to this parable, Wisdom in Proverbs also sends out her servants:

---

1. A. J. Droge, "Call Stories," *The Anchor Bible Dictionary* (New York: Doubleday, 1992), vol. 1, 822. John's Gospel follows a slightly different pattern: at least some of the disciples take the initiative before Christ invites them to follow (John 1:35-50). Though disciples take the initiative, John emphasizes the importance of Christ's acceptance of them and their initiatives.

> She has sent out her servant girls,
> she calls from the highest places in the town,
> "You that are simple, turn in here!"
> To those without sense she says,
> "Come, eat of my bread and drink of the wine I have mixed."
>
> (Prov. 9:3-5)

According to Psalm 19, the entire cosmos is calling:

> The heavens are telling the glory of God;
> and the firmament proclaims his handiwork.
> Day to day pours forth speech, and night to night
> declares knowledge.
> There is no speech, nor are there words;
> their voice is not heard;
> yet their voice goes out through all the earth,
> and their words to the end of the world.
>
> (Ps. 19:1-4)

Jesus of Nazareth was the mediator of God's call to the first twelve disciples. God used an otherwise obscure Ananias to pray for Saul of Tarsus, restoring his sight and filling him with the Holy Spirit (Acts 9:10-19). The call to become a Christian is mediated by the preaching, teaching, and ministry of the church. With very few exceptions, God's call comes through mediators.[2]

---

2. In some of the most remarkable calling stories in the Bible, God speaks directly to the one called. God told Abram to leave his country and kin and go to a land God would show him (Gen. 12:1). God spoke to Moses from a burning bush (Exod. 2:23-4:17). God called Samuel's name (1 Sam. 3:4). The voice of the Lord said to Isaiah, "Whom shall I send, and who will go for us?" (Isa. 6:8). The Lord came to Amos and told him to prophecy to Israel (Amos 7:15). In God's freedom, God may or may not use mediators, but by far the prevalent pattern is making use of some part of creation to mediate God's call. It is also possible that even in these exceptional calling stories, the terse phrases about the Lord speaking could be a kind of shorthand for what in fact was a process in which mediating elements were present.

Is God's Call Effectual?

Many, but not all, biblical accounts of vocation stress the point that God's call is effectual. As Dietrich Bonhoeffer says, "In the life of Peter grace and discipleship are inseparable. He had received the grace which costs."[3] When God called, Abram left Ur of the Chaldeans and traveled in obedience to God's command, Moses left his flocks to humble the mighty Pharaoh and lead Israel out of Egypt, David left his sheep and took up his royal duties, Amos left Tekoa to prophesy to the northern tribes of Israel, and the sons of Zebedee left their nets and followed Christ. When the Word of God is mediated by the faithful work of the church, and when the Spirit of God fills that work with divine power, God's call is effectual. Individuals experience the grace of God in a life-altering way, and they offer the God of all grace their grateful obedience. Though in its broadest sense vocation includes grace and obedience, gift and task, indicative and imperative (e.g., 1 Cor. 1:26), its specific sense centers on the task and the imperative. The fitting and spontaneous response to God's grace and mercy is to devote one's whole life to God and God's mission in the world.

Another side of biblical teaching strongly suggests that human beings can resist or reject God's call. In the parable of the wedding banquet, those who first received the king's invitation "made light of it and went away," and some even "seized his slaves, mistreated them, and killed them" (Matt. 22:5-6). One man to whom Jesus said "Follow me" forfeited his chance to become a disciple because he wanted first to bury his father (Luke 9:59-60).[4] Jesus denied this man a leniency Elijah granted Elisha, when Elisha asked to say farewell to his parents before leaving all in response to God's call through Elijah (1 Kings 19:19-21). The same preached gospel that changes one person's life falls on the

---

3. Dietrich Bonhoeffer, *The Cost of Discipleship,* rev. ed., trans. R. H. Fuller (New York: Macmillan, 1963), 49.

4. Failure to bury a fellow Jew, a relative, and especially a parent was thought to be a supreme impiety. To bury a fellow Jew or relative, especially if doing so involved great risk as in times of war, was the mark of a pious, honorable Jew. See, for example, the book of Tobit, where the holy Jew, Tobit, buries numerous Jewish victims of Sennacherib in Nineveh. He also has to flee and have all his possessions confiscated (Tobit 1:16-20). See also Antigone's horrified response to Creon's decree not to bury her brother, and her courageous act of civil disobedience in Sophocles' play *Antigone.*

deaf ears of another person. The call of Wisdom and the voice of all creation are speaking everywhere and always, but "their voice is not heard" (Ps. 19:3).

Why is God's call effectual in some but not others? Why do some reject the gospel and others accept it? Why does God choose Jacob but reject Esau? Attempts to answer these questions raise the complex and much debated issues of how human freedom relates to God's sovereign will, the power of sin to resist grace, the mystery of evil, predestination, and more. To these profound questions, the Gospels give only terse responses. "For many are called, but few are chosen" (Matt. 22:14).[5] "You did not choose me, but I chose you" (John 15:16).

When Paul exhorts the Christians at Corinth to "consider your own call," he observes that not many of them, by worldly standards, were wise or powerful when God called them. He discerns a divine pattern: "But God chose what is foolish in the world to shame the wise; God chose what is weak in the world to shame the strong . . . so that no one might boast in the presence of God" (1 Cor. 1:26-29). Paul acknowledges that all depends on God's election, and that part of what God is revealing is the primacy of a grace that overturns worldly powers and prestige.

Paul wrestles mightily with these issues in Romans 9-11. Paul is so vexed by the Jewish rejection of Christ and the gospel that he wishes he were accursed and cut off from Christ if it would somehow enable Jews to come to Christ. He affirms that it all depends "not on human will or exertion, but on God who shows mercy" (9:16). God chose Jacob and not Esau even before either one had done anything good or bad "so that God's purpose of election might continue, not by works but by his call" (9:11-12). He also discerns God's purpose in giving the Jews "eyes that would not see and ears that would not hear" (11:8): "[T]hrough their stumbling salvation has come to the Gentiles," which means "riches for the world" (11:11-12). As more and more Gentiles enter into God's covenant, it will "make Israel jealous" until they turn to Christ and are saved (11:11, 15). "I want you to understand this mystery: a hard-

---

5. These words appear to separate at least some of the "called" from the "chosen." But since they follow a story about a guest who was thrown out of the wedding feast because he was not wearing a wedding robe, one could argue that he was never one of the "invited ones" *(keklemenois)*.

ening has come upon part of Israel, until the full number of the Gentiles has come in. And so all Israel will be saved" (11:25-26). In regard to the gospel, unbelieving Jews are "enemies of God for [Gentiles'] sake" but in regard to their election "they are beloved, for the sake of their ancestors, for the gifts and the calling of God are irrevocable" (11:28-29). God has "imprisoned all in disobedience so that he may be merciful to all" (11:32).

Though vexed by the rejection of the gospel, Paul's predominant responsive note is that the church rejoice in the "good pleasure of God" that "chose us in Christ before the foundation of the world to be holy and blameless before him in love," and who "destined us for adoption as his children through Jesus Christ" (Eph. 1:4-5). The call of God rests on the foundation of a gracious election that stands more secure than the very structures of the universe. The central concern of Paul with freedom is not its relation to divine sovereignty. It is that the freedom of the gospel not be lost in a return to slavery to the law of salvation by works. The freedom of the gospel deepens the motive and enhances the effectiveness of love for God and neighbor (Gal. 5:13–6:10). Paul exhorts believers to "work out your own salvation with fear and trembling, for it is God who is at work in you, enabling you both to will and to work for his good pleasure" (Phil. 2:12-13). Not knowing who would heed the call, the apostle Paul preached the gospel far and wide to all, confident that in the end God would be "merciful to all."

Can You Know You Are Called?

What if a person desires God's grace and calling, but feels that he or she has not experienced God's effectual call? First, it is important not to misunderstand the nature of God's call. God is not likely to speak to us from a burning bush, or to strike us blind, like Paul. Signs and wonders do not have to be present in order to experience God's call. In fact, very few believers experience such dramatic encounters with God, and churches seeking ministers rightly worry about candidates who claim to have had them. In subsequent chapters I will say more about how specific experiences and practices can evoke and sustain a sense of vocation. The concern here is that the extraordinary nature of some call stories should not prevent Christians from sensing their own call.

Many, like Timothy, experience an awakening to the gospel in a slow, steady process of learning the Christian faith from a mother, who learned it from her mother. The awareness of God's grace in Christ and the desire to turn away from sin and toward God often dawn slowly, but they surely make their presence known nonetheless.

Others may find a second response more appropriate to their condition. Jesus says, "'Ask, and it will be given you; search, and you will find; knock, and the door will be opened for you. For everyone who asks receives, and for everyone who knocks, the door will be opened'" (Matt. 7:7-8). Those who feel they have asked over and over again without receiving an answer should consider what it means to ask. Is this asking the central passion of your life, the pearl of such great price that you are willing to sell everything you have to possess it (Matt. 13:45-46)? Bonhoeffer affirms two propositions: "only he who believes is obedient; only he who is obedient believes."[6] Obedience is not the chronological consequence of belief. Rather, faith is the condition of obedience, and obedience is the condition of faith. In fact, obedience is not only the consequence of faith; it is the presupposition of faith.[7] Bonhoeffer says that in response to God's call a person must take the "first step," which brings one into a "situation where faith is possible." Peter had to leave his nets. Levi had to leave his tax collecting. This "first step" is an "external work" that is "within everyone's capacity, for it lies within the limits of human freedom." The Lutheran confessions "show their awareness" of such a situation, though they "soft-pedal it as though they were almost ashamed of it." Bonhoeffer advises a person who wants to believe to accept the "invitation to come to the Church where the word of salvation is proclaimed." He adds, "You can do that of your own free will." You can leave home, go into the church, and listen to the sermon. "If you will not, you are of your own free will excluding yourself from a place where faith is a possibility."[8] Eventually, repentance must come as well:

> No one should be surprised at the difficulty of faith, if there is some part of his life where he is consciously resisting or disobeying the commandment of Jesus. Is there some part of your life which you are refusing to surrender at his behest, some sinful passion, maybe, or

6. Bonhoeffer, *The Cost of Discipleship*, 69.
7. Bonhoeffer, *The Cost of Discipleship*, 70-71.
8. Bonhoeffer, *The Cost of Discipleship*, 70-71.

some animosity, some hope, perhaps your ambition or your reason? If so, you must not be surprised that you have not received the Holy Spirit, that prayer is difficult, or that your request for faith remains unanswered. Go rather and be reconciled with your brother, renounce the sin which holds you fast — and then you will recover your faith! If you dismiss the word of God's command, you will not receive his word of grace.[9]

As with Peter, who obeyed the call of Jesus by stepping out of the boat onto the water, the "first step of obedience proves to be an act of faith in the word of Christ." If you believe, "take the first step, it leads to Jesus Christ. If you don't believe, take the first step all the same, for you are bidden to take it."[10]

Bonhoeffer was well aware that his approach here ran dangerously close to "works righteousness." But he accepted that risk to do battle with the greater danger he saw in his complacent fellow German Lutherans, who said they had faith, or wanted to have faith, but did not live that faith out in their lives or seek it with all their heart. For my purposes, his insights about faith and obedience pose both a challenge and a hope for those who say they want to experience God's effectual call. The challenge is to obey, to wrestle against sin and to put oneself into places where the word of God is taught, preached, discussed, and prayed. Sometimes it is precisely in and through the struggle against sin that God calls. The hope is that all, whether obedience or faith or the call, is grace.

The Two Forms of the Call

Drawing from these biblical themes, we need to distinguish two forms of calling. There is a *general form* in which the mediators of God invite, summon, or call everyone to turn away from sin and turn toward the cross of Jesus Christ so that they may receive forgiveness of sins and the gift of the Holy Spirit. This call takes the form, for example, of the weekly homilies and sermons that go forth around the

9. Bonhoeffer, *The Cost of Discipleship*, 72-73.
10. Bonhoeffer, *The Cost of Discipleship*, 73.

world. It also occurs in the voices of wisdom, conscience, and creation as they invite sinners to new lives of glory to God. There is also a *specific form* of the call when, by the power of the Holy Spirit, the call becomes a living reality in the life of each individual. Saul heard the general call in the preaching of Stephen, even as he witnessed Stephen's martyrdom and assisted the murderers by watching over their coats (Acts 7:58). But it was not until Jesus confronted him individually and personally that the general call became a living reality in his life (Acts 9:1-18). It is one thing to know that all humans die; it is quite another to know that I am having a heart attack and will die in a few short seconds. So too the knowledge of the general form of the call differs qualitatively from knowledge of the specific form. The specific form of the call is effectual, reshaping a life. Saul the Pharisee was quite different from Paul the Apostle. Few people have such a dramatic and radical conversion, but all must experience in some way the turning away from sin and the turning toward God. The struggle with sin endures as long as we are in the body. But through the power of God's call, the basic stance of the heart shifts from suspicion and disobedience to trust and obedience.

Particular Callings to Places of Responsibility

Nearly all I have said so far about the biblical idea of vocation concerns the call to become a Christian and lead a life worthy of that calling. This calling is a "heavenly calling" and a "holy calling" (2 Tim. 1:9). It is the call all Christians have in common, a call to exhibit the fruit of the Spirit (Gal. 5:22-23). It is what Luther called a "spiritual vocation" *(vocatio spiritualis)*.

Does God also call individuals to particular callings, what Luther called "external vocation" *(vocatio externa)?* To be the husband of a particular wife, the wife of a particular husband? To be an engineer, mechanic, carpenter, or to take on any other form of paid work? To our particular places in the family and in varied relational locations with friends and others? Is Luther on firm biblical ground when he insists that all such stations are vocations? If so, does God call people to and within such stations in the same way that God calls people to salvation?

Recent Challenges to Traditional Affirmation of Particular Callings

Many criticize the Lutheran and Reformed tradition for designating specific relational spheres as vocations or callings. One central concern behind the criticism is a distortion that periodically emerges: justification of conservative conformity to a corrupt status quo by claiming that one's vocation is to do whatever one's stations require. This view equates vocation with the duties of one's stations. Miroslav Volf, in part because of this concern, rejects Luther's view of vocation and turns to the New Testament language of gifts instead.[11] A related concern is that identifying one's paid work, and other special relations, as particular callings departs from how the Bible uses the term vocation. Gary Badcock, for example, argues that in the Bible, "the call is generally to a sacred rather than a secular role, a role that is discontinuous with the ordinary social sphere, and even with natural human existence as such."[12] In this view, God does call people to particular vocations, but those are restricted to offices and activities in the "religious sphere" of the church. For Badcock, lay ministry is a vocation, but firefighting is not.[13]

Though these and others rightly oppose a simple and total equation of one's relational spheres with vocation, and the conformism that results, they wrongly reject the classic Protestant view of particular callings. To jettison the idea of particular vocations from Christian ethics, or to restrict its applicability to church-related activities, neglects the potential of vocation to inspire and guide Christian obedience in the varied life of the world. As Karl Barth demonstrated, one can honor both the emphases in the biblical usage and the concern that all of life, in its particularity, should be interpreted in relation to God's calling.

---

11. Miroslav Volf, *Work in the Spirit* (New York: Oxford University Press, 1991), 104-19.

12. Gary Badcock, *The Way of Life* (Grand Rapids: Eerdmans, 1998), 83. See also, for example, *Theological Dictionary of the New Testament*, vol. III, ed. G. Kittel, trans. and ed. G. W. Bromiley (Grand Rapids: Eerdmans, 1965), 487-501.

13. Badcock, *The Way of Life*, 106.

Karl Barth's Qualified Affirmation of Particular Callings

Barth distinguishes sharply the vocation to be a Christian from one's stations in life. The primary meaning of vocation in the New Testament, says Barth, is the call to be a Christian and to lead a life worthy of that call. This call is a "heavenly calling" (Heb. 3:1), and is "from above." As such, it is not synonymous with one's duties or, as Karl Holl says, with an "inner call" and an outer voice of "things and their necessity."[14] It is shared by all Christians, for "There is one body and one Spirit, just as you were called to the one hope of your calling, one Lord, one faith, one baptism, one God and Father of all, who is above all and through all and in all" (Eph. 4:4-6). Volf and Badcock would agree with Barth on this point.

But Barth continues to use vocation in a qualified sense, to designate "places of responsibility" one occupies concretely, and which give particular form to what God's call and command require for that person.[15] These "places of responsibility" are not limited to the "religious sphere" of the institutional church, as Badcock would have it, but are comprehensive in scope and include all significant special relations. Barth insists that vocation should not and cannot be simply equated with what social roles and relations may require. But vocation also must never be severed from them either. As Barth says, the call does not float abstractly above the stream of life, but rather it meets people in all their concrete, situated existence — as this particular person and no other.

Perceiving one's places of responsibility as one's vocations does not merely baptize the status quo. As Barth says,

> [I]n the light of this calling he will not merely find himself summoned to be what he is; he will also find himself summoned as the

---

14. Karl Barth, *Church Dogmatics* 3/4, ed. and trans. G. W. Bromiley (Edinburgh: T&T Clark, 1961), 602.

15. Barth, *Church Dogmatics* 3/4, 602-7. Barth says that vocation "comes into all human spheres and cuts right across them" (602), sharply distinguishing vocation from one's stations. But he insists that this call meets a person already situated by God's providence in her concrete existence. This forms her "place of special responsibility" where she hears God's call and its implications personally. Barth calls this "place" a person's vocation (598, 607).

one he is to new existence and action. Saul as the one he is and has been is to become Paul. This means that the previous state of his vocation is to undergo an expansion. . . . He is invited to a journey to new harbours in which he will again be himself. . . .[16]

In a similar vein Bonhoeffer notes that, for Luther, "the Christian's worldly calling is sanctified only in so far as that calling registers the final, radical protest against the world." Relational spheres are callings only when they are "exercised in the following of Jesus."[17] This is why Bonhoeffer says, "Luther's return from the cloister to the world was the worst blow the world had suffered since the days of early Christianity."[18]

Every time, then, a Christian refers to the spheres of spouse, parent, friend, citizen, lawyer, pastor, etc., as callings or vocations, the Christian is challenged to interpret the activities undertaken in those spheres in the light of the call to love God and neighbor. If the duties and obligations of these spheres serve the neighbor, they should be fulfilled "as to the Lord." Doing so is a faithful response to God's calling in a person's particular situation. If the duties and obligations of these spheres harm the neighbor, they should be rejected for the sake of the Lord, who died for all. Those spheres should be transformed, if at all possible, so that they issue in actions that serve the neighbor. One is not called to be a Christian "in general"; one is called to be a Christian in the concrete social locations one presently occupies, as this mother to these children, this citizen of this country, and so on. One is not called merely to be a wife, a husband, or a mechanic; one is called to be a wife, a husband, or a mechanic as a Christian "in the Lord." Particular duties are callings or vocations insofar as the vocation or calling to be a Christian is expressed through them.

Particular Callings in the Community of the People of God

Though the Bible may not often use the terms *klēsis* and *qara'* for particular callings, there are good biblical reasons for doing so. There is lit-

---

16. Barth, *Church Dogmatics* 3/4, 606.
17. Bonhoeffer, *The Cost of Discipleship*, 52.
18. Bonhoeffer, *The Cost of Discipleship*, 51.

tle dispute that God calls believers to particular tasks and offices for service in the church or, as Badcock says, in the "religious sphere." The New Testament is clear on this point. In the church there are varieties of gifts, services, and activities. But the same God "activates all of them in everyone" (1 Cor. 12:4-6). These are "manifestations of the Spirit for the common good" (v. 7). Paul identifies his apostleship as both a calling (Rom. 1:1) and a gift (Eph. 4:11). By using "calling" and "gift" interchangeably Paul implies, or at least strongly suggests, that "gifts" of apostles, prophets, evangelists, pastors, teachers — and all specific offices and services of the church — are also callings (Eph. 4:11; 1 Cor. 12; Rom. 12:3-9).[19] Not all will be apostles, all prophets, all miracle workers (1 Cor. 12:29). Members of the body of Christ must discern the gifts each has been given, as well as the best way to use these gifts to meet the needs of the body. The members of the body that seem to be weaker are "indispensable" (1 Cor. 12:22), and God gives greater honor to the "inferior member" (12:24). Christians should not covet or demean another's gifts and callings; rather, they should perceive the importance of them all, always with a view to the common good. Callings in this context do not refer to a special kind of life — say, a celibate one — but to functions, offices, or services that make use of gifts to contribute to the common good of the church. They are not the same as the call to be a Christian, but they do designate specific ways members of the church express their response to that call.

There is a similar pattern in the Old Testament — indeed, the comprehensive reach of vocation into every sphere of life is more obvious there than in the New Testament. God calls all of Israel to a covenant with the purpose of blessing all the inhabitants of the earth. Within

---

19. Miroslav Volf's pneumatological approach to work and calling develops a view of vocation based on gifts in a very fruitful manner. Unfortunately he develops this as an *alternative* to creation-oriented views of vocation as found in Luther and Calvin. Protestant vocation frequently associates gifts with vocation, especially in the Puritan forms, but does so in relation to doctrines of creation and providence, and with far less attention to eschatology and pneumatology. Volf's work here constitutes a significant contribution to the doctrine of vocation. For an exchange on the topic of how the doctrines of creation and eschatology relate to work and social ethics, see Miroslav Volf, "Eschaton, Creation, and Social Ethics" in *Calvin Theological Journal* 30/1 (April 1995): 130-43 and my response to Volf, "Creation, Eschaton, and Social Ethics: A Response to Volf" in *Calvin Theological Journal* 30/1 (April 1995): 144-58.

this covenantal community "each person has a responsibility to perform whether it be that of king or soldier or craftsman or shepherd."[20] God calls some individuals to special, extraordinary tasks and offices: Moses to liberate Israel and lead her out of Egypt into the promised land; Deborah and the judges to free Israel from her oppressors; David and other kings to establish Israel in the land and protect her from enemies; Amos and the prophets to warn Israel of judgment and to call Israel back to covenant fidelity; Ezra and Nehemiah to guide Israel from exile and lead in rebuilding the temple and the cities. But these extraordinary callings do not cancel, or in any way demean, the ordinary roles, services, tasks, and activities governed by God's commandments and oriented to God's purposes.

Callings in the Old Testament also correspond with gifts — skills and abilities needed for the task. When the tabernacle was built, God said to Moses, "I have called by name Bezalel . . . and I have filled him with divine spirit, with ability, intelligence, and knowledge in every kind of craft, to devise artistic designs, to work in gold, silver, and bronze, in cutting stones for setting, and in carving wood, in every kind of craft. Moreover, I have appointed with him Oholiab . . . and I have given skill to all the skillful, to that they may make all that I have commanded you" (Exod. 31:2-6). Everyone whose spirit was willing "brought the Lord's offering to be used for the tent of meeting, and for all its service, and for the sacred vestments" (Exod. 35:21). "All the skillful women spun with their hands, and brought what they had spun in blue and purple and crimson yarns and fine linen; all the women whose hearts moved them to use their skill spun the goats' hair" (Exod. 35:25-26).

Though ordinary Israelites may not have been conscious of being called to their places of responsibility, the comprehensive character of the covenant relationship evident in the scope of the commandments certainly warrants identifying these places as callings. The extraordinary nature of some particular callings does not mean that ordinary tasks and roles are not callings. The Law of Moses, which constituted the life of Israel, connects the will and purpose of God to every conceivable aspect of life (Exod. 20-23). Each and every member of the covenant community has a sacred duty to heed God's law and contribute to God's purpose. The Israelites have a sense that the success

---

20. Donald R. Heiges, *The Christian Calling* (Philadelphia: Fortress Press, 1958), 22.

of all activity depended ultimately on God's favor. Therefore the Psalmist confesses,

> Unless the Lord builds the house,
> those who build it labor in vain.
> Unless the Lord guards the city,
> The guard keeps watch in vain.
>
> (Ps. 127:1)

And the Psalmist prays,

> Let the favor of the Lord our God be upon us,
> And prosper for us the work of our hands —
> O prosper the work of our hands!
>
> (Ps. 90:17)

God calls Israel to a comprehensive, communal existence in the land of Palestine. This includes not only those who serve in the tabernacle and temple; it includes farming, building, tending flocks, marrying, raising children, and more — all the ordinary activities that constitute the life of a community.

Particular Callings in Secular Spheres

But is this same, comprehensive scope also evident in the New Testament? After all, the Christian church is not the theocratic society and nation that Old Testament Israel was. The New Testament speaks of specific tasks, services, roles, and relations *in the church* as particular callings through which individuals express their distinctive ways of responding to the general calling. It is one thing to acknowledge as callings our special places in the church, our ecclesiastical roles, as callings. It is another to identify our places in the secular orders as callings. Is it legitimate to extrapolate, by analogy, from what Paul says about the gifts and callings in the church and apply it to our "places of responsibility" in marriage, family, economic and political life, and elsewhere?

At least three aspects of the biblical view of these matters justify an affirmative answer to this question. The first is one passage that clearly does use the word *klēsis* to refer to a Christian's social locations, 1 Corinthians 7:17-24:

> [L]et each of you lead the life that the Lord has assigned, to which God called you. . . . Was anyone at the time of his call already circumcised? Let him not seek to remove the marks of circumcision. Was anyone at the time of his call uncircumcised? Let him not seek circumcision. . . . Let each of you remain in the condition [*klesei*] in which you were called. Were you a slave when called? Do not be concerned about it. . . . For whoever was called in the Lord as a slave is a freed person belonging to the Lord, just as whoever was free when called is a slave of Christ. You were bought with a price; do not become slaves of human masters. In whatever condition you were called, brothers and sisters, there remain with God.

Here Paul uses "call" [*klēsis*] in two different ways. One is the call to fellowship with Christ, a call that meets people in diverse circumstances of life — as married or unmarried, slave or free, circumcised or uncircumcised. The other identifies these very circumstances as callings, the constitutive features of a life that "the Lord has assigned" (v. 17). Since it is clear that Paul is not giving an exhaustive list of the features of a life in which "each one" must "remain with God," but is mentioning only those that sparked controversy at Corinth, it is reasonable to conclude that all defining spheres of social life are by implication "callings" assigned by the providence of God. To have "each one" "remain with God" in each and all of life's circumstances is to shape activities in those places with a view to the will of God in Christ Jesus, and to interpret such activities as service to the Lord and to the neighbor. Though this is a rare usage for the term *klēsis* in the New Testament, the fact remains that it is so used. But even if there were no such use of the term, it does not necessarily follow that it would be unbiblical for Luther and others to do so. The Bible never uses the term "Trinity" for God, for example, but that alone does not mean it is unbiblical to worship God as Trinity.[21]

21. Dan MacDougall, in a seminar discussion of this chapter at Covenant College, pointed out that the parallel between the terms "trinity" and "calling" breaks down. The New Testament never uses the term "trinity" at all, though what the church means by trinity faithfully embodies what the New Testament teaches about Father, Son, and

The second reason for including all one's places of responsibility under the term particular callings is the pattern discernable in New Testament exhortations relating to wives, husbands, masters, slaves, parents, children, and subjects. This pattern extends beyond what is normally thought of as the church in the world. The apostle Paul begs the Christians at Ephesus to "lead a life worthy of the calling to which you have been called" (Eph. 4:1), a life of humility, gentleness, patience, love, unity, peace, and truthfulness (Eph. 4:2-6, 25). Though the focus here is on life within the church, it is not exclusively so. It includes marriage, family, and work as well. Thus wives are to be subject to their husbands "as you are to the Lord" (Eph. 5:22). Husbands are to love their wives, "just as Christ loved the church and gave himself up for her" (Eph. 5:25). Children are to obey their parents "in the Lord" (Eph. 6:1), and parents are to bring their children up in "the discipline and instruction of the Lord" (Eph. 6:4). Slaves are to obey earthly masters "as slaves of Christ, doing the will of God from the heart," and render service with enthusiasm "as unto the Lord and not to men and women" (Eph. 6:5-7). Masters are to "do the same" with their slaves in the knowledge that "both of you have the same Master in heaven" (Eph. 6:9). Peter urges Christians "for the Lord's sake" to accept the authority of every human institution, including emperors and governors "as sent by him to punish those who do wrong and to praise those who do right" (1 Pet. 2:13). Peter exhorts slaves to accept the authority of their masters even when they are harsh. When, as slaves, they suffer for doing what is right, they have God's approval. "For to this you have been called, because Christ also suffered for you, leaving you an example, so that you should follow in his steps" (1 Pet. 2:21).

"In the Lord." "For the Lord." "As unto the Lord." "With the Lord!"

Holy Spirit. The New Testament does, however, use the term "calling" frequently, and almost exclusively to mean what I've described above as "general calling," or as church-related tasks and offices. Therefore to use the term to refer to one's places of responsibility" in the broader social orders runs against the grain of New Testament usage. His point is well taken. But, as I try to show in this discussion, the lack of clear demarcation between Christians "in the church" and Christians "in the broader society," the almost interchangeable way Paul uses terms for "gifts" and "callings," and the insistence that social roles are callings, not in themselves but "in the Lord," constitute solid grounds for continuing to refer to one's places of responsibility in the social orders as callings or vocations.

God's call to be a Christian must qualify every aspect of life: marriage and family, employment relationships, political life, as well as the life of the church. The call to love and serve the Lord, made active in a person's life, transforms all spheres and activities into so many callings. The church is indeed central to the New Testament view of vocation; Donald Heiges rightly says, "unless Christians take their calling seriously within the church there is not much hope of their taking it seriously in the world."[22] The church is central, but it is not the exclusive domain of Christian vocation, and certainly not in the sense of what many Christians today think of as church. As Paul Minear points out,

> Early Christians did not much speak of a person going to church, but more often thought of the church as being present with each person at his place of daily employment. To the degree that his work represented the Spirit's call and the Spirit's response, to that extent the Church was actively fulfilling its mission through him. In his chores were embodied its repentance and forgiveness, its struggle with temptation, its victory.[23]

According to Minear, New Testament Christians saw the "frontier of God's war along the line of human associations and decisions encountered in their day-to-day living," producing a "quiet revolution in all their attitudes." He rightly suggests it is this revolution "which the Reformation partially re-enacted, and which may yet again in our own day break out with its pristine power."[24]

A third reason to describe Christians' places of responsibility as callings is the larger theological pattern of the Bible. "For from him and through him and to him are all things" (Rom. 11:36). God created and sustains heaven and earth. Women and men are images of God as they are fruitful and as they are responsible stewards who represent God's reign on earth (Gen. 1:26-28). God's intention at creation was for human beings to delight in responsible fellowship with God, mutuality and interdependence with one another, and stewardship over their natural

---

22. Heiges, *The Christian Calling,* 41.

23. Paul S. Minear, "Work and Vocation in Scripture," in *Work and Vocation: A Christian Discussion,* ed. and intro. John O. Nelson (New York: Harper & Brothers Publishers, 1954), 67.

24. Minear, "Work and Vocation in Scripture," 67-68.

environments. Sin perverts each relationship. It causes men and women to disobey and hide from God; to dominate, blame, and envy other persons; and to toil vainly with a natural environment that now resists their efforts (Gen. 3). The purpose of God's redemptive covenants is to restore all these relationships. As each and every central part of life stands under the divine blessing at creation, and becomes warped by sin, so too each and every part is being redeemed in Christ Jesus. The New Testament declares that Christians hope for a comprehensive renovation, a "new heavens and a new earth where righteousness is at home" (2 Pet. 3:13; see also Rom. 8:18-25). This is why the kingdom of God is comprehensive, extending beyond the organized church into all of life. This is also why what people do in the home, workplace, and community — in all aspects of life — must be permeated with the Spirit of Christ. What Christians do in these spheres to bring about justice, love, and peace exhibits the influences of the kingdom of God, providing both parables of and building blocks for the New Creation.[25]

This larger theological perspective, in which God's purpose includes the redemption of human life in its entirety, including institutions, and even the cosmos, encourages Christians to sense God's purpose and call in all of life. The Spirit of God not only gives "spiritual" gifts to be employed in the service of the community of faith; it also gives "natural" gifts for the benefit of the wider human community. In light of the comprehensive character of God's kingdom and purposes, it is legitimate to extend the New Testament emphasis upon gifts and callings in the church into gifts and callings in the broader society. The same applies to needs and obligations. As they give rise to particular callings in the church, so too they give rise to particular callings beyond the Christian community. In the parable of the separation of the sheep and the goats, the Son of Man is incarnate in the hungry, the thirsty, the stranger, the naked, the sick, and the imprisoned of the world. Whatever is done or not done for them is done or not done for Christ.

This extension of callings into the broader society may have been easier in a more pervasively Christian era, where it was widely assumed

---

25. Miroslav Volf, *Work in the Spirit*, 88-102, 117-19. Volf argues that the work of Christians and non-Christians, outside the church as well as within it, has eschatological value because of continuity between New Creation and creation. His convincing argument can easily be extended to all "secular" activities.

that the "body" commonwealth, and its varied parts, have Christian purposes. But this extension still applies. Its original New Testament development was for a minority community in a world in which they considered themselves strangers. In the absence of a consensus about what is "Christian" about relational spheres, Christians are compelled to exercise greater discernment as they seek to determine what their call means for their callings. In exercising this discernment, Christians will be less likely to conform passively to the duties of their stations as they grapple with how to express their call in their callings.

How God Calls People to Particular Callings

Though there are exceptions, generally God uses mediators to call individuals to particular places of service. God rarely speaks directly to a human being from the heavenly throne or a burning bush. Like the larger call to faith and obedience, particular callings are mediated. As the church grew and complaints arose because Hellenic Christian widows' needs were being neglected, "the twelve called together the whole community" and directed them to "select from among yourselves seven men of good standing, full of the Spirit and of wisdom, whom we may appoint to the task" of daily distribution of food (Acts 6:1-4). The seven were selected and stood before the apostles, "who prayed and laid their hands on them" (6:6). The Spirit used a vision to convince Peter that hitherto "unclean" Gentiles were to hear the gospel and receive the Holy Spirit (Acts 11:1-18). At the direction of the Holy Spirit, the church at Antioch laid hands on Barnabas and Saul and sent them off on Paul's first missionary journey (Acts 13:2-3). After the church formally resolved the controversy about whether to accept Gentiles into the Christian community, the apostles and elders "with the consent of the whole church" selected Judas and Silas and sent them to Antioch, where Paul and Barnabas were working, to deliver a letter spelling out the conclusions of the first church council (Acts 15:22-35). The core of the letter said "it seemed good to the Holy Spirit and to us" not to impose the burden of Jewish law upon believing Gentiles. After Judas and Silas strengthened and encouraged the church at Antioch "for some time," that church "sent them" back to their senders in the Jerusalem church (Acts 15:33-34).

Though the New Testament does not provide a formula for discerning God's callings, it does indicate key elements often present in this process. They are gifts, needs, obligations, discussion, and prayer. The callings of apostles, pastors, teachers, or administrators are "gifts" of the Holy Spirit for the welfare of the body of Christ (I Cor. 12, Rom. 12, Eph. 4). When a member of the body of Christ has gifts needed for particular forms of service, that member has a particular calling to use those gifts in that service. The duties bound up in various services are to be fulfilled as responses to God's callings. Though the process certainly includes the individual's self-assessment and willingness to serve, the process of discernment has communal aspects that are essential to discovering one's callings. Though Saul's encounter with Christ on the road to Damascus was intensely private, it was Ananias who laid hands on him and prayed that Saul would be healed and filled with the Holy Spirit. Afterward the community baptized him (Acts 9:17-19). Though Paul received the gospel as a revelation (Gal. 1:12), he set his gospel before Peter and other church leaders in Jerusalem "to make sure that I was not running, or had not run, in vain" (Gal. 2:2). With some exceptions, the process is communal, flexible, and dynamic.[26] As new needs and gifts are recognized, the Spirit — most often through the Christian community — selects and commissions individual Christians in their callings.

Though the New Testament speaks of these gifts and callings as "spiritual" gifts given through grace and acted upon in faith, they are related to the natural abilities of the members who receive and utilize them. Saul's intelligence, passion, and comprehensive grasp of the Hebrew Bible and Jewish tradition were not cancelled by his call and callings. Rather they were redirected and transformed into fruitful service to the church and the world. The spiritual gift, and its related calling, brings something genuinely new to an existing individual, but assessing

---

26. Sometimes a particular calling, or a particular course of action within a calling, is communicated by a vision to an individual. When Peter fell into a trance, the voice of the Lord told him to accept the Gentiles as clean rather than unclean (Acts 10:9-16). The "holy angel" told Cornelius to send for Peter and hear what he had to say (Acts 10:22). In a dream Paul saw a Macedonian beckoning, and heard God calling him to go there to preach the gospel (Acts 16:9-10). When they had a sharp disagreement about whether to take Mark with them on what became Paul's second missionary journey, Paul and Barnabas parted ways. Barnabas took Mark with him to Cyprus, and Paul took Silas with him to Syria and Cilicia and beyond (Acts 15:36-41), indicating that the Spirit's callings work even through sharp controversy among church leaders.

natural gifts can help in the discernment of spiritual gifts and related callings. The redeeming God who calls to new service is the same God who created and providentially situated a person in her places of responsibility. Accordingly, "The Apostle Paul was not a Pharisee plus a new interest; the whole focus and purpose of his life was changed. The religious motive of a sense of vocation works upon the raw material of secular circumstances and the character of the agent. The subsequent behavior is not a creation *ex nihilo*."[27] Therefore one should "be able at least to orientate himself by what he has already been and become as he is all ears for what is now, to-day, demanded of him."[28] An individual's natural gifts and existing relations mediate particular callings, helping her to discern what tasks belong to her in the broader society as well as in the Church.

Because, like Christ, Christians are to love the world and be agents of its redemption, God's callings also relate to human needs, whether those needs are in the church or beyond it. When a Christian perceives a genuine human need and has the abilities needed for attending to it, that need becomes a spark of God's calling to him. To the extent that the duties of one's many places of responsibility also contribute to meeting human needs, those duties also are God's callings.

The Purpose of God's Call

> For you were called to freedom, brothers and sisters; only do not use your freedom as an opportunity for self-indulgence, but through love become slaves to one another. For the whole law is summed up in a single commandmant, "You shall love your neighbor as yourself." (Gal. 5:13)

The Bible describes the purpose to which God elects and calls people in a variety of ways. Already at the call of Abram, God promised, "in you all the families of the earth will be blessed" (Gen. 12:3). The apostle Peter puts it this way: "But you are a chosen race, a royal priesthood, a holy nation, God's own people, in order that you may proclaim the mighty acts of him who called you out of darkness into his marvelous

---

27. W. R. Forrester, *Christian Vocation: Studies in Faith and Work* (New York: Charles Scribner's Sons, 1953), 207.

28. Karl Barth, *Church Dogmatics* 3/4, 596.

light" (1 Pet. 2:9). God calls people out of the darkness of sin — a domain of bondage to the powers of evil — and into God's marvelous light — a domain of freedom, joy, peace, and love. As children of the light, Christians are called to "proclaim the mighty acts" of God. Like Jesus, Christians are called to devote their entire lives to God's will and purpose. "'As the Father has sent me, so I send you'" (John 20:21). And what did the Father send Jesus into the world to do? Luke's account of Jesus' inaugural sermon sums it up in this way:

"The Spirit of the Lord is upon me
because he has anointed me to bring good news to the poor.
He has sent me to proclaim release to the captives
and recovery of sight to the blind,
to let the oppressed go free,
to proclaim the year of the Lord's favor."

(4:18-19)

This mission challenges the powers of sin, bondage, injustice, and spiritual blindness. It calls for a rearrangement of everything from one's own heart to political powers, bringing them in line with the Lordship of Jesus Christ. Sometimes this ministry is summed up as "proclaiming the good news," or as a "ministry of reconciliation," or as a holy partnership "in a heavenly calling" (Heb. 3:1), or as striving for the kingdom of God and God's righteousness (Matt. 6:33). Because the Christian calling challenges the powers of injustice, sin, and evil, it brings Christians into conflict with the principalities and powers of this fallen world. Therefore, like Christ, Christians are called to suffer when the powers of this world oppose doing what is right in the name of Christ (1 Pet. 2:21). Whatever the particular calling may be, the activities undertaken within it must contribute in some way to God's mission, to the care and redemption of all God has made.

Summing up, then, the Bible has two basic meanings for vocation or calling. Each of these has two forms. The first is the one call all Christians have to become a Christian and live accordingly. Of this there is a general form, where the proclaimed word echoes the voice of creation calling all away from folly and into the wisdom that is Jesus Christ, and there is a specific form, where this call becomes existentially and personally felt. The second meaning is the diverse spheres of life in and through which Christians live out their faith in concrete ways. Of this there is a more general form, such as being a husband, wife, child, parent, citizen, preacher, etc., "in the Lord." And there is a specific form, where it refers to the actual duties each of us takes on in our concretely occupied places of responsibility "in the Lord."

Call and Commandments

The biblical notions of calling and command, callings and commandments, overlap but they are not synonymous.[29] Because God is the *source* of both call and command, and because God's call and command alike direct people to participate in God's purposes and to conform themselves to God's will, they overlap. The command and commandments articulate the *content* of what God calls all Christians to be and to do. God's callings will never finally contradict God's command and commandments. God calls all to love God with all their heart, soul, strength, and mind; and to love their neighbors as themselves (Matt. 22:37-39). God calls all to "live by the Spirit" (Gal. 5:17). They are to develop, by the power of the Spirit, virtuous characters so that all they do is qualified by "love, joy, peace, patience, kindness, generosity, faithfulness, gentleness, and self control" (Gal. 5:22-23). Such a Spirit-filled life is the "freedom" to which God calls believers (Gal. 5:13). When Christ says "follow me!" the goal and content of his call is the trail of love and

29. Gary D. Badcock, in *The Way of Life,* equates vocation with the love commandment, in part because he wants to correct the version of Christian piety in which he was nurtured. This version sees vocation in terms of God's "heavenly blueprint" that makes every detail of life "of supreme importance to God." One must seek God's will in every detail, for the blueprint contains decisions such as "whether to do the shopping in the morning or in the afternoon." He suggests that God doesn't really determine how Christians should decide such matters, and asks, "Perhaps, then, we ought to say the same of the decision between becoming a mechanic and becoming a postal worker" (p. 9). Christian vocation has nothing to say about such particulars because "The Christian calling is nothing less than to love God and one's neighbor, as Jesus teaches — or alternatively, to respond to the Word of grace with faith and obedience, to use a more characteristically Pauline expression" (p. 10). The will of God "as the Bible presents it is mainly general rather than specific; for on the whole it relates to humanity in general rather than to particular individuals" (p. 82). Vocation and command are synonymous and, aside from supplying literary variety, one or the other is superfluous.

obedience he himself has blazed. The other commandments give more specific applications of the twofold love command, and what it means to live by the Spirit. In doing so they give further specification of what God calls all Christians to be and to do. In obedient response to God's call, Christians love God and neighbor as they strive to hallow God's name, honor their parents, speak the truth in love, live faithfully in their marriages, uphold their neighbors' good names, and heed other commands and exhortations of God.

Some have suggested that God's call and callings can contradict God's commandments. When I was in graduate school, I had a friend and fellow student whose marriage was in dire trouble and who was having extramarital sex with several women, some of whom had been victims of severe sexual abuse. He told me God was calling him to a healing ministry, helping these rape victims by enabling them to experience good sex. For him the calling overrode the command not to commit adultery. The Libertines of Calvin's day used the idea of particular callings to justify theft, marital infidelity, and other violations of God's revealed commandments. They argued that Christ was the end of the law, and that pimps and thieves should "remain in their callings" as the apostle Paul recommended (1 Cor. 7:20). Calvin opposes these "wretches" who not only excuse such iniquity, but "adorn it with the honorable title of 'vocation,' as if God were calling us to it."[30] They act as if "God had given His law in vain for discerning between good and evil."[31] Calvin appeals to natural reason and the revealed commandments of God to oppose the Libertines, who had wrongly supposed that God's callings could contradict and trump God's commands. Beneath Calvin's argument is the deep assumption that God does not call people to violate God's commands. This rightly presupposes that God's call and callings do not contradict any command or commandments.

But some biblical accounts of God's call seem to imply that the call sometimes contradicts at least some of the commandments.[32] Com-

---

30. *John Calvin: Treatises Against the Anabaptists and Against the Libertines*, ed. and trans. B. W. Farley (Grand Rapids: Baker Books, 1988), 277.

31. Calvin, *Treatises*, 250.

32. Perhaps the clearest and most commented upon case of conflict is when God told Abraham to sacrifice Isaac (Gen. 22). Technically, this is not so much a conflict between vocation and command as it is between a specific command of God and the general command not to commit murder.

menting on the man who wanted to bury his father before following Christ (Luke 9:58ff.), Dietrich Bonhoeffer says that in this case a "legal ordinance," presumably, the command to honor one's parents, is a barrier between Jesus and the man he has called. He comments,

> But the call of Jesus is stronger than the barrier. At this critical moment nothing on earth, however sacred, must be allowed to come between Jesus and the man he has called — not even the law itself. Now, if never before, the law must be broken for the sake of Jesus; it forfeits all its rights if it acts as a barrier to discipleship. . . . Only the Christ can speak in this fashion. He alone has the last word."[33]

The would-be disciple has to choose between obeying the command to honor his parents by burying his father and obeying the call to follow Jesus. Normally the commandments should be obeyed. But when they become a barrier to discipleship, and when it is God in the form of Christ who calls, whatever actual obligations they impose dissolve.

But perhaps there is another way to view this conflict. The conflict may be resolved by seeing the moral commands in the second table of the Ten Commandments as *prima facie* duties. Under normal circumstances these commands are and should be followed. But when two or more "first glance" duties are in conflict in a rare but complicated situation, only one of the conflicting *prima facie* duties really is one's "actual duty."[34] In the case of the would-be disciple, there is a conflict between the apparent duty to honor one's parents and the apparent duty to have no other gods before God — that is, to give one's ultimate loyalty and allegiance to the God who in Christ is calling him. Since it is God in Christ who is calling for ultimate allegiance, following Jesus is that person's "actual duty" even though it means he will be unable to fulfill his apparent duty to bury his father.[35] The command to love God above all and to love

---

33. Bonhoeffer, *The Cost of Discipleship*, 65. See also his comments on the rich young man (81-82).

34. See W. D. Ross, *The Right and the Good* (Oxford: Clarendon Press, 1930), 19ff. How this approach would apply to the first table of the Law is less clear.

35. In Matthew 15:1-9 and Mark 7:6-13 Jesus sharply criticizes the Pharisees for breaking the commandment, "honor your father and your mother," when they demand a religious tax (the Corbon in Mark. 7:11) that would force children to divert money that ought to be used to support their parents, and to use it instead for an alleged offering to God. Jesus calls this hypocrisy, a direct and culpable breaking of God's commandment

one's neighbors as oneself, in morally complex circumstances, sometimes requires a suspension of duties that would otherwise define the paths of love. In such cases, one who heeds the call and forsakes family to follow Jesus is fulfilling the spirit of the law by obeying the command to love God above all, even though this requires neglecting duties to parents. There is a great danger here for self-deception; I will explore this danger at greater length in Chapter Four. At this point I will only suggest that if anyone "hears" a call directing him or her to violate God's commandments, that person should make sure it really is from God by requiring at least two miracles to confirm its divine origin.

If the source of call and command is the same, and if God never calls anyone to disobey God's commandments, then is there any difference between them? One difference is that the call is *prior* to the commandments in two ways: (1) On the corporate level, God first calls Abram and Israel and then gives the commandments; (2) on the individual level, God's personal call first activates the awareness of God's love and grace, which then enables the commandments to function as they ought. The same love commandment becomes a "new" commandment when believers love one another just as Jesus loved them (John 13:34). On both levels, the call indicates the priority of electing grace over obedience to commandments. This is in part why the apostle Paul proclaims that the covenantal promise — to Abraham and through Christ to believers — precedes the law, and that therefore faith in Christ frees believers from the prison of the law (Gal. 3:15-26). The call, closely linked as it is to election and grace, provides enabling power to resist the flesh and to live by the Spirit. Such a life is "not opposed" to the law, and actually fulfills its true intent (Gal. 3:21, 5:13-14, 23). This is also why, to the extent that a person feels personally graced and called by God, she experiences God's commandments not as burdensome duties, but as "permissions" to do what she loves, or as guidance for a life of gratitude.[36]

Another difference concerns the relation of particular callings to

---

for the sake of tradition, in which people honor God with their lips but "their hearts are far from" God (Matt. 15:8).

36. This is not to say that a sense of vocation eliminates all sense of duty and burden. Jesus himself had to "set his face" toward Jerusalem. But still, as Calvin stressed, filial obedience is qualitatively different from slavish obedience. That difference relates to greater love and desire to do what is commanded, because of who is commanding it and because of growth in loving what God loves and wills.

Christian freedom. There is an ancient Christian tradition that distinguishes *adiaphora,* or "indifferent things," from things God requires and forbids. Christians are not morally free to fail to do what God requires or to do what God forbids. These matters are governed by God's revealed commandments, which must be obeyed. But many actions and responsibilities relating to stations in life are neither commanded nor forbidden — whether to remain single or get married, to become a lawyer or a carpenter, to invest oneself in this friendship or in that one, to live in New Jersey or in Minnesota, to exercise one's professional skills in this institution or that one. All Christians should make whatever choices they make about these and other *adiaphora* "for the Lord's sake," and live out their lives "as unto the Lord," but the particular choices they make are not dictated by God's commandments. Such choices are shaped by God's particular callings, so that one feels called to roles and relations when he would have been free to do otherwise without violating a commandment of God. Particular callings, then, invite persons into contexts and projects that "go beyond" the commandments in the sense of directing lives and decisions not explicitly commanded or forbidden by the commandments.

Frequently the freedom associated with calling puts vocation at odds with a sense of duty. Parker Palmer, for example, contrasts vocation as duty with vocation as gift. He says that "'oughts' had been the driving force in my life — and when I failed to live 'up' to those oughts, I saw myself as a weak and faithless person." He never stopped to ask, "'Is such-and-such truly my gift and call?'"[37] Then he began to see matters in a new light:

> Today I understand vocation quite differently — not as a goal to be achieved but as a gift to be received. Discovering vocation does not mean scrambling toward some prize just beyond my reach but accepting the treasure of true self I already possess. Vocation does not come from a voice "out there" calling me to become something I am not. It comes from a voice "in here" calling me to be the person I was born to be, to fulfill the original selfhood given me at birth by God.[38]

37. Parker Palmer, *Let Your Life Speak: Listening for the Voice of Vocation* (San Francisco: Jossey-Bass, 2000), 67.
38. Palmer, *Let Your Life Speak,* 10.

Palmer oversimplifies this complex matter; it was not so much the "true selves" that Abram, Moses, Samuel, Amos, Jesus, and Saul already possessed that they discovered when God called them. God's call and callings do come, as Barth says, "from above," and they carry with them an element of summons and of duty, which can become burdensome, as Jonah discovered when he tried to thwart God's call. But it remains the case that freedom, deliberation, and discernment of the individual and the community play a larger role in determining what God is calling someone to do than they play in determining what God is commanding her to do. For this reason the Christian tradition throughout the ages has associated vocation with gifts, and used it to refer aspects of Christian existence that are in some sense "optional." It is also why vocation, more so than commands, guide Christian decisions by way of "invitation" as well as by demand.[39]

A related difference between vocation and commandments is the way vocation treats the particularity and individuality of God's will for a given person. Vocation includes the belief that God's providence governs our lives in general and in detail. In the love and nurture I give my three children, God's love and nurture are actually expressed for them. We are who we are, ultimately, not by fate or fortune, but by God's providence. God calls us to obey the commandments in our particular and total circumstances. Those very circumstances thus become part of our vocation, as the places in and through which we love God and neighbor. Vocation's relation to particularity ought not be seen in terms of an inflexible "blueprint" in which God predetermines every detail of life, such that we can "miss our calling" by failing to find *the* right spouse or *the* right career. Rather, God's providence provides comfort by leading us to the humble self-understanding that as finite, limited beings God calls us only to do our part, at this time and in this place. If God's providence can triumph over the evil actions of Joseph's brothers to save the world from a famine, it can certainly prevail over mistakes and sins we make as we prayerfully discern our callings.

39. The Greek *entellomai* is translated as "to command" or "to commission" and the noun *entolē* is translated as "command," "commission," or "order." Except for the one place in the New Testament, where the term likely refers to the entire proclamation of Jesus (Matt. 28:20), commandment connotes imperative demand. The terms *kaleō* and *klēsis* can mean either "to summon" or "summons," which does carry imperative force, or "to invite" or "invitation," which does not, or at least carries less such force.

Robert M. Adams discerns a similar sense of vocation when he says vocation is the term aptly used to refer to a task that belongs to someone "in a way that relates to them personally and not just to their situation."[40] As finite, limited, providentially situated individuals, we are presented with particular goods that are "offered to us to love in a more particular way." These goods lead us to choose specific projects, which in turn contribute in a limited way to God's project. Vocations "answer to our need for responsibilities proportioned to our capacities."[41] They are tasks in the universe that are *"mine in a morally valid way."*[42] The particular goods we nurture through our specific places of paid work, domestic life, neighborhoods, and friendships guide and fulfill our callings. Once taken on, the duties of these projects become part of our callings, but we are free in many cases to have chosen differently, with no moral disapproval stemming from one of God's commandments.

Conclusion

The Bible provides ample support for vocation as articulated in the three themes described in chapter one. If my distillation of the early reformers' view of vocation is accurate, then its central thrust is that all of life's relational spheres — paid work included — are religiously meaningful as places for service to God and neighbor. Like the New Testament authors, Luther and Calvin recommend deference and respect for the authority of social structures and those who exercise power in their offices. One's total and particularized situation in life is not a result of caprice, fate, or blind forces of nature and history; rather, God's providence has situated individuals in their respective social locations, their time in history, with diverse gifts and opportunities for service. The general call of God in Christ is to take specific form in one's life. As a prism refracts light into a variety of colors, so too one's relational settings refract God's general call into the variety of particular callings in the life of an individual or a community.

---

40. Robert M. Adams, *Finite and Infinite Goods: A Framework for Ethics* (New York: Oxford University Press, 1999), 300.
41. Adams, *Finite and Infinite Goods,* 303.
42. Adams, *Finite and Infinite Goods,* 292.

CHAPTER THREE

Theology for Vocation — Religious Affections and Vocation

As we saw in Chapter One, the division and specialization of labor, capitalist reduction of value to exchange value, secular neglect or denial of religious or supernatural reality, pluralist relativizing of public expressions of Christian faith — all make it exceedingly difficult to see mundane relations and activities as responsive to God's call. Little in our society reminds us of God's presence and purpose; much militates against awareness of God's reality. How many auto mechanics see their work as part of God's providential kindness toward motorists? How many parents think of themselves as God's agents and representatives for their children when they hear them cry at 3:30 a.m. or when they break up warring siblings for the tenth time in one morning? Even the pastoral calling — perhaps the one most clearly linked to a sense of God's call — is often described in terms of therapy, grief management, and number-crunching. The fact that so much work is drudgery, or actually ends up harming others, also impairs the religious sense that one is called by God to serve the neighbor in a particular role or set of relations.

Christians respond to these features of American society in several ways. Some Christians *conform* to the social milieu. Christian faith and the church then become instrumental to economic, political, or therapeutic ends. Faith then becomes meaningful, and churches grow, because they lead to economic success, self-fulfillment, healthier marriages, and psychological wholeness. Other Christians *criticize* and *retreat* from aspects of social and cultural life that have been taken over by hostile forces. People here find genuine religious meaning, or their vocation, in "voluntary" institutions, or perhaps in the nuclear family, instead of in their economic, political, and public settings. Life is experienced as vocational when participating in a "Big Brother" or "Big Sister" program or volunteering for the local food bank. Often vocation is attached to church-related activities, rather than to "secular" pursuits. Some call this a communitarian response.[1]

As we saw in Chapter Two, many Christian theologians and Bible scholars say we should not view our roles in society as "callings" in the first place. According to them, the reformers were wrong to confer so much religious value upon mundane activities and roles, since their approach had no basis in the Bible. I tried to show that there are indeed firm biblical foundations for the reformers' view. In this chapter I explore some of the theological and experiential roots of vocation. My focus here concerns how it is that people feel called by God at all; it is upon the "general calling" more so than upon "particular callings."

In the first part of this chapter I will focus upon common human experiences that, when interpreted through the lens of faith, are integral to one's awareness of being called by God. I use the term "religious affections" in the tradition of Jonathan Edwards, who used it to refer to experiences of God's power and grace. In the second part of the chapter I will identify practices and institutional structures that help provoke and sustain a lively sense of vocation. My aim in treating these theological foundations for vocation is to clarify the experiential roots of vocation, and so to help spark and sustain awareness of God's callings and to direct Christians toward faithful participation in all relational fields.

---

1. See, for example, Douglas F. Ottati, "The Spirit of Reforming Protestantism," in *The Christian Century*, Dec. 16, 1992, 1,164. See also Ottati, *Reforming Protestantism: Christian Commitment in Today's World* (Louisville: Westminster/John Knox Press, 1995) and Moltmann's discerning analysis of forces leading some to pit "society" over against "community" and to ascribe religious value to the latter but not the former in Jürgen Moltmann, *Theology of Hope: On the Ground and the Implications of a Christian Eschatology*, trans. James W. Leitch (New York: Harper & Row, 1967), 316-21. The "communitarian" description fits Hauerwas and Ellul better than Barth, whose revised understanding of vocation as the "place" for Christian "freedom in limitation," a place given by providence and in which one obeys God's command, restores at least some of the wider range of the classic view of vocation. See Barth, *Church Dogmatics*, 3/4, ed. and trans. G. W. Bromiley (Edinburgh: T&T Clark, 1961), 607-47.

Vocation and God's Mission

One of the deepest theological roots of Protestant vocation is the *comprehensive* nature of God's mission in this world. The God who created the cosmos will not permit the forces of sin and evil to destroy it. The Psalmist declares, "The earth is the Lord's and all that is in it, the world, and those who live in it; for he has founded it on the seas and established it on the rivers" (Ps. 24:1-2). God's eschatological goal, like the creational beginning, is all encompassing. Paul says, "We know that the whole creation has been groaning in labor pains until now; and not only the creation, but we ourselves, who have the first fruits of the Spirit, groan inwardly while we wait for adoption, the redemption of our bodies" (Rom. 8:22-23). And Peter says, "[I]n accordance with his promise, we wait for a new heavens and a new earth, where righteousness is at home" (2 Pet. 3:13). The "righteousness" indwelling this "new earth" includes the renewal of society and cosmos, as well as of individuals.[2] According to the New Testament, God is already working toward this comprehensive renewal through Christ and the Church.

Cornelius Plantinga Jr. vividly describes the goal of God's activities in terms of shalom:

> Put together all the wonders and intricacies of creation; all the graces of redemption; all the delights and surprises of love; all the beauties of music and arts; all the blended power and freedom of a concert pianist doing a fortissimo run in octaves or a basketball player making a dynamic spin move in the lane; put together all the quiet reassurances and wisdoms passed along the generations; every dwelling together of all races and both sexes in harmony with non-human creation; all the deep satisfactions and fulfillments of life in God's world — put all this together and call it shalom. Shalom is God's design plan for creation and redemption; sin is human vandalism of these great realities and therefore an affront to their architect and builder, and a stupid fouling of our own nest.[3]

---

2. See Moltmann, *Theology of Hope*, 334; Nicholas Wolterstorff, *Until Justice and Peace Embrace* (Grand Rapids: Eerdmans, 1983), 69-72.

3. Cornelius Plantinga, Jr., "Fashions in Folly: Sin and Character in the 90s," January Series Lecture, Calvin College, 1/15/93, 19-20.

God created all things; sin infects all things; God redeems all things through Jesus Christ. Christians, like the Christ whose name they bear, share in God's redemptive and creative purposes in all things. *Therefore Christian vocation includes all aspects of cultural and social life.* The Puritan preacher Thomas Case, in a sermon originally addressed to the English House of Commons in 1641, was well aware of the comprehensive nature of the Christian calling:

> Reformation must be universal . . . reform all places, all persons and callings; reform the benches of judgment, the inferior magistrates. . . . Reform the universities, reform the cities, reform the countries, reform inferior schools of learning, reform the Sabbath, reform the ordinances, the worship of God . . . you have more work to do than I can speak. . . . Every plant which my heavenly father hath not planted shall be rooted up.[4]

It is not surprising that a seventeenth-century English writer would say, "I had rather see coming toward me a whole regiment with drawn swords, than one lone Calvinist convinced that he is doing the will of God."[5] Though this rousing rhetoric conjures up military imagery, the primary form of Christian obedience should fit the pattern of suffering love displayed in the life and death of Jesus Christ.[6]

Religious Affections and Vocation

The objective narrative of God's mission in this world through Christ and the church, and the stirring example of a Thomas Case, however,

4. As cited by Wolterstorff, *Until Justice and Peace Embrace*, 8-9, from Michael Walzer, *The Revolution of the Saints: A Study of the Origins of Radical Politics* (Cambridge: Harvard University Press, 1965), 10-11. Case's sermon was one in a series of sermons by Puritan divines, delivered at the invitation of the English government.

5. Wolterstorff, *Until Justice and Peace Embrace*, 9.

6. The central means Christians use in this ambitious project should be non-coercive. Unfortunately, all too often coercive, even violent means have been used. Thus James M. Gustafson rightly warns, "Perhaps no one is to be feared more than a devout Christian or a Muslim behind a gun (or nuclear weapon) who is absolutely certain that his cause is God's cause" (*Ethics From a Theocentric Perspective: Theology and Ethics,* Vol. 1 [Chicago: University of Chicago Press, 1981], 107).

will not alone revive the vocational sense evident in Thomas Case's passionate sermon. We must move from the objective domain of God and the story to the subjective domain of how we internalize the story so that it becomes existentially meaningful for our experience of God, ourselves, and our world. This is the realm of religious affections, and of the practices that give rise to them and sustain them.

Theology construes the world with "'an intention to relate to all things in ways appropriate to their belonging to God.'"[7] A faith-informed construal interprets the powers that bear down upon us and sustain us in their relatedness to God. The main effort of Christian theology is not to convince atheists or agnostics of the truth of the Christian claims, important as that task may be. Rather, it is to help Christians interpret the world in light of their faith in the God manifested in Jesus Christ, who renews of all creation. For the Christian, theology is reflection in the service of "faithful participation" in God's universal commonwealth.[8] If Christians are to become faithful participants in the purposes and processes of creation and redemption, it is essential that they hold together both the "sacred" and the "secular," the "religious" and "non-religious" aspects of experience, and that they do so in a way that affirms the importance and integrity of each. This unity of life under God's reign is brought about by a vital sense of life as vocation.

Gustafson describes six "senses" expressive of human experience, which Christians interpret in relation to God. These are senses of dependence, gratitude, obligation, remorse, possibility, and direction.[9] By building upon what Gustafson says about these senses and by relating them to central aspects of vocation, I will try to locate areas of experience where Christians feel a sense of God's presence and calling. In this way the more abstract theological claims made above become visible in our own experiences of God "in, with, and under" all creation. The whole universe is a sacrament of God's grace and power, if only we have the eyes to see and the ears to hear.

7. Gustafson, *Ethics From a Theocentric Perspective,* 1:158. Here Gustafson is following Julian N. Hart, "Encounter and Inference in Our Awareness of God," in *The God Experience,* ed. Joseph P. Whalen, S.J. (New York: Newman Press, 1971), 51-54.

8. Ottati, "The Spirit of Reforming Protestantism," 3-4.

9. Gustafson, *Ethics From a Theocentric Perspective,* 1:129-36. See also Gustafson, *Can Ethics be Christian?* (Chicago: University of Chicago Press, 1975), 82-116.

A Sense of Dependence

Perhaps never before has the global human community been so aware of its interdependence. A widely published advertisement begins with a butterfly flapping its wings in the Amazon, creating a subtle breeze that spreads pollen. The pollen causes a caribou to sneeze, sending a massive herd into a stampede. This adds wind and dust to a storm, which then becomes a hurricane. The hurricane alters the global pattern of weather. So the wings of a butterfly influence the weather of the globe.

Humans depend upon the natural environment; the natural environment depends upon human beings. The economy of one nation depends upon economies of other nations. Interdependence invites us to expand our awareness of the communities in which we knowingly or unknowingly participate. This can deceptively blur accountability by concealing the fact that some causal factors are much more influential than others, for good and for evil. Interdependence also can provoke extreme anxiety: If I depend on so many other human and non-human factors, what if one or more of them runs afoul? What if this whole tenuous economic web rips apart? What if global warming floods the world's coastal cities? What if some mad, warmongering tyrant uses nuclear weaponry? A group of terrorists hijack passenger jets, smash two of them into the World Trade Center and one of them into the Pentagon, and our world will never be the same. Letters infested with anthrax arrive in the mail sorting rooms and offices of American political, judicial, and media powers, killing innocent people along the way. The powers of government temporarily shut down and freedom, along with its presupposed security, is threatened. Since September 11, 2001, anxiety and a sense of insecurity have risen to one of their highest levels in American history.

The sense that we exist, when we could very well have never been born, and that we continue to live, when at any moment we could die — gives rise to a profound sense of dependence. Our individual identity depends upon the sexual activity of our parents at a particular time, as well as upon hundreds of thousands of pieces of genetic material configuring the three trillion cells composing each body in a specific way. Any one of a vast number of minor chemical shifts, accidents, or sicknesses could end our lives at any time. The resilience and ingenuity of viruses give rise to alarm at the fragility of life. The pervasive presence of this fear brings in millions of dollars for movies that stir up the deep anxieties lurking in our nascent awareness of life's precarious contingency. Plagues, wars, floods, famines, and earthquakes have always threatened. In the winter of 1991 Saddam Hussein had a nightmare, and the stock market plummeted. Our sense of dependence is augmented by modern awareness of the vast and intricate web of life.

Apart from grace, under the influence of sin, this dependency provokes profound anxiety over the specter of our demise, or deep resentment toward all the limits and threats to our existence. Sin leads people to believe the illusion that human powers can provide absolute security in our inherently uncertain world. Seen theologically, anxiety and resentment are ultimately failures to trust in the God in whom we live and move and have our being.

The doctrine of vocation encourages us to interpret our sense of dependence as a reminder of the various ways in which we are called to love God and neighbor. Faith confesses that God's providence "sustains, nourishes, and cares for, everything [God] has made, even to the last sparrow."[10] It is because of God's providential purposes that we exist, and do so in this era rather than in another, and continue to exist as long as we do. Precisely how God's providence operates amid natural and social causes is a complex and difficult question. The Bible teaches that God's wisdom, care, and power are active in every part of creation, and active in ways that do not violate the integrity of human and natural agencies. Our sense of contingency and dependence, our anxiety that we might at any time cease to exist, invite us to discern the unique opportunities for service of God and neighbor that we have in this time and place. As image bearers of God, human beings consciously participate in God's providence by being provident themselves — caring for the people whose lives touch ours and for the natural environment in which we live.

Rather than humbly affirming our dependence and trusting in God, the giver of life, we live in fear of death and loss. Or we deny our insecurity and our finitude, and we foolishly believe that we will live forever. Or, as feminist Christians have insightfully shown, we collapse

---

10. John Calvin, *Institutes of the Christian Religion*, ed. John T. McNeill, trans. Ford Lewis Battles (Philadelpha: Westminster, 1960), 1.16.1.

our identity into self-abnegating patterns of excessive dependence upon others. We reject the call God extends to us in the very depths of our existence, so that eventually we become deaf to the voice of God in creation and providence. The Psalmist says,

> The heavens are telling the glory of God;
> and the firmament proclaims his handiwork.
>
> Day to day pours forth speech,
> and night to night declares knowledge.
>
> There is no speech, nor are there words;
> their voice is not heard;
> yet their voice goes out through all the earth,
> and their words to the end of the world.
>
> (Ps. 19:1-4)

God's redemptive grace opens deaf ears to hear again the voice of God calling through creation. By the power of the Holy Spirit, men and women enter into Christ's sense of absolute dependence upon God the Father. Jesus says, "[D]o not worry about your life. . . . Look at the birds of the air; they neither sow nor reap nor gather into barns, and yet your heavenly Father feeds them. Are you not of more value than they?" (Matt. 6:25-26). In Christ there is freedom from anxiety and fear, and freedom for a pervasive and profound sense of dependence. Our dependence is both a gift and a task: a gift because sin has not totally destroyed God's good creation, and a task because creation calls us to add our voices to the chorus declaring God's glory. The ethical imperative attached to our sense of dependence is to preserve and enhance life, and to resist the powerful forces bent on destroying creation.

As we continuously receive God's gifts of life and sustenance through all those persons on whom we depend, so we give of ourselves to others through our participation in God's callings. Although the persons upon whom we depend have an integrity of their own, and though sin infects them all, faith discerns the loving hands of God's providence working through them all and hears in them God's call.

A Sense of Gratitude

A sense of gratitude usually accompanies a sense of dependence. When we pause to reflect upon the "gifted" character of our lives, we not only realize our dependence, we also feel thankful. The sheer beauty, complexity, and mystery of the universe and ourselves inspire grateful awe and delight in the Creator. Calvin, overwhelmed by "this most vast and beautiful system of the universe" and by the "storehouse overflowing with inestimable riches" that God has implanted in each human being, exclaims, "wherever you cast your eyes there is no spot in the universe wherein you cannot discern at least some sparks of his glory."[11] Calvin's delight in God's wisdom evident in creation finds its goal in giving heartfelt thanks to God, the creator and giver of gifts.

Everything that contributes to life and its flourishing is a gift freely given from God. Capacities for feeling, willing, and thinking are God's gifts. Food and drink, and the biological processes transforming these into nourishment are given to us moment by moment. Beauty and harmony, music and the arts, and the ability to marvel in wonder at the unimaginable expanse and complexity of the universe, or of the atom, are the Creator's gifts. Parents and children, friends and acquaintances, all the good effects of cultural, social, economic, and political life — these too are gifts bestowed by the Father of all blessings. All the efforts that have gone on before us, creating the institutions through which we are nurtured, and in which we discover our callings, are also sustained by God's gracious power. Indeed, every single example of truth and goodness, wherever it may be found, is made possible by God, the creator and sustainer of a world God created "very good."

Calvin was convinced that unless people learned to see that every good thing they have is a gift bestowed upon them by the Source of all gifts, they would never worship God as they ought. True piety, he says, is "reverence joined with love of God which the knowledge of his benefits induces." For Calvin this kind of piety can only be experienced through heartfelt awareness of God's benevolence:

> For until men recognize that they owe everything to God, that they
> are nourished by his fatherly care, that he is the Author of their every

11. Calvin, *Institutes*, 1.5.2-3.

good, that they should seek nothing beyond him — they will never yield him willing service. Nay, unless they establish their complete happiness in him, they will never give themselves truly and sincerely to him.[12]

For Calvin, God as "father" and "fountain of good" are the most central of all metaphors for God, partly because they point so directly to God's caring, giving nature.[13]

Of course, the "giftedness" of life is not unmixed, but "This life, however crammed with infinite miseries it may be, is still rightly to be counted among those blessings of God which are not to be spurned. Therefore, if we recognize in it no divine benefit, we are guilty of grave ingratitude toward God himself."[14] We find evil, as well as good, in our parents, children, friends, spouses, colleagues, political, educational, and economic institutions, and all the rest. Gustafson writes,

> We understand why some persons commit suicide, deciding that it is better not to be than to be. But the primal experience of most persons most of the time is that it is better to be than not to be, whether this is explained as the desire to survive or more grandly as a heartfelt response to the wonder of one's own existence and of the marvels of the world of which we are a part. And except in the most desperate of human circumstances there are indications of reasons for gratitude along with reasons for enmity and despair.[15]

Genuine gratitude is never deaf to the cries of those who suffer and are oppressed. It rather is the deepest impulse for bringing relief, healing, and justice to those who suffer. One of the truly demonic aspects of war, and of crime-plagued inner cities, is that these contexts seem to

12. Calvin, *Institutes,* 1.2.1. See also Brian A. Gerrish, *Grace and Gratitude: The Eucharistic Theology of John Calvin* (Minneapolis: Fortress Press, 1993), which argues that God as giver of every good gift is the theological center of Calvin's thought.

13. See Gerrish, *Grace and Gratitude,* esp. 21-49. Another reason for Calvin's preference was the centrality of the familial imagery in New Testament, and especially Pauline, views of God and salvation. For Calvin we are saved by being "adopted" into God's family by the work of the Son, and so receive all the benefits as free gifts bestowed by the Father rather than as earnings of a servant.

14. Calvin, *Institutes,* 3.9.3.

15. Gustafson, *Ethics From a Theocentric Perspective,* 1:131.

utterly blot out all traces of the goodness of Creator and creation. But faith confesses that, by God's grace and power, the goodness of God will finally prevail over sin and evil. Faith recognizes the gifted character of life, and it trusts that God will sovereignly overrule suffering and adversity, perhaps in this life and surely in the life to come.

If the general sense of gratitude for gifts received evokes a sense of God's call to devote one's entire life to serve the Giver of gifts, then the specific awareness of particular gifts leads to diversity of callings. According to Romans 12 and 1 Corinthians 12, the Spirit distributes gifts to various individuals so that they will devote these gifts to the good of the whole Church. If the Spirit gives one the gift of prophecy, then that person is called to be a prophet. So too, gifts of ministry, teaching, exhorting, money, administration, compassion, faith, miracles, speaking in tongues, and all the rest help people discern the particular ways the Spirit is calling them to serve "the common good" (1 Cor. 12:7).

Ingratitude is a chief obstacle to experiencing life as vocation. Ingratitude is the blind refusal to acknowledge with thanks the gifted character of life and of God. With King Lear, many feel "more sinned against than sinner." Instead of thanking God, ingratitude blames God; it views accomplishment and prosperity as rightful earnings rather than as unmerited gifts. It views one's own failures and adversity as unmerited affliction, and the failures of others as rightly deserved. As Brian A. Gerrish put it, "We now sit like blind spectators in the theater of God's glory. We enjoy the gifts but ignore the giver, or ascribe his bounty to fortune or to nature itself. . . . [I]n the place of the true God we set up idols of our own fancy."[16] Like Penelope's suitors, who consumed Odysseus' food and wine and hoped to marry his wife while he was delayed at sea, we squander God's bounty.[17] Ingratitude, blind as it is to God's gifts, also deafens us to the callings which otherwise arise out of God's generous and diverse gifts.

Were it not for the Gift of God's own Son, "given over" to the world to save it from sin, we would never be able to see the gifted character of all creation. Paul proclaims, "For while we were still weak, at the right

---

16. Brian A. Gerrish, *Grace and Gratitude,* 46. Here Gerrish is summarizing Calvin's view.

17. See Book XXII of Homer's *Odyssey* for the kind of punishment the ancient Greek poet and his readers thought such disloyalty and ingratitude justly deserve.

time Christ died for the ungodly. . . . But God proves his love for us in that while we were still sinners Christ died for us" (Rom. 5:6, 8). And again, "If God is for us, who is against us? He who did not withhold his own Son, but gave him up for all of us, will he not with him also give us all things?" (Rom. 8:31b-32). It is indeed right and fitting that the sacrament of the Lord's Supper is also known as the "Eucharist," from the Greek word for "giving thanks." The stunning clarity of the gift of God's own Son jars our eyes open, enabling us to see the rest of reality anew, so that its extraordinarily gifted character is finally recognized. Not unlike the way the Rosetta stone unlocked an otherwise unintelligible system of hieroglyphics, or the way working through an example in mathematics causes the more general principle to lock into its now understood place, so too the manifestation of God's giving character in Christ opens our eyes to God's gifts in all creation. As in our sinful state we believe the serpent's lie that God selfishly withholds gifts (Gen. 3:1-5) and accordingly respond to reality with suspicion and selfishness, so in our redeemed state we trust the gospel's promise of divine mercy and respond to reality with trust and generosity: "The truth is that God has given himself from the beginning; now he gives himself again, to be beheld more clearly in the face of his Christ."[18] Once trust in Christ's death and resurrection assures the anxious heart that God is gracious and giving, then the scales blinding our eyes fall away and we begin to see and feel that God's goodness and grace are everywhere at work to sustain and renew the world. And we give thanks.

A sense of vocation is a constitutive element in the sense of gratitude arising from a faith-inspired view of the gifted character of God and the world. To behold the grace of God in the face of Christ is to offer oneself in loyal service to God in Christ. When Paul met the risen Christ on the road to Damascus his response was, "What am I to do, Lord?" (Acts 22:10). The heart-stabbed cry of Jewish listeners at Pentecost is to the point: "Brothers, what should we do?" (Acts 2:37). Heartfelt gratitude opens up the depths of our being to God's common call to all humanity: "Love God with all your heart, soul, strength and mind, and love your neighbor as yourself." Gifts lead to gratitude, which leads to renewed desire to love God and neighbor. If a vital sense of calling is not based upon God's grace and gifts, then it easily slides

---

18. Calvin, as cited by Gerrish, *Grace and Gratitude*, 88.

into a form of works-righteousness and arrogance whose end is spiritual destruction.

When the political and social orders were more pervasively "Christian," it was natural to extrapolate from what Paul says about gifts given for the "common good" of the body of Christ (I Cor. 12, Rom. 12), so that all aptitudes and abilities were seen as giving rise to callings to serve the body politic, the commonwealth of society as a whole. Though, as we saw in Chapter Two, some Christian theologians recently have challenged this extrapolation, there are good reasons to defend it as vital to Christian discipleship in the world. The New Testament rarely uses the term *klēsis* to refer to one's places of responsibility in "secular" spheres, but there are nonetheless sound biblical and theological principles that warrant it.[19] Miroslav Volf suggests that Christians use gifts by extension when they serve outside the church, and that non-Christians use gifts by analogy when they use their abilities to serve others.[20] Ultimately it is the comprehensive scope of God's purposes mentioned above, and the unity of God's works in creation and redemption, that justify this extension. All gifts are given by the Spirit and are to be used to express love of God and neighbor, whether inside or outside the church. In the parable of the separation of the sheep from the goats, those rewarded and punished are surprised and ask when it was that they saw Jesus hungry, thirsty, a stranger, or naked. Jesus replies that what is done, or not done, to "the least of these" is done or not done to Jesus (Matt. 25:40, 45). If all of life is to be service to God, and if most of life is lived within social spheres other than the institu-

19. Lee Hardy, *The Fabric of This World: Inquiries into Calling, Career Choice, and the Design of Human Work* (Grand Rapids: Eerdmans, 1990), esp. 44-76. Hardy recognizes that in the New Testament the gifts leading to particular callings have ecclesiastical rather than societal roles in mind (cf. Rom. 12, I Cor. 12, Eph. 4). Hardy appeals to tradition and alludes to theological principles that need further articulation: "For although the Bible concentrates on the spiritual gifts and their employment in the community of faith, the Christian tradition has generally extended the Biblical principle, confessing that our 'natural' gifts also come from God and are to be employed for the benefit of the wider human community" (81-82). I agree with Hardy, but (as I argue in Chapter Two) I think there is a stronger biblical and theological basis for this extrapolation than even he supplies.

20. See Miroslav Volf, "Eschaton, Creation, and Social Ethics," *Calvin Theological Journal* (April 1995), esp. 138-43, and Volf, *Work in the Spirit: Toward a Theology of Work* (New York: Oxford University Press, 1991), 111-21.

tional church, then the religious significance of these spheres is particularly important. For this reason Calvin said, "a vocation is the principal part of human life and the part that means most to God."[21]

A Sense of Obligation

The sense of obligation arises out of our experiences of being sustained by others, recognizing our own dependence on orderly processes, knowing that orderly processes require our participation, and realizing that others depend upon our attention and care. We experience the pull of our obligations as parents, children, spouses, friends, workers, church members, and citizens in local, national, and global communities. We have contractual obligations, job descriptions, social roles, voluntary commitments, and obligations arising out of the numerous ways we entrust ourselves to others and accept their trust in return.[22] When we neglect or violate our obligations, we experience moral conflict, regret, and repentance. Though there are degrees of moral awareness, the vast majority of human beings feel the pull of obligations and the discomfort of failing to meet them. Gustafson rightly discerns that a sense of "having done some wrong, of not fulfilling some ideal" is part of common human experience.[23]

Vocation construes these obligations theologically. In the general sense of being obligated to others, one senses God's call to love God and neighbor. In the particular obligations emerging from our implicit or explicit acceptance of what others have entrusted to us, we discover the particular actions to which God is calling us specifically. Through

21. *John Calvin: Treatises Against the Anabaptists and Against the Libertines,* ed. and trans. B. W. Farley (Grand Rapids: Baker Books, 1988), 78.

22. See Joseph Allen, *Love and Conflict: A Covenantal Model of Christian Ethics* (Nashville: Abingdon, 1984), 32-39, for a discerning treatment of entrustment and obligation. Allen distinguishes entrustment from trust and from being trustworthy. "To entrust is not merely to trust in the inner sense of being *disposed* to entrust ourselves to the other, but actually to place ourselves or something we value in the other's hands. . . . To entrust is to take a risk — to risk that we might be betrayed" (33). When obligations derive from entrusting oneself, or from acceptance of the entrustments of others, then social life is quickly seen as teeming with moral obligations.

23. Gustafson, *Ethics From a Theocentric Perspective,* 1:133.

my obligations to provide for the physical, emotional, social, and spiritual flourishing of my children, for example, I experience God's call to serve Christ as he is represented in the needs of my children. Since our lives are rife with obligations, life in its particularity and in its general shape is a life of vocation.

Sometimes obligation is experienced as an inescapable demand to which one yields grudgingly out of fear, or beneath which a tormented conscience groans in guilt and even despair. But the power of God's law is here working to drive a person toward forgiveness and renewal discovered in union with Christ in his death and resurrection. Few theologians of the Christian church have seen this aspect of vocation as clearly, or have articulated it as forcefully, as Martin Luther. For him, though they are earthly in nature, callings relate to faith as part of God's law. The duties of one's stations fuse the general law of God with one's own life. God uses their demands to drive individuals to their knees at the foot of the cross, and to provide avenues for service born of the love and freedom that faith creates. Gustaf Wingren insightfully sums up Luther on this point:

> Through vocation God's presence is really with man. As the God of the law, he places himself above man's self-will, and drives man to prayer, which is answered by God's love and care. In vocation works are constrained to move toward one's neighbor, toward the earth; and faith alone, trust, prayer, all without works, ascends heavenward. In all this one is incorporated into Christ; the cross in the vocation is his cross, and the faith which comes forth from that cross in the vocation is his resurrection.[24]

In its accusatory role, God's law joins forces with the obligations we have as spouses, parents, children, friends, pastors, teachers, or any other moral field in which we are placed, to convict us. The law is an

---

24. Gustaf Wingren, *Luther on Vocation*, trans. C. C. Rasmussen (Philadelphia: Muhlenberg Press, 1957), 33. See also Einar Billing, *Our Calling*, trans Conrad Bergendoff (Philadelphia: Fortress Press, 1964), 4-21. Luther, unlike Hauerwas and Yoder, sees the death of Christians to their own sinful natures to be a participation in the sufferings of the cross of Jesus Christ. Because vocations are ordered, by God's providence, to serve others rather than to fulfill oneself, participation in them involves suffering of all sorts. This was one reason for Luther's rejection of the monastic life: it chose the way of ease rather than the sorts of suffering service as mother or father involve.

abstraction. "Thou Shalt Not Steal" lacks force until it combines with the duties of our stations. Only when one realizes, for example, that one's alcoholism, or sloth, or perhaps even penchant for golf, robs affection from spouse and children, squanders energy that might be devoted to one's profession, incapacitates one for worship — only then does one begin to see oneself as a sinner who needs God's forgiveness. The duties of our stations are numerous and existentially felt. After the Spirit uses the law's demand to spark awareness of vocational failings, leading to despair and finally God's forgiveness, the other side of vocation emerges: a welcoming invitation to serve God and neighbor.

This experience of obligation is quite different from that of the relentless demand of law. When the gift of forgiveness is experienced, it creates in the forgiven an awareness of gratitude and a new freedom for serving the neighbor in love. As Barth says, commands become permissions to enter into the freedom of obedience. At this point, Calvin's "third use" of the law comes to expression as concrete obligations involved with a person's callings. Our duties as children, parents, spouses, employers, employees, friends, and citizens are particular expressions of God's command to love God and neighbor. In the pull of conscience, faith hears the voice of God calling individuals and groups to particular acts of obedience within the varied contexts of life. Here the call is experienced in the form of a "permission" or a welcome "invitation" to apply one's gifts here rather than there. In their purest form, God's callings are not "summons" of a divine "Commander," whom the obedient soldier strenuously and reluctantly obeys. Rather they are impulses of the indwelling Spirit, calling us forth to discover our lives anew in loving service to God and neighbor. In Christ the energies of the Spirit make the yoke easy and the burden light (Matt. 11:30). Gift and task seem to flow together in redemption. As Einar Billing discerns, the gift of forgiveness can renovate our view of our tasks:

> [T]he power of the forgiveness of sins to organize positively the call, to open new vistas beyond the old duties and tasks and expand their circle with new opportunities of one's calling, that is lost. In the measure in which the forgiveness of sins degenerates into an opiate, the call shrinks into a job.[25]

25. Billing, *Our Calling,* 15.

In experiences of particular obligation the will of God becomes concrete and specified as God's will for an individual in a specific time and place. In the same way the knowledge that we will all die someday takes on a whole new light when the doctor says, "You have inoperable cancer and can expect at best six months to live," so too the knowledge that God so loved the world that he gave his only begotten Son takes on a whole new meaning when the Spirit assures the repentant heart that Christ died to forgive you. So also we should interpret God's general call to love others in relation to particular obligations God calls us to fulfill in our friendships, paid work, marriages, and families. In all of them God's general call is applied and made specific, showing where and how God wants each of us to love our neighbor.

Christians construe their experiences of dependence, gratitude, and obligation in terms of God's will and presence. These experiences spark an awareness of God's call, for the eyes of faith see God's goodness and grace where unbelief sees nothing, or perhaps only blind forces of fate or fortune. The prevailing culture in North America is in many ways in flight not only from God, but also from the very experiences Christians construe in relation to God. The lottery and the rapid expansion of legalized gambling in the United States illustrate this. For many, the dream leading them to squander money on gambling is rooted in the desire to become independent, never to need to thank anyone for anything, and to be liberated from all obligations.[26] Rather than flee from the fundamental structures of moral life, Christ invites us to find in them life full and abundant.

A Sense of Meaning

The fourth, and final, experiential aspect of piety I will relate to vocation is the sense of meaning.[27] Questions concerning our place in the universe, the purpose and meaning of things, spring spontaneously

26. Pastor Rick Porter pointed this out after hearing an earlier version of this material at "Interpreting the Faith," a conference for pastors at Union Theological Seminary, Richmond, Virginia, Summer 1991.

27. Gustafson identifies two other "senses," the sense of possibility and the sense of direction. What I will say about the sense of meaning overlaps what he says about these senses.

from little children and preoccupy the world's most learned and thoughtful philosophers. Human beings have a fundamental need to understand the ordering principles of the realities and processes of which they are a part. Whether the subject of concern is the growth of a tree or the origins of the universe, human beings question, "How?" "Why?" "What?" We seek to understand the patterns, purposes, origins, and natures of things. We try to connect the parts of our lives to larger frames of meaning, trying to make sense of our lives. We wonder what happens during and after the moment of death, and are intrigued by movies like *Flatliners* that dramatically speculate on the singular experience of the death of the body. Many scientists cannot "shrug aside the breathtaking ingenuity of the laws of physics, the extraordinary felicity of nature, and the surprising intelligibility of the physical world" as merely a naturalistic "given."[28] The lawful harmony of nature points to an intelligent, purposeful creator. Some dullards have no curiosity or sense of wonder at the harmony and beauty of creation; others have had it drummed out of them by suffering or deadening educational systems. But traces of the sense of wonder and the quest for meaning survive in most human beings.

We find meaning by identifying parts and linking them to each other, forming larger wholes. In the realm of human actions these wholes are goods, ends, values that give meaning and purpose to life. For some, the size of the larger whole is small, as small as one's individual well being; all the rest of life and thought find meaning by contributing to one's own pleasure. For some, the family unit is that which measures the meaning of all; they work for the family, go to church for the family, vote for candidates who promise to make it easier for the family to flourish, and so on. For others, the source of meaning is the local church; work, family, friends, citizenship are all meaningful in terms of how they come to bear upon that church. For others, the largest frame is one's ethnic group, gender, or nation. Causes, worthy and unworthy, give life meaning. Resisting pollution, saving the planet's atmosphere, preserving any and all species, or removing racial injustice, for example, provide meaning by ordering activities to serve their respective ends.

We find meaning for our present lives by seeing them in some co-

---

28. Paul Davies, "Physics and the Mind of God" (Templeton Prize Address, 1995), *First Things: A Monthly Journal of Religion and Public Life*, 55 (August/September 1995): 34.

herent connection with past and future. Meaningful paid work, for example, is to some degree a fulfillment of previous training and preparation as well as part of a person's larger purposes and plans for her or his life. A meaningful marriage is based on a past history of promises and activity as well as future goals.

It is widely lamented that fragmentation, not integral wholeness, characterizes most modern life. Paid work is fragmented from home life and recreation; businesses pursue short-term profits rather than larger goods; value is dominated by instrumental concerns for means rather than ends; human life and identity lack integrity. A paid job, marriage, friendship, relationship, or an entire life becomes meaningless when it cannot be coherently connected with past and future. Some believe that contemporary American culture no longer has meaningful connections with its moral moorings in Enlightenment and Judeo-Christian traditions, and that people no longer hope to contribute to the common good. If they are right, this crisis of meaning is a major factor in the decline and eventual demise of our institutional life. When cultures, friendships, careers, marriages, families, and other significant relational contexts are cut off from past and future they become meaningless, and when they become meaningless they eventually die.

The doctrine of vocation encourages us to connect all aspects of our present, past, and future to God's plans and purposes. In doing so it provides a solid, integrative center for all of life. The gospel is the gospel of reconciliation. "[I]n Christ God was reconciling the world to himself" (2 Cor. 5:19). Christ brings healing and wholeness to our otherwise broken lives. The energies of the Spirit unite us not only with the Life of God in whom we live and move and have our being; they also unify our past, present, and future as a liturgy of sin, forgiveness, and renewal. God's call to devote everything we are and do to Christ and to service of God and neighbor brings unity to our lives. Paid work, home life, recreation, friendships are all particular callings in response to this one call. Thus Paul writes, "Therefore, my beloved, be steadfast, immovable, always excelling in the work of the Lord, because you know that in the Lord your labor is not in vain" (1 Cor. 15:58).

Vocation views present life as shaped by past operations of our Creator and Redeemer so that we can better serve God's purposes for the future. Life is not a tale told by an idiot, a brief candle, full of sound and fury, signifying nothing; it is participation in the life of God,

Maker of heaven and earth and Redeemer of the whole cosmos. In these postmodern times, when so many people are casting about for sources of meaning, God's call invites everyone to discover their lives in the larger context of God, the Alpha and Omega of the universe.

Because the outworking of God's purposes is mediated, Christians interpret the institutional contexts of life as arenas of God's activity to sustain creation and to overcome sin and its effects. Natural, cultural, political, economic, educational, familial, and ecclesial contexts then become theologically meaningful as the powers that bear down upon us and sustain us by God's purposeful providence. God's callings come to us in and through them, inviting us to serve God and our neighbors, working toward God's shalom. In this way fragmentation is overcome within the meaningful harmony and integrity of a life embedded in God's callings. God's grace in Christ brings reconciliation, healing, and wholeness to lives that are broken by the power of sin.

Helps for a Piety of Vocation

The theological foundations for vocation include a comprehensive vision of the mission of God in this world and a theological interpretation of our senses of dependence, gratitude, obligation, and meaning in light of vocation. Though in an increasingly secular, pluralistic society there are fewer overtly Christian institutional supports for this sense of life as vocation, faith affirms God's presence and providence working in, and through all things. A central task of the institutional church is to inspire a piety that sees all of life in relation to God. Word and sacrament, prayer and liturgy, fellowship and music revive and sustain the sense that God is present in and through our world. With Saint Augustine we ask "the whole mass of the universe" about God and hear it reply, "'I am not God. God is he who made me.'"[29] This vision of creation is a gift of the Spirit, who blows wherever she wills.

There are, however, some institutions and disciplines that may help people hear God's call in their senses of dependence, gratitude, obligation, and meaning. These can become "helps" which the Spirit uses to

---

29. Augustine, *Confessions,* trans and intro by R. S. Pine-Coffin (London: Penguin Books, 1961), Book 10, Sec. 6 (212).

spark, confirm, strengthen, and redirect our sense of God's call and callings. Because so much of our culture and institutional life either neglects or opposes the "vocational" nature of life, renewed attention to strategies for maintaining a sense of life as calling is needed. Many books have been written recently that provide numerous useful suggestions for preserving a "spirituality" for daily life. While this book is more about the theological and ethical aspects of vocation than it is about particular strategies, it is also important to discuss some promising forms of individual and group activities.

Prayer and Meditation

Regular times for prayer and meditation remind us of God's presence and calling in and through all the "senses" articulated above. According to one survey, 73 percent of respondents who reported feeling God's calling in their paid work also said they regularly engaged in devotional reading of the Bible.[30] Traditionally prayer and meditation on Scripture or a devotional took place before and after meals, at many workplaces, and in schools. Until the 1950s, American public schools began the day with prayer. Many hospitals still contain chapels that once were regularly occupied by the staff for prayer and meditation. Many business offices likewise included prayers in daily routines. Church attendance two or even three times on Sundays and again during the workweek reinforced daily prayer and meditation. The United States Constitution's guarantee of religious freedom combined with renewed sensitivity to the need for tolerance and religious pluralism have removed many "helps" to vocational piety.

I am fortunate enough to have daily chapel available to me throughout the academic year. Often a hymn, a prayer, a stained glass window, a particular part of the liturgy, a portion of Scripture, the homily, or the pastor's benediction provokes a sense of God's grace and power in the world, and does so in a way that affects how I view my students and my work for the rest of the day. I am one of relatively few people who work in a Christian context.

---

30. William E. Diehl, *In Search of Faithfulness: Lessons from the Christian Community* (Philadelphia: Fortress Press, 1982), 38.

As society becomes more and more secular, Christians must become more intentional and disciplined in prayer and meditation. Family prayer, reading and discussion of Scripture are especially valuable helps in these times when so many churches never really teach youth even the basic storyline of the Bible or how to pray. Dual careers of parents, excessive demands on single parents, and an inordinate number of structured after-school activities for children make family meal devotions the exception rather than the rule in most homes. Many parents never bother to study the meaning of Christian faith themselves, leaving that to "experts," and so are not competent to discuss it with their children. Individuals and parents exhaust massive amounts of time and energy in their paid work, and in preparing their children for paid work, but often pay almost no attention to the roots of Christian vocation. Jesus says, "[W]hat does it profit them if they gain the whole world but forfeit their life?" (Matt. 16:26). We are so busy talking that we never really listen. If we are to be followers of Christ, we have to order our priorities differently.

The Christian tradition is vastly rich in resources for anyone who wants help in prayer and meditation. The Psalms, the challenging words of the prophets, the stories of the Bible, proverbs and parables, and apostolic letters — the whole biblical canon is rich with resources. The liturgies of Eastern and Western churches, the writings of Christian mystics, and the theology and sermons of past church leaders all contain an inexhaustible reservoir for anyone who wants to come and drink from it. Prayer and meditation can spark and sustain a sense of life as calling.

Exemplary Christians

Because so much Catholic tradition venerates Christians who forsake sex, marriage and family, and "secular" life, a polemical rejection of "saints" sometimes accompanies Protestant vocation. Luther criticized and ridiculed monastic vows and those who put so much value on the monastic life.[31] In spite of this needed critique, the fact remains that in-

---

31. See Martin Luther, "The Judgment of Martin Luther on Monastic Vows, 1521" trans. J. Atkinson, in *Luther's Works: Vol. 44: The Christian In Society,* ed. J. Atkinson (Philadelphia: Fortress Press, 1966), 243-400.

dividuals and groups can and often do inspire a sense of vocation. Sometimes exemplary Christians remind us of the call to serve others, a call all Christians have in common. Thus Paul says, "Be imitators of me, as I am of Christ" (1 Cor. 11:1). What, more precisely, are the Christians at Corinth to imitate? "[W]hatever you do, do everything for the glory of God. Give no offense to Jews or to Greeks or to the church of God, just as I try to please everyone in everything I do, not seeking my own advantage, but that of many, so that they may be saved" (1 Cor. 10:31-33). The biblical stories about Abraham, Sarah, Jacob, Joseph, the midwives, Moses, the kings, the prophets, and the apostles are an instructive and at times inspirational legacy for Christians today. The genius and extraordinary accomplishments of exemplars like Mother Teresa, Dorothy Day, Dietrich Bonhoeffer, Albert Schweitzer, and so many others remind us of God's grace and power at work in the world.

But in our warranted admiration for such noteworthy service, we must not forget all the "ordinary saints" with which God has graced our lives.[32] Grandmothers and mothers whose loving care sustains the lives of their dependents; grandfathers and fathers who faithfully and loyally give of themselves to their children; children who care for their aged parents; honest politicians, businesspeople, and mechanics; friends whose constancy and care sustained us in our hour of need; predecessors whose honest work and generosity created and developed the institutions on which we depend — so many can sharpen our sense of vocation.

Recently, at an adult education forum on "Saints" at my home church, the moderator of the panel asked those in attendance to identify the "saints" who influenced their life of faith. It was amazing to me that not one person mentioned a "famous" person. Parents were mentioned most often, but members of churches whose lives of faith and service were also noteworthy, though they were unknown outside this small community. They were Sunday school teachers, deacons, and elders. Sometimes at the mention of a person's name, others who had been members of this community for some time would knowingly nod their affirmation as they recalled the strong faith and good deeds of this or that person.

32. Robert Benne, true to his Lutheran heritage, emphasizes this point very fruitfully in his book *Ordinary Saints: An Introduction to the Christian Life* (Minneapolis: Fortress Press, 1988).

Often the choice of paid work, and the whole ethical tenor of one's activities within paid work, are greatly influenced by a "saint" who formed an influential example. As a professor I write many letters of recommendation, sometimes years after a student has left St. Olaf College. I am especially diligent in this task because I continue to be grateful to my former teachers, particularly Richard J. Mouw and James M. Gustafson, who were so faithful and diligent in recommending me when I was a student. I cannot repay them, but I can show my gratitude by being faithful and diligent in this part of my work. Exemplars function in similar ways in other occupations. By reflecting on especially exemplary mothers, friends, fathers, husbands, wives, carpenters, mechanics, pastors, and businesspeople, our sense of vocation can be sparked and deepened.

Parachurch Groups

William Diehl, speaker and writer on faith and daily life, emphasizes the need for group settings outside the institutional church. His own practice has been to form or join a group of Christians who meet regularly in homes to read and discuss Scripture, share sorrows and joys, and pray together.[33] If the predictions of Robert Wuthnow are on target, in the future more and more Christians will form small "household churches" to express and develop their faith.[34] Though I believe the institutional church is more important than Diehl thinks and more likely to remain primary than Wuthnow predicts, I do think that their recognition of the importance of households is on target. These groups can become vital avenues for renewing Christian sense of vocation in all of life.

Meeting with other Christians to discuss specific work settings is also a good way to sustain a sense of calling. Many professions have been doing this for some time. Christian lawyers and Christian businesspeople meet regularly to discuss faith and daily life, and sometimes have regional and national conferences whose primary objective

---

33. Diehl, *In Search of Faithfulness*, 65, 69.

34. Robert Wuthnow, *Christianity in the Twenty-first Century: Reflections on the Challenges Ahead* (New York: Oxford University Press, 1993).

is to discern the relation of faith to their professions. Organizations such as these can become very helpful for discerning how one's calling to be a Christian can be expressed in one or another field of paid work. These groups should be encouraged and expanded to include occupations such as carpentry, auto repair, secretarial work, and many other valuable jobs not usually considered "professions." Christians should organize regularly to discuss their faith and its bearing on their paid work.

Unpaid activities in significant relational contexts also should be seen as ways of helping to sustain life as calling. Christian parents should meet to discuss their vocations as parents and how they work this out in their homes. Spouses should meet with other spouses to discuss faith and the vocation of marriage. Single parents should discuss their vocation with other single parents; single adults without children should discuss how to use their context as a place for living out God's calling. Retreat centers provide special circumstances in which people are free to discuss faith and life in a relaxed setting. Many lives have taken a pivotal change as a result of a retreat or fellowship group.

Sympathy for the Needy and Vulnerable

Awareness of human need and vulnerability often inspires a profound sense of calling. Children spontaneously express concern and desire to help the starving children in other places when they see pictures of them in need. As we open ourselves up to the needs of the world, we gain and regain a sense of calling. By being mindful of the needs we are meeting in all our relational contexts, we can gain and sustain a sense of calling. Needs for safety, health, education, food, clothing, housing, entertainment, nurture, and creativity underlie most professions. Needs for emotional support, a safe context for communication and vulnerability, feeling that one is a valued contributor to common projects, to be trustworthy — these needs underlie many relational contexts such as marriage and friendship.

In the cries of our own children and the children of the world, we hear the cries of the infant Jesus; in the pain of victims of oppression and injustice, we perceive the suffering of Christ. Needs that are especially pressing include the pervasiveness of poverty, inhuman working conditions, lack of safety, domestic violence, and poor or nonexistent medical treatment. Christians who do not feel called to direct participation in programs specifically aimed at removing these needs should transform all their callings to bend them in some way to meet them. Parents should raise children who will be sensitive to these needs and committed to striving to remove or reduce them; teachers should teach in ways that inform students of these needs and lead to their removal; pastors should choose liturgies and hymns, and write sermons, in ways that heighten Christian commitment to justice; medical doctors should, if at all possible, donate some of their skills to reduce these needs; and so forth. Rather than callously turn a deaf ear to the world's need, all callings must be transformed in its light.

Kairos Experiences

Christians should reflect upon those times in their lives during which God's grace and calling were more deeply and clearly sensed than at other times. The Greek word *Kairos* refers to times especially full of God's purpose and presence. The New Testament refers to the "time" of God's sending Christ into the world as a time of *Kairos* (Eph. 1:10). *Kairos* refers to the time of the inbreaking of God's kingdom (Mark 1:15), the time of decision (2 Cor. 6:2). Unlike *Chronos*, which merely marks the passage of hours, days, and years, *Kairos* is time as it is filled with meaning and sets the basic direction of individual and communal history.

Each of us has times of personal *Kairos*, times of decision and insight, times that set the basic stance of our lives in other times. These may be more dramatic and more definite for some Christians than for others, but to some degree nearly all Christians eventually have some experiences like these. Remembering these times, meditating upon them, and sharing them with others can renew a sense of calling.

Often we seem to need "extraordinary" examples and experiences to shake us out of our unbelieving stupors. Flannery O'Connor used the grotesque and the extreme in her novels because in our secular culture "you have to make your vision apparent by shock — to the hard of hearing you shout, and for the almost-blind you draw large and startling figures."[35] The problem with "extraordinary" examples and experiences is that they can as easily conceal as reveal the sacred, sacramental character of the "ordinary." So we must beware that our reflection upon *Kairos* experiences does not result in further distancing God from mundane life but rather leads to a faith that sees God's hand at work in all circumstances of life.

I'll close this chapter with two examples from the life of a member of the Church of the Savior in Washington, D.C. This member felt God calling him out of paid work to become a fund-raiser for "Jubilee Housing," an ambitious project that renovates dilapidated urban apartment buildings and then invites homeless people to purchase units and trains them to become responsible homeowners. This member had lost his previous job as president of a prosperous Chicago insurance firm because of a hostile takeover by wealthy stockholders. His experience of being called out of the world of paid work is indicative of a pattern:[36]

> Then, at my lowest point in our married life, I found myself at Wellspring, the retreat center of the Church of the Savior. There was a 24-hour period of silence during this retreat when I had my dialogue with God and asked him to help me get rid of my pride and all the other baggage I was carrying. It was at that point I experienced a *kairos* moment when I knew with absolute certainty that I must leave the business world, though I had no idea what I would do in its place. That was a scary, exhilarating moment I shall never forget.

The second example illustrates how times of tragedy are often part of *Kairos* experiences. Several years after devoting himself to Jubilee Housing, this same person attended a funeral for two children, six and ten years old, who were brutally murdered by their own father. Many of the themes noted above are powerfully present in his response:

> As I stood in the hallway of the funeral home, a jumble of thoughts went through my mind. I thought about my own grandchildren and how loved they are; I thought about our own children and the legacy

---

35. Flannery O'Connor, *Mystery and Manners: Occasional Prose,* selected and ed. Sally and Robert Fitzgerald (New York: Farrar, Straus & Giroux, 1957), 34.

36. This quotation and the next are from the diary of Richard Schuurman, shared with me in a letter.

Ann and I have given them. . . . I thought about the heritage both Ann and I have in the parents we had; and I remembered standing in the cemetery in Makkum a few days ago where my grandfather is buried, reflecting on what a good and honest man he was.

And I thought to myself: none of us has any choices about any of this: the genes we inherit; the love and nurture we receive; the moral values we are taught — all these and much, much more, are gifts to us, passed on from one generation to the next. We had nothing whatsoever to do with it. How can anyone say, then: "I deserve everything I have in life, because I did it on my own."

But what about these innocent children? They, too, had nothing to say about who *their* father would be or the circumstances of *their* lives. Is this some cosmic game of tossing the dice? If God loves us equally, why are not his gifts shared equally? How much easier it is to ask the questions than to give the answers. Instead of answers which used to come so easily, at this point in my life I now make choices and live without the why: I choose order over chaos; I choose purpose over meaninglessness; I choose a God who suffers pain with our pain, over a God of retributive justice.

Shortly thereafter, he established a new venture called "Free the Children," an innovative program that supplies money to help pay for the education of inner-city children through their college graduation and links them with Christian community organizations to help provide the social and moral context that helps these children benefit from the educational help.

A tragedy, a powerful experience of human need, a deep sense of being gifted and called, and a creative response to problems our larger society either ignores or fails to solve — these were primal elements in one person's experience of being called. Not everyone faces such dramatic moments of calling, and these dramatic examples should not be used to downplay the importance of smaller acts of change and less remarkable callings. Through prayer, Bible study, meditation on Scripture, having good models to follow, cultivating networks of fellow Christians beyond our church lives, and cultivating our sympathy for others, as well as through more extraordinary times of change and leading, we can become more aware of and faithful to God's will for our vocation in our daily lives.

CHAPTER FOUR

Abuses and Proper Uses of Vocation

Evil rolls across the ages, but so does good. Good has its own momentum. Corruption never wholly succeeds. . . . Creation is stronger than sin and grace stronger still. Creation and grace are anvils that have worn out a lot of our hammers.

CORNELIUS PLANTINGA JR.[1]

It has been, and ever shall be, one of the tasks of Christian ethics not only to touch the depths of the human soul but also to frame the oecumene with institutions that preserve freedom, aid evaluations, and enhance the possibilities of just and loving relationships in the very fabric of civilization.

MAX STACKHOUSE[2]

Introduction

Sin not only deafens us to God's voice in our senses of dependence, gratitude, obligation, and meaning; it also corrupts the use of vocation

---

1. Cornelius Plantinga Jr., *Not the Way It's Supposed to Be: A Breviary of Sin* (Grand Rapids: Eerdmans, 1995), 199.

2. Max Stackhouse, "The Vocation of Christian Ethics," *The Princeton Seminary Bulletin* 16/3 (November 1995): 304.

language itself, conscripting it into the service of kingdoms of sin and evil. The ways sin attempts this are legion, and it is no small matter to reflect on them so as to aid discernment of what is right and so promote good and avoid evil.

People who feel called to do the will of God sometimes perform shocking and morally reprehensible acts:

> On May 25, 1989, a 23-year-old white Afrikaner, Barend Strydom, was found guilty of murdering eight black people and was sentenced to death by the Supreme Court in Pretoria. Strydom killed all but one of his victims one morning in downtown Pretoria, shooting them in cold blood. . . . Strydom's father, an elder in the Nederduitse Hervormede Kerk, testified that his son was a devout Christian who had himself told the court that before he went on his killing spree he had spent three days and nights alone meditating and praying to ensure that he was doing God's will. In his summing up, the judge mentioned that Strydom was well read in the Bible.[3]

The rogue pilots who hijacked airliners on September 11, 2001, and slammed them into the World Trade Center also prepared for their action with a season of sustained prayer. They felt they were responding obediently to God's will. In a chapter entitled "On What the Libertines Understand by the Vocation of Believers, and How Under This Guise They Excuse Every Form of Villainy," Calvin condemns Christians who claim they have a "vocation" to be pimps, thieves, and adulterers.[4] Lies, treachery, and even murder are sometimes deemed justifiable for those called by "destiny" or "necessity."

Vocation is more often abused to justify immorality in less obvious ways. Calvin's and Luther's respect for "order" and "office" is easily twisted by the powerful to perpetuate abuse of the weak and subordinated members of society — the poor, minorities, and women. Luther's transvaluation of the dairy maid's work — as important to God as the service of princes and preachers — can slide into slothful neglect of the Spirit's gifts, avoidance of opportunities for more

---

3. John W. de Gruchy, *Liberating Reformed Theology: A South African Contribution to an Ecumenical Debate* (Grand Rapids: Eerdmans, 1991), 140-41.

4. *John Calvin: Treatises Against the Anabaptists and Against the Libertines*, ed. and trans. B. W. Farley (Grand Rapids: Baker Books, 1988).

needed service elsewhere, and quietist acceptance of a corrupt but changeable status quo. Recognition of finitude in meeting special obligations to spouse and children may conceal idolatrous constrictions of love and loyalties. Or, on the opposite side, a person may use his or her "calling" to, say, foreign missions as a cover for neglecting a spouse, parents, or children. For some it is easier to love humanity "in general" than to love their spouse. Admiration for extraordinary callings of Albert Schweitzer or Mother Teresa (or even Jesus of Nazareth) can fuel a spiritual hubris that belittles ordinary obligations to family, local church, and neighborhood. Abuses of vocation seem as slippery and treacherous as sin itself.

Basic Consideration for Rightly Using Vocation

The Call and Callings

The main way to resist abuse of the notion of calling is to insist that life amid individuals' varied callings or places of responsibility be governed by the common Christian calling to serve God and to follow Christ. Calvin holds that "all callings *that serve the common good* of human beings are lawful and holy."[5] Puritan William Perkins says, "A particular calling must give place to the general calling of a Christian when they cannot both stand together . . . because we are bound unto God in the first place and unto man, under God."[6] Perkins rejects occupations such as usury, gambling, and maintaining houses of gaming, arguing that "God is the author of lawful callings, and an unlawful calling is really no calling at all."[7] Lawful callings serve the common good. As Douglas F. Ottati puts it, any activity or practice that fails to restrain evil and promote good "is a practice out of accord with the dynamic movement beyond resignation toward reconciliation and renewal. By structure, design, or intractable circumstance, a calling or practice that cannot stand with the calling of a Christian

5. Calvin, *Treatises*, 81.

6. William Perkins, *The Works of William Perkins,* ed. Ian Breward (Abingdon: Courtneny Press, 1970), 457.

7. Perkins's view as summarized by Ottati in his *Reforming Protestantism: Christian Commitment in Today's World* (Louisville: Westminster/John Knox Press, 1995), 124.

seeks an end contrary to the public good and well-being of God's all-inclusive commonwealth."[8]

Love

The North Star for right use of the doctrine of vocation, and for conforming one's callings to the call to follow Christ, is Christian love. *The* primary Christian calling is to love God with all one's heart, soul, strength, and mind, and to love one's neighbor as oneself. The norm of love should govern Christian action and character in each and every calling, though love may take different forms as its requirements and the needs of the neighbor are refracted through diverse vocational fields. The respect a youth should have for a parent differs from the respect a friend should have for a friend, though both are forms of love for God and neighbor. The privileges and obligations a father has for his own children differ from those he has to children of other fathers, though fulfilling both may express love. The proper and fair use of coercion exercised in a parent's discipline, a professor's grades, or a jury's verdict differs from the forgiveness of sins proclaimed from pulpits throughout the world, but they all can be expressions of Christian love.

Any obligation of one's paid work, political life, or any other relational field that violates Christian love must be rejected as contrary to Christian vocation. Any felt urge to act contrary to love, whether in keeping with the duties of one's station or contrary to them, whether experienced during prayer or after days of prayer and fasting, has nothing to do with God's call. It is instead the voice of sin masquerading in religious guise.

Shalom

If love is vocation's guiding moral norm, then shalom is its orienting ideal. Shalom, or peace, is much more than the absence of hostility. As Nicholas Wolterstorff points out, shalom includes joy and delight:

8. Ottati, *Reforming Protestantism*, 129.

Shalom at its highest is *enjoyment* in one's relationships. A nation may be at peace with all its neighbors and yet be miserable in its poverty. To dwell in shalom is to *enjoy* living before God, to *enjoy* living in one's physical surroundings, to *enjoy* living with one's fellows, to *enjoy* life with oneself.[9]

He continues, "And of course there can be delight in community only when justice reigns, only when human beings no longer oppress one another":

> When "justice shall make its home in the wilderness,/and righteousness dwell in the grassland" — only then will it be true that "righteousness shall yield shalom,/and its fruit be quietness and confidence for ever" (Isa. 32:16-17).[10]

Shalom is a condition of wholeness, of health and flourishing to the fullest extent.

What Barth says about the "will for health" under "respect for life" applies to the Christian calling to long and work for God's shalom:

> The will for health of the individual must therefore take also the form of the will to improve, raise and perhaps radically transform the general living conditions of all men. If there is no other way, it must assume the form of the will for a new and quite different order of society, guaranteeing better living conditions for all. Where some are necessarily ill the others cannot with good conscience will to be well.[11]

Shalom includes, but goes beyond, justice.[12] Shalom expresses God's original will for life in creation, and God's ultimate goal for life in the

---

9. Nicholas Wolterstorff, *Until Justice and Peace Embrace* (Grand Rapids: Eerdmans, 1983), 69-70.

10. Wolterstorff, *Until Justice and Peace Embrace*, 70.

11. Barth, *Church Dogmatics*, 3/4, ed. and trans. G. W. Bromiley (Edinburgh: T&T Clark, 1961), 363.

12. Shalom is closer to what Paul Ramsey calls "righteousness" (inclusive of *mishpat, tsedeq, chesed*) in *Basic Christian Ethics* (Chicago: University of Chicago Press, 1978), 2-24, than to justice understood as primarily or exclusively a political or legal matter. One important difference between biblical "righteousness" and "shalom" is that the former more than the latter shows how God's will ought to be embodied in the totality of fallen human existence, whereas shalom depicts the embodiment of God's will in its perfected condition.

eschaton. Shalom is both a divine gift and a human task. God is already working toward this comprehensive renewal through Christ and the Church.

Even as every Christian is called to love God and neighbor, so each Christian is called to offer her or his life to serve God's Shalom. In all their callings — home and extended family, friendships, paid work, cultural activity, and political life — Christians must strive to establish justice, contribute to the common good, and promote enjoyment of life in creation under God's reign. Particular "callings" that cannot be used to serve this calling are not from God and must be forsaken. Christians should see all relational spheres of life as contributing somehow to God's shalom.

Discernment in a World Created but Fallen

A fourth orienting concept for right uses of vocation is the need for discernment amid the ambiguity of all callings. In general, all significant relational fields express both God's good creation and human corruption, glimmerings of the "already" of God's glorious re-creation and signs of the "not yet" of the sinful age that is still with us. Institutional forms of life, and the large dynamics on which they rest, are ambiguous mixtures of creation and fall, and so from a moral point of view they include potential for good and evil. The energies and activities of the Creator and Redeemer are operative in them. Human beings discover themselves within them and preserve, reshape, or destroy them. History and nature provide some givens, but human beings shape the particular institutional forms in which we experience marriage, family, state, business, church, and culture. They are "ordering processes and patterns of interdependence" through which God sustains and bears down upon us.[13] Though God's providence places particular individuals in diverse familial, economic, social, cultural, and political matrices, human beings exercise agency within and through them. In their callings Christians must discern what is good and what is evil, and promote what is good and resist what is evil. Vocation thus

13. James M. Gustafson, *Ethics From a Theocentric Perspective: Theology and Ethics,* Vol. 1 (Chicago: University of Chicago Press, 1981), 219-22.

calls for "faithful participation" in the life of this world. It is realistic about the corruption of the world and its stations, but also about traces of God's good creation and the possibilities for transformation. It calls for continual reformation of personal and institutional life.

When life amid one's callings is governed by the common Christian calling to serve God and follow Christ, when it is guided by love, shaped by shalom, and tested by discernment, then vocation will be used properly; it will be abused when it contradicts these principles. Difficulties emerge when one tries to apply this understanding of vocation to concrete action and character amid one's callings. What does love of neighbor mean, for example, for a Christian who is a SWAT-team sharpshooter, a lawyer assigned to defend a corporation with racist employee practices, an artist or musician balancing demands of the creative process over against other pressing obligations, or a parent who has enough to feed his or her own children, but not those of a neighbor in need? Is shalom directly relevant to our fallen condition? In the shalom of the new creation, the lion will lie with the lamb, but this does not mean we can put lions and lambs together right now. Christians hope for a day when a child will play in the snake pit without fear, but this does not mean that in this age we place vipers in our children's cribs. If hope for shalom does not lead us to place snakes in our children's cribs, should it rule out Christian participation in the coercive institutions of political life? When does ambiguity move so far into a dark area that the appropriate stance is not attentive discernment and compromise, but prophetic critique, insubordination, or withdrawal? As thoughtful Christians respond to these questions, they understandably differ in their particular judgments and directives.

With these basic considerations in mind, it is important to recognize three ways in which the Protestant doctrine of vocation has been abused: (1) to justify idolatry of work, (2) to encourage illicit constrictions of love, and (3) to provide a cover for injustice. Consideration of these abuses brings to the fore some of the more trenchant Christian criticisms of the doctrine of vocation, so we need to identify aspects of the doctrine of vocation that help avoid abuses and support its proper uses.

Idolatry or Piety?

The French Reformed theologian/ethicist Jacques Ellul emphasizes the fallen character of modern work. He argues that there is nothing in the Bible allowing us to equate *work* with *calling*. "It is an imperative of survival," says Ellul, "and the Bible remains realistic enough not to superimpose upon this necessity a superfluous spiritual decoration."[14] Work is an unavoidable requirement of existence, which one does not enjoy, but endures. "[W]ork has no ultimate value, no transcendental meaning. Before God, it is that which draws us to survive and which characterizes us as human beings."[15] Ellul says that work is permissible and necessary, but of no deeper religious meaning. Seeing work as expressive of Christian vocation "reflects in the ideological realm the growing importance of work in the capitalist economy during the sixteenth and seventeenth centuries."[16]

Stanley Hauerwas echoes similar concerns in his essay, "Work as Co-Creation: A Critique of a Remarkably Bad Idea." The target of his attack is Pope John Paul II's encyclical *Laborem Exercens,* but his criticisms apply to the classic Protestant view of vocation as well. He criticizes the pope's use of Genesis 1:27-28 to support the idea that through their work human beings become co-creators with God, arguing that this idea is "exactly opposite" to this text: "The good news of the creation account is that God completed his creation and that mankind needs do nothing more to see to its perfection." Hauerwas holds that the *Imago Dei* consists in being a representative of God, and a "representative is not a co-creator."[17] The claim that human beings achieve fulfillment and become more human through work fails to account for the fallenness of work and refuses to recognize that work is at best a way to earn a living. Although work may have periods of intrinsic pleasure and interest, "most work is not intrinsically fulfilling, but a neces-

14. Jacques Ellul, "Work and Calling," in *Katallagete,* 4/2-3 (Fall-Winter, 1972): 8.

15. Ellul, "Work and Calling," 14.

16. Lee Hardy, *The Fabric of This World: Inquiries into Calling, Career Choice, and the Design of Human Work* (Grand Rapids: Eerdmans, 1990), here summarizes Ellul's views (p. 104).

17. Stanley Hauerwas, "Work as Co-Creation: A Critique of a Remarkably Bad Idea," in *Co-Creation and Capitalism: John Paul II's Laborem Exercens,* eds. J. W. Houck and O. F. Williams (Lanham, Md.: University Press of America, 1983), 45-46.

sity for survival as well as contributing to our interdependence as social beings." The one grace Hauerwas might ascribe to work is that we do not need to find "any great significance or salvation" in our work:

> Our work does not have to have or contribute to some grand plan. . . . Work gives us the means to survive, be of service to others, and, perhaps most of all, work gives us a way to stay busy. For while work may not be ultimately fulfilling, it is at least a great gift — a hedge against boredom. Attributing greater significance to work risks making it demonic as work then becomes an idolatrous activity through which we try to secure and guarantee our significance, to make "our mark" on history.[18]

In the original creation our task was merely to till and keep the garden. "Our sin was and is exactly to try to make it more' than that."[19]

For Hauerwas the story worsens when John Paul II speaks of work as a sharing of Christ's work, and of the suffering endured in work as "carrying the cross of Christ." The pope and Protestant vocation view the sleepless nights of parents and professors, the tedium and danger of work, as participation in Christ's sufferings.[20] For Hauerwas, "Such a claim comes very close to trivializing the cross of Christ by identifying every kind of suffering or onerous task with Jesus' cross." With John H. Yoder, Hauerwas sees the cross representing particular suffer-

---

18. Hauerwas, "Work as Co-Creation," 48.

19. Hauerwas, "Work as Co-Creation," 48.

20. Pope John Paul II's claims here bear a close resemblance to those of Luther. For Luther the whole structure of all legitimate offices or stations is self-sacrificial service to the neighbor, linking all related sufferings implicitly to the cross. Thus he describes the duties of the Christian prince in this way: "'I will do likewise, seeking from my subjects not my own advantage but theirs. I will use my office to serve and protect them, listen to their problems and defend them, and govern to the sole end that they, not I, may benefit and profit from my rule.' In such manner should a prince in his heart empty himself of his power and authority, and take unto himself the needs of his subjects, dealing with them as though they were his own needs. For this is what Christ did to us [Phil. 2:7]; and these are the proper works of Christian love." (*Luther's Works, Vol. 45,* ed. J. Atkinson (Philadelphia: Fortress Press, 1966), 120). For analogous claims with special reference to the suffering incurred by being persecuted for obeying God's word through one's offices, particularly public ones, see Luther's sermons on "The Sermon On The Mount," *Luther's Works,* 21:44-50. See also John Howard Yoder, *The Politics of Jesus* (Grand Rapids: Eerdmans, 1972), 97, 132.

ing "when the power of non-resistant love challenges the powers that would rule this world by violence."[21] For Hauerwas, it is not only misleading to confer so much religious significance upon work, it is hubris and idolatry.

According to Ellul and Hauerwas, vocation refers to the call of the gospel to become a Christian to one's functions and services in the Church. They agree with the classic Protestant insistence that God's call comes to human beings without regard to social position, and that any mundane occupation can become a place from which to serve God and neighbor. But they oppose interpreting work or such roles as spouse, child, or parent as vocations because doing so idolatrously elevates the significance of our activity to divine status of God's work as creator and/or redeemer. They restrict the idea of vocation to the Church, or perhaps (as in Ellul's case) to extracurricular volunteer activities.

In Response

Let me begin by noting that Ellul and Hauerwas rightly point to a very real danger in the Protestant doctrine of vocation. If vocation is twisted so that human activity usurps divine activity in creation and redemption, then it must be challenged. Ultimate significance belongs to God, who is Creator, Judge, and Redeemer, and to God alone. The clamoring demands of domestic, political, economic, and other fields must never displace the call of God in Christ to faith and new life. What finally matters is not whether we are male or female, married or single, prince or pauper, parent or child, Italian or Dutch; what finally matters is whether or not by faith, through baptism, we have been united with Christ in his death and resurrection. If vocation contradicts or clouds this fundamental truth of the Gospel, then it must be corrected.

A second point, which must follow the first, is that vocation does not view work as redemptive or self-fulfilling. Luther is emphatic about the fact that works of one's callings cannot save. The righteousness received by faith is separate from the justice achieved amid one's stations. Gustaf Wingren faithfully represents Luther on this point: "Works belong to the earthly realm, in service to others, directed downward in vo-

21. Hauerwas, "Work as Co-Creation," 50.

cation which bears altogether the stamp of the earthly realm. And vocation is most purely and really served when through the gospel it has become clear that vocation has nothing to do with salvation."[22] For Luther there will be no vocations or orders in the world to come; their existence is temporary, fleeting, and transitory. Even if some later Calvinists did turn work into a means of redemption, for the early reformers it was not so.

A third point is that Ellul and Hauerwas strip mundane life of religious meaning it ought to possess. They tend to follow the modern pattern of first constricting the idea of vocation to paid work, and then severing paid work from religious meaning. What is lost, and what must be recovered, is the powerful way vocation integrates all spheres and relations of human life into a religious vision of love and service to God and neighbor. Finally it is Jesus Christ who lives in and with the needs of our sisters and brothers — the teething pain of the infant crying out in the middle of the night, the broken and anxious heart a friend has trustingly opened, or the hunger of the homeless. God's provident and redemptive care is a *mediated* care; under vocation's sacred canopy, all experiences of life take on a sacramental quality.

There are many theological presuppositions and implications of these claims that must be reconsidered, notably doctrines of providence and its relation to redemption, and what used to be called the "orders" of creation and their relation to the church and the order of redemption.[23] At this point I only note that vocation in its better forms avoids idolatrous valuation of paid work, widens the scope of what is religiously meaningful, and infuses all of life with a sense of service to God and neighbor.

Vocation — A Cover for Constrictions of Love?

Many Christian ethicists argue that Protestant vocation encourages Christians to disobey Jesus' command to love their neighbor, and more

---

22. Gustaf Wingren, *Luther on Vocation,* trans. C. C. Rasmussen (Philadelphia: Muhlenberg Press, 1957), 14.

23. See Douglas Schuurman, "Creation, Eschaton, and Social Ethics: A Response to Volf," *Calvin Theological Journal* 30/1 (Spring 1995): 144-58, for general directions in which I think this should be developed.

specifically his command to love their enemies.[24] Those who make this criticism often object to "Christendom" aspirations in Christian theology and practice. According to these critics, a world ruled by the church is not a positive outcome of the leaven of the gospel in the world, but rather a sinful pattern of accommodating Christian beliefs and practices so as to legitimate corrupt political, social, cultural, and economic powers.[25] These critics argue that the doctrine of vocation promotes conservative conformity to the coercive powers of this evil age and selfish constrictions of Christian love.[26] Protestant vocation thus contributes to the loss of genuine Christian witness and discipleship. Because these criticisms are numerous, serious, and trenchant, they merit closer examination. Though these criticisms reveal abuses of the idea of vocation, they do not convincingly make the case that Protestant vocation should be rejected. Rather, it should be re-articulated, with emphasis upon the four principles elaborated above, to ensure its proper use.

John H. Yoder and Leo Tolstoy argue that a central feature of Protestant vocation encourages selfishness, or constrictions of love to a specific group, such as family, race, or nation. Martin Luther expresses a feature central to Protestant vocation when he limits the scope of Jesus' command to "Give to everyone who begs from you, and do not refuse anyone who wants to borrow from you" (Matt. 5:42). According to

24. See, for example, John H. Yoder, *The Priestly Kingdom: Social Ethics as Gospel* (Notre Dame: University of Notre Dame Press, 1984), esp. 138 and 210 n.9; Hauerwas, "Work as Co-Creation," 45-48; Dorothee Soelle, *To Work and to Love: A Theology of Creation*, with Shirley A. Cloyes (Philadelphia: Fortress, 1984), 1-54; Miroslav Volf, *Work in the Spirit: Toward a Theology of Work* (New York: Oxford University Press, 1991), 102-13.

25. For an interesting debate about whether Christendom is a positive expression of the mission of the Church or a perversion of it, see Oliver O'Donovan, *The Desire of Nations: Rediscovering the Roots of Political Theology* (Cambridge: Cambridge University Press, 1996), 193-242, and Stanley Hauerwas and James Fodor, "Remaining in Babylon: Oliver O'Donovan's Defense of Christendom" in Hauerwas, *Wilderness Wanderings: Probing Twentieth-Century Theology and Philosophy* (Boulder, Colo.: Westview Press, 1997), 199-224.

26. According to critics, the medieval doctrine of vocation did this by transforming the radical demands of Jesus into "counsels" for those who opt for a more perfect Christian life, and sequestering them within the walls of the monastery. The Protestant doctrine did this by distinguishing two "kingdoms," a spiritual one governing inner and interpersonal life and a temporal one governing social life, and then restricting the radical ethical teachings of Jesus to the spiritual kingdom. In either case, the doctrine of vocation effectively removes Christ's ethical teachings from society and encourages Christians to conform to the patterns of life as they are determined by the world.

Luther, "Christ is not telling me to give what I have to any scoundrel that comes along and to deprive my family of it or others who may need it and whom I am obliged to help, and then to suffer want myself and become a burden to others."[27] Instead, because parents have a calling to meet the needs of their children, they have a moral obligation not to give to others what God has entrusted to them to meet the needs of their own children. According to Luther, giving essentials to beggars would be theft: stealing from one's own children and giving it to others. The more general principle behind Luther's advice is that we have a special obligation to meet the needs of those brought near by God's providence through our various callings. Beneath this principle is trust that God's providence has placed us within our callings, and that duties of love are to be given structure by the refracted obligations of our callings. This includes humble acknowledgment of our finitude, recognizing that as finite beings we are unable to meet the needs of the whole world. But we can serve our neighbor by serving our children.

Leo Tolstoy objects to this view, arguing that giving privileged treatment to persons in a special relation violates Christian love. He defines Christian love as a preference for others over ourselves. He holds that "before a man can love he must 'cease from preferring some people to others *for his own personal welfare.*'"[28] Love bombards Christians with its scattering of demands:

> The demands of love present themselves *constantly* and *simultaneously* and *without any order*. Here is a hungry old man for whom I have a little love and who has come to ask for food which I am keeping for the supper of my much-loved children: how am I to weigh the present demand of a feebler love against the future demand of a stronger?[29]

Tolstoy observes that once this restriction is granted, it is a small step to withhold clothes from a freezing child out of consideration for future children one may have some day:

27. Luther, "The Sermon on the Mount (Sermons)" in *Luther's Works*, vol. 21: *The Sermon on the Mount and the Magnificat*, ed. J. Pelikan (St. Louis: Concordia Publishing House, 1956), 117.

28. Leo Tolstoy, *On Life*, World's Classics edition, trans. Aylmer Maude (London: Oxford University Press), 102-3, as cited by Paul Ramsey, *Basic Christian Ethics* (Chicago: University of Chicago Press, 1978), 155.

29. Tolstoy, *On Life*, xxiii, 97, as cited by Ramsey, *Basic Christian Ethics*, 156.

If a man may reject the present demands of a feebler love for the sake of the future demands of a greater love, is it not evident that such a man, even if he wished it with all his might, will never be able to judge to what extent he may reject present demands in favour of future demands; and therefore, not being able to decide that question, *will always choose the manifestations of love which please him best* — that is, he will yield not to the demands of love but to the demands of his personality. [Such a man] *deceives himself and others and loves no one but himself.*

Tolstoy concludes, "Future love does not exist. Love is a present activity only."[30]

John Howard Yoder makes a similar critique in the context of his reply to the common counterexample to pacifism: What would you do if you had to protect your family from an intruder who broke into your house at night? On Luther's view, the father's vocation includes representing God's provident protection of his wife and children, and so the father should risk harming the intruder, if necessary, to prevent the intruder from injuring his family.

Yoder rejects priority of the well-being of one's children and wife over that of the intruder. In addition to noting the sexism implied by the counterexample, Yoder says, "It is an altruistic form of egoism when I defend *my* wife or *my* child because they are precisely *my own.*" To use force in this case is to engage in an act of selfishness; "though covered over with the halo of service to others, it is still self-oriented in its structure."[31] According to Yoder, Jesus' call to forsake house, land, parent, spouse, and child loosens social bonds: "Any consideration of what this means must at least make us question the assumption that the first test of moral responsibility . . . is the readiness to kill in defense of one's family."[32] Yoder's position directly implies that Protes-

---

30. Tolstoy, *On Life*, xxiii, 97-98, as cited by Ramsey, *Basic Christian Ethics*, 156.

31. John H. Yoder, et al., *What Would You Do? A Serious Answer to a Standard Question* (Scottdale, Penn.: Herald Press, 1983), 20. Yoder's main point is that it is a very long stride from this counterexample to justification of war, though many ethicists assume the step to be self-evident. He also rightly points out that ethical legitimacy depends upon many assumptions (one knows for certain the intent of the intruder, that one's efforts to use force against the intruder will succeed, etc.) that are highly questionable.

32. Yoder, *What Would You Do?* 39.

tant vocation, by endorsing preferential treatment of persons in special relations — such as friends, children, or parents — perversely reverses the true meaning of the call of Christ. It becomes a cover for egoism, nationalism, racism, and other tribalisms.

In Response

There are two distinct features of vocation and "special relations" that need further consideration in light of this criticism. Further consideration of them will help avoid abuses of vocation and establish its proper use. The *first* is whether it is contrary to Christian love to give privileged treatment to persons with whom one is in a special relation; the *second* is whether it is contrary to Christian love to give privileged treatment to oneself. For Tolstoy and Yoder, the former is merely a hypocritical cover for the latter. For Luther and Calvin, there is a vast moral and religious difference between self-love and selfless care for those whom God's providence has placed under our care through our vocations.

Neighbor-Centered, Theocentric, Preferential Loves

According to Luther and Calvin, Christians experience self-sacrifice *primarily* in their callings to serve spouse, children, subordinates, and superiors. In "On Temporal Authority," Luther says, "A Christian should be so disposed that he will suffer every evil and injustice without avenging himself; neither will he seek legal redress in the courts but have utterly no need of temporal authority and law for his own sake. On behalf of others, however, he may and should seek vengeance, justice, protection, and help, and do as much as he can to achieve it."[33] Luther held similar views on the command to lend or give to anyone who asks. If the goods belong only to you, then lend and give as others ask. But if the goods have been entrusted to you to use in your calling as a father, then do not rob from your children to give to a beggar.[34] Callings are

33. Luther, "On Temporal Authority: To What Extent It Should Be Obeyed," *Luther's Works,* 45:101.
34. Luther, *Luther's Works,* 21:117.

places for self-sacrifice in faithful service to the neighbors God's providence brings near.

Rather than constricting love of neighbor to be perverted into self-love, vocation expands the love from within special relations outward into ever widening circles, and finally to God. Luther says that the estate of marriage "redounds to the benefit not alone of the body, property, honor, and the soul of an individual, but also to the benefit of whole cities and countries. . . ."[35] Without faith, a husband and father sees marriage to be "bitterness and drudgery" and asks, "What, should I make such a prisoner of myself?" Christian faith sees marriage and fatherhood as callings:

> [Faith] opens its eyes, looks upon all these insignificant, distasteful, and despised duties in the Spirit, and is aware that they are all adorned with divine approval as with the costliest gold and jewels. It says, "O God, because I am certain that thou hast created me as a man and hast from my body begotten this child, I also know for a certainty that it meets with thy perfect pleasure. I confess to thee that I am not worthy to rock the little babe or wash its diapers, or to be entrusted with the care of the child and its mother. How is it that I, without any merit, have come to this distinction of being certain that I am serving thy creature and thy most precious will?"[36]

Notice that, in vocation, the child is not *my* child, but the child *thou hast begotten*. The father is not serving *himself*, or even *my child*, but *thy creature*. Though Luther thought monastic "callings" were rife with selfishness and hypocrisy, he believed secular callings in the domestic, economic, and political orders were places of self-sacrificial service.

If we follow Luther and Calvin here, the basic movement of vocation is theocentric. The doctrine of vocation directs humans to recognize that God created each of us as finite, and has providentially gifted and situated persons to serve these particular neighbors here and now. God's Spirit sees all and works through all; human beings serve in particular places, trusting and hoping that their service has a positive influence on the whole.

Luther rightly opposes a spirituality that leads others, in God's

---

35. Luther, "The Estate of Marriage," *Luther's Works*, 45:44.
36. Luther, "The Estate of Marriage," *Luther's Works*, 45:41.

name, to neglect their own parents, spouse, and children for the sake of the monastery or of humanity "in general." The proximity of the needs of those nearby combines with the availability of resources to place priority on service to those close at hand when there is a definite conflict. And service to those nearby need not exclude others that are more remote. Through loving those close, and through receiving their love, God's love and care redound to the benefit of all creation.[37] Though there is no room for self-love in Luther's view, there is room, indeed a sacred obligation, to give privileged treatment of the needs of one's children and dependents when they conflict with the needs of those who do not stand in such a special relation.

Paul Ramsey agrees with Luther. He says, "Itself non-preferential so far as concerns only the agent's own 'personal welfare,' Christian love *for the neighbors' sake* may actually prefer certain persons to others." When making judgments of this sort, there is "great peril" of self-deception. But one "may also make the choice actually required for maximum service to his neighbors. In short, there may be a 'neighbor-centered preferential love' replacing 'self-centered preferential loves.'"[38] Christian ethics is based on "a radically unselfish love, but it is an '*enlightened* unselfishness.'"[39] It is "enlightened" by giving weight to need and special relations when the demands of more than one neighbor press upon the moral agent. Here Ramsey rejects Tolstoy's assumption

37. Many interesting and complex issues are at stake here. Gene Outka argues that agape is "the guardian in rather than the direct inspiration of every special relation" and that special obligations cannot be "simply derived from or founded directly upon agape" (*Agape: An Ethical Analysis* [New Haven and London: Yale University Press, 1972], 274). Stephen G. Post in *A Theory of Agape: On the Meaning of Christian Love* (Lewisburg, Pa.: Bucknell University Press, 1990), challenges Outka on these points (esp. 79-90). See also William Werpehowski's illuminating analysis of this topic in "'Agape' and Special Relations," in *The Love Commandments: Essays in Christian Ethics and Moral Philosophy,* eds. Edmund N. Santurri and William Werpehowski (Washington, D.C.: Georgetown University Press, 1992), 138-56; and Stephen J. Pope's fine essay, "Proper and Improper Partiality and the Preferential Option for the Poor," *Theological Studies* 54/2 (June 1993): 242-71. See also Stephen J. Pope, *The Evolution of Altruism and the Ordering of Love* (Washington, D.C.: Georgetown University Press, 1994). For a philosophical account of issues relating to special responsibilities, see Robert E. Goodin, *Protecting the Vulnerable: A Reanalysis of Our Social Responsibilities* (Chicago: University of Chicago Press, 1985).

38. Ramsey, *Basic Christian Ethics,* 158-59.

39. Ramsey, *Basic Christian Ethics,* 160.

that the demands of love meet us in a constant, unordered scattershot. They rather come to us through our callings.

Self-Love and Vocation

Unlike Luther, who has almost nothing affirming to say about self-love, Ramsey tries to include it within the more fundamental love of neighbor. He says that duties to self must be defined "vocationally in terms of duties to others." Legitimate self-love springs from trust that one is created, justified, and loved by God, and it is controlled by its dependence upon love of neighbor:

> While the positive will to be one's self does not contest the ground with neighbor-love, nevertheless, an individual existing with gratitude and faith "before" God and out of love "for" another has abundant reason to be "willing" to be himself and to develop his own capacities to their maximum. After the leap to the neighbor's side has been effected, on the basis of self-acceptance there may be (indeed, there must be) a derivation of duties to one's self.[40]

Joseph Allen adds a useful distinction between self-abasement, opposed by Barbara Hilkert-Andolson and many feminists, and sacrifice of one's interests to those of others when they conflict. Because we have been created and forgiven by God, we should not be self-abasing, but instead have a wholesome sense of our own worth. Like Ramsey, Allen gives priority to neighbor love while making room for self-love. His guiding principle is that Christian love gives a "strong but not absolute" priority to the interests of the neighbor when they conflict with self-interest.[41]

Tolstoy and Yoder rightly object to selfishness and sinful constrictions of affection and loyalty. There is good reason for so many gospel texts to call people to forsake sinful attachments to family and the familiar. Gustafson, following Augustine and Edwards, sees "contraction" as the core metaphor for the human fault. He says the human fault is a shrinking of self and community "into a little space, circum-

---

40. Ramsey, *Basic Christian Ethics*, 161.
41. Joseph Allen, *Love and Conflict: A Covenantal Model of Christian Ethics* (Nashville: Abingdon, 1984), 120-30.

scribed and closely shut up within itself. . . . [It] keeps us from proper understanding of our proper relations by contracting our trusts and loyalties, our loves and desires, our rational construing of the world and our moral interests."[42] Because of the power and pervasiveness of this tendency, constant vigilance is needed to affirm the neighbor-directed and ultimately theocentric movement of vocation.

If vocation leads to affirmation of special relations in ways that hold a danger of concealing selfishness and callous disregard for distant neighbors, the view of Yoder and Tolstoy holds an equally serious danger in the opposite direction. As Valerie Saving-Goldstein, Barbara Hilkert-Andolsen, and other feminists ethicists argue, the notion of agapic love as self-sacrifice pure and simple often leads women to self-abnegation, and to slothful neglect of their agency and gifts for the broader community.[43] We need legitimate self-love that attends to the interests of the self as an image bearer of God redeemed by Christ, and of potential service to others.

Neglect of Special Relations: An Expression of Hubris

Another danger of Yoder's and Tolstoy's view is neglecting one's special relations in the name of serving some larger, seemingly more important "religious" cause. It is sometimes a sinful temptation to neglect one's spouse, children, local church, and community ostensibly to serve an abstract "cause" or humanity "in general." The same Jesus who calls disciples to forsake family (Matt. 12:47-50) also criticizes the Pharisees for imposing a religious tithe even when it would deplete resources needed to care for aging parents:

> And why do you break the commandment of God [to honor your mother and father] for the sake of your tradition? For God said, 'Honor your father and your mother,' and 'Whoever speaks evil of father or mother must surely die.' But you say that whoever tells father

42. Gustafson, *Ethics From a Theocentric Perspective,* 1:306.

43. Barbara Hilkert-Andolson, "Agape in Feminist Ethics," *Journal of Religious Ethics* 9 (Spring 1981), 69-83, and Valerie Saving-Goldstein, "The Human Situation: A Feminine View," in *Womanspirit Rising: A Feminist Reader in Religion,* ed. Carol Christ and Judith Plaskow (San Francisco: Harper & Row, 1979), 24-42.

or mother, 'Whatever support you might have had from me is given to God,' then that person need not honor the father. So, for the sake of your traditon, you make void the word of God. You hypocrites! (Matt. 15:3-7)

According to Jonathan Edwards, the obligation to love one's family is even stronger than the obligation to love the rest of humankind, because the family "is more peculiarly our own, and is more appropriated to ourselves. . . ." He says, "a great proportion of the wickedness of which men are guilty, and that will be brought out at the day of judgment, will be the sin which they shall have committed in the families to which they belong."[44] Albert Schweitzer usually discouraged people who wanted to follow his example by doing something "extraordinary." He felt that a "restless spirit" drove most people who came to him for advice. He comments, "Such persons wanted to dedicate themselves to larger tasks because those that lay nearest did not satisfy them. . . . Only a person who can find a value in every sort of activity and devote himself to each one with full consciousness of duty, has the inward right to ask as his object some extraordinary activity instead of that which falls naturally to his lot."[45]

Calvin puts the point very well. Commenting on the parable of the Good Samaritan, he says,

> I do not deny that the more closely a man is linked to us, the more intimate obligation we have to assist him. It is the common habit of mankind that the more close men are bound together by the ties of kinship, of acquaintanceship, or of neighborhood, the more responsibilities for one another they share. This does not offend God; for

---

44. Jonathan Edwards, *The Works*, 2 vols., rev. Edward Hickman, with essay by Henry Rogers, memoir by Sereno E. Dwight (London: Ball, Arnold, and Co., 1840), vol. 2, 182. In his sermon on "Self-examination respecting the families to which we belong," Jonathan Edwards warns against neglecting special relations: "There are many persons who appear well among their neighbours, and seem to be of an honest, civil behaviour in their dealings and conversation abroad; yet if you follow them to their own houses and to the families to which they belong, there you will find them very perverse in their ways; there they live in ways which are very displeasing to the pure all-searching eyes of God."

45. Albert Schweitzer, *Out of My Life and Thought: An Autobiography*, trans. C. T. Campion, postscript by Everett Skillings (New York: Henry Holt and Co., 1949), 91.

his providence, as it were, leads us to it. But I say: we ought to embrace the whole human race without exception in a single feeling of love; here there is no distinction between barbarian and Greek, worthy and unworthy, friend and enemy, since all should be contemplated in God, not in themselves.[46]

Respect for God's providence and creational limits creates a humble acknowledgment of one's finitude. Vocation encourages Christians to live out their calling in and through the special relations in which they have been placed by God's design. Many times it is precisely this service that, as Luther saw, redounds to the welfare of the larger society. Luther also insists that any surplus a Christian may have — of money, talents, energies — once they have fulfilled their obligations to their dependents, should be generously given to distant neighbors. For finally God's kingdom reaches to the ends of the earth, and from God, through God, and to God are all things (Rom. 11:36).

Callings: A Cover for Injustice?

PRINCE [HENRY]: "I see a good amendment of life in thee; from praying to purse-taking."
FALSTAFF: "Why, Hal, 'tis my vocation, Hal; 'tis no sin for a man to labour in his vocation." (Shakespeare, *Henry IV*)[47]

Vocation is easily abused to support injustice. Some Christians in the United States felt the nation had a divine "calling" to fight Soviet communism through military means, and so supported American military involvement in Vietnam, Central America, and elsewhere. Founders of nations and empires appeal to "destiny" and "fate," concepts closely related to vocation, to justify their acts of murder, theft, and expansion. Many American Christians have an eschatology in which Israel has a divine right to establish a nation, to the point of utter disregard for the human rights of Palestinians. Some Christians feel

---

46. Calvin, *Institutes of the Christian Religion,* ed. John T. McNeill, trans. Ford Lewis Battles (Philadelphia: Westminster, 1960), 2.8.55.

47. Henry IV, Part I, Act I, Scene ii, ll. 114-117, as cited by Dorothee Emmet, *Function, Purpose, and Powers* 2d ed, fwd. Victor Turner (London: Macmillan 1972), 253.

called by God to bomb abortion clinics, violating the rights of doctors and medical staff. The criteria for right use of vocation stated above imply that in these cases the language of vocation is being abused. When vocation is used in such cases, it is really a self-serving justification for the will to power, to follow one's own inclinations and urges.

Calvin criticized the Libertines as "wretches" who "overturn" the apostle Paul's injunction to continue in their vocation (1 Cor. 7:17-24) in order to allow each person to "follow the inclination of his own nature and to work and live according to what advances his profit or pleases his heart":

> And not only under this guise do they approve of all these vocations which are repugnant to the truth of Scripture, but also of those which pagans condemn by their natural reason. Let a pimp, they say, do his job! Let a thief rob boldly! For it is right for everyone to pursue his calling. If anyone replies to the contrary how villainous these matters are, and that nature itself teaches us to regard them with horror, they respond that it is enough for everyone "to remain in his calling."[48]

In the seventeenth century, Gerrard Winstanley also condemned similar misuses of vocation, and eventually turned away from the notion of calling itself. He writes,

> Surely this power [of laws] is the burden of the creation . . . for though it pretend justice, yet the judges and law officers buy and sell justice for money, and wipes their mouths like Solomon's whore and says "It is my calling," and are never troubled at it.[49]

Unlike Winstanley, who rejects vocation altogether, Calvin retains it and eventually turns it against the aims of the Libertines, restoring it to its proper use. If an occupation or practice does not conform to the Bible or natural law, it is not one's calling. In such cases, the language of calling is a hypocritical cover for injustice and corruption.

But not all cases of injustice are this clear. The doctrine of vocation

---

48. Calvin, *Treatises*, 277.

49. Winstanley, "A New Year's Gift Sent to the Parliament and Army," January 1650, cited by Paul Marshall, *A Kind of Life Imposed on Man: Vocation and Social Order from Tyndale to Locke* (Toronto: University of Toronto Press, 1996), 80. According to Marshall, Winstanley by this time had "acquired a jaundiced view of callings."

can be easily abused to promote injustice in public and private spheres. It can encourage inaction in the face of injustice, and actions that harm neighbors. There are three aspects of the doctrine of vocation that are especially prone to misuse in perpetuating injustice: its acknowledgment of corruption within callings, its view of relations among social spheres, and its affirmation of a hierarchical order.

Acknowledgment of Corruption

Because Protestant vocation calls for participation in this fallen world in the hope of the world's redemption, realistically acknowledging ambiguity, it can easily be used to promote too much tolerance of and participation in injustice. From its inception, Protestant vocation affirms a sober realism about the corruption of the world into which Christians are called to serve. Only in the world to come will there be freedom from corruption; until then, every institution and vocation bears the marks of sin as well as of the good creation. Against the Libertine claim that there is no evil in the worldly estates, Calvin says,

> We know today that the world is so depraved that in all estates, even in those that are legitimate, there are so many bad incidents that it is a pity. . . . For example, the nobility is full of vanity, of excessive pomp, of pride, of licentiousness and insolence, of blasphemy, and of ambition. Justice is full of favors, of avarice, of tricks, and even from time to time of fleecing people. Merchandising is full of lies, of crooked deals, of perjury, of deceptions, and of rapine and cruelty. In brief, there is no vocation in which a great deal of abuse is not committed.[50]

Calvin explicitly condemns the Libertines for using the language of vocation to justify participation in these sinful practices. But he also affirms Christians are called into these estates in order to bend them to serve the common good.

More recently, Emil Brunner too has recognized the fallen character of life in this world:

50. Calvin, *Treatises*, 278.

All the orders . . . are, in their historical form also revelations of sinfulness and godlessness. . . . It is, of course, true that they are indications of the will of God for community, but they are at the same time instruments of an evil, violent, collective egoism, instruments of tyranny, by means of which the collective body holds the individual in bondage, and degrades him to be the mere instrument of egoistic collective ends. Precisely on account of their obvious necessity and utility they are at all times in danger of becoming idols by being transformed into absolutes.[51]

Brunner warns against "a certain kind of Lutheranism" that holds "the disastrous dogma that various 'orders' are not subject to the command of Jesus Christ, but only to the rule of reason."[52] Brunner agrees that the "characteristic legality" of the orders "can only be understood by means of reason." But, he says, "it is totally false to draw the conclusion that in the sphere of the 'orders' Christ 'has nothing to say.' Just as the Christian can never forget whose subject he is, so also he can never forget that obedience to this King means love, and he has no right to close his eyes or shut his heart to anything by means of which love is injured by the 'orders.'"[53]

This acknowledgment of ambiguity in a world created good but fallen into sin, and of a kingdom "already but not yet," can easily be misused to justify slothful neglect of possibilities for transformation or arrogant assertion of the will to power. In its proper use vocation calls for "faithful participation" in society, rather than withdrawal, and discernment of good from evil, obedience from disobedience, within this fallen world. To the extent that the world is fallen, vocation generates a spirit of continual reform of all of life's institutional forms, so that they more fully conform to justice, love, and shalom.

This perspective rules out *triumphalism*, which sees the present order — or a given part of it (e.g., nuclear family, church, volunteer group) — as the full embodiment of God's will. Our "places of responsibility" contain evil as well as good, and as long as we await the Return of Christ it shall always be so. This perspective also rules out *cynicism*,

51. Emil Brunner, *The Divine Imperative*, trans. Olive Wyon (Philadelphia: Westminster, 1937), 216-17.
52. Brunner, *The Divine Imperative*, 217.
53. Brunner, *The Divine Imperative*, 218.

which sees the present order as utterly corrupt and incapable of re-demption. Our stations express something of God's good creation, and it is the genius of providence as well as redemption to wrestle good from the jaws of evil. It also rules out *moral paralysis,* which sees the am-biguity as so complex and irresolvable that one should do nothing, or perhaps anything. For the most part, the moral ambiguity characteris-tic of callings is not gray, but a spiral of black and white. Inaction is in-appropriate to this kind of ambiguity. Some institutional patterns are more corrupt and corrupting than others are. A given institution can become more fully conformed to God's purposes than it currently is. An occupation may be found, or reshaped, to provide more effective means of service.

There are exceptions to this stance of discernment amid ambiguity. Some institutions and practices become so corrupt that the proper Christian response is to criticize, condemn, and forsake. In political life, these are times of *status confessionis,* situations in which politics be-comes so corrupt that to participate, compromise, or fail to challenge, is to contribute to evil. These are situations where the heart of the gos-pel and the very life of the Church are at stake. Two recent examples of such situations are the racist politics of the Nazis before and during World War II, and of the South African government under Apartheid.[54]

54. For a superb discussion of the meaning of *status confessionis* with special refer-ence to the situations in Germany and South Africa, see Dirk J. Smit, "What Does *Status Confessionis* Mean?" in *A Moment of Truth: The Confession of the Dutch Reformed Mission Church 1982,* ed. G. D. Cloete and D. J. Smit (Grand Rapids: Eerdmans, 1984). Smit says, "There comes an hour in which general truths and timeless principles, all neatly bal-anced with a 'yes' and a 'but,' in their very balance fail to understand the demand of the hour; they then become false doctrine, an escape from the urgent need for prophecy" (p. 18). Also, "the expression *status confessionis* means that a Christian, a group of Chris-tians, a church, or a group of churches are of the opinion that a situation has developed, a moment of truth has dawned, in which nothing less than the gospel itself, their most fundamental confession concerning the Christian gospel itself, is at stake, so that they feel compelled to witness and act over against this threat" (p. 16). And again, "*In status confessionis nihil est adiaphoron.* Precisely the abnormal situation itself causes viewpoints and arrangements which are adiaphora or neutral matters under normal circumstances to lose the innocence and neutrality" (p. 16). Here I take it Smit does not mean that be-fore the 1980s Apartheid rightly was a matter of "adiaphora," but rather that it was not yet clear how the church should act in light of Apartheid until that time. Later in the es-say (p. 18), Smit draws an analogy with family life, saying that "normally" the fifth com-mandment means parents should be free to determine how to discipline their children

Though the language of *status confessionis* has largely been applied to political life, it can also be fruitfully used to refer to other social spheres. In normal circumstances, Christian freedom rules Christian decisions in the concrete life of families, businesses, the arts, and schools. But these too can, in some circumstances, be so overtaken by the forces of evil that Christians must take a stand against them, or at least against certain practices and institutions within them.

Though there are these important exceptions, most Christian existence in this fallen world must, in the words of the apostle Paul, "discern what is the will of God — what is good, acceptable, and perfect" (Rom. 12:2). As individuals and communities, Christians must discern God's will and callings anew in relation to changes in their situations, their places in the life cycle, and the needs and opportunities of the communities in which they live. The general stance, accordingly, is one of attentive discernment to the perils and possibilities for good in all callings.[55]

Relations among Social Spheres

Injustice is not only caused by improper discernment of ambiguity and corruption; it can also be promoted by distorting the relations among social spheres. The relations among social spheres can be distorted in two ways: (1) isolating one sphere from another to insulate it from outside interference and critique, and (2) collapsing two or more spheres together to usurp another sphere's God-given autonomy. The Puritan

---

(i.e., *adiaphora*), but when abusive parents appeal to the fifth commandment to perpetuate their abuse, the matter is no longer "indifferent" or a matter of freedom; it become a kind of *status confessionis* in which the parents must be stopped. He quotes as follows: "'Separate houses of worship and structures of administration may be neutral in themselves,' says Buthelezi, 'but when racism sets up its idolatrous shrines in them they lose their neutrality, they become confessional symbols of a counter-church within the church of Christ'" (p. 20).

55. Although the stance I am recommending is sometimes associated with the wisdom traditions of the Bible and the Church, in distinction from prophetic traditions, I want to emphasize that the need to resist evil once discerned is no less courageous and determined in the sage than in the prophet. There is thus a prophetic element in the discernment needed for life in vocation. See James M. Gustafson, *Varieties of Moral Discourse: Prophetic, Narrative, Ethical, and Policy,* 1988 Stob Lectures, Calvin College and Seminary.

directive to "remain within one's calling," originally used to deter irresponsible restlessness and meddling in others' affairs, can be used to insulate victims of injustice in one sphere from help they might otherwise receive from another. When the "public-private" split, for example, is twisted so that pastors, physicians, police officers, or judges who know of serious domestic abuse fail to intervene out of respect for the "private" sphere of the home, the separation of spheres reinforces injustice.[56] Or, to take another example, when pro-Apartheid Calvinists used Abraham Kuyper's doctrine of "sphere sovereignty" to immunize the state from critique by South African churches, the separation of sphere was abused to promote the injustice of Apartheid. In God's creative providence, the spheres of social life are interdependent, yet distinct. At times one will need the other to avoid injustice and promote the common good.

On the other hand, one sphere can usurp the rightful functions of another. The clearest example of this is state totalitarianism. In the name of the need to maintain order and avoid chaos, the state controls the economy, church, family, media, and education, and so seeks to usurp not only the legitimate autonomy of social spheres but also God, who alone rules all social spheres through the mysteries of providence. It is also possible for the institutional church to interfere with, and even dominate, other social spheres. Perhaps today the greatest danger is the ever-growing power of corporations, whose power seems to know no regional or social bounds.

The difficulty of proper relations among spheres is compounded by the fact that at times temporary interventions are needed of one sphere into another, to avoid injustice or supply the conditions necessary for the common good. The state, for example, ought not usurp the role of business as it seeks to create conditions conducive to a productive economy. But if an important corporation, crucial to the common good, is in grave danger of collapse, the state might rightly decide to intervene to give assistance. Or, if working conditions violate basic human rights, state authorities rightly intervene to curb the powerful tendencies of capitalism to exploit workers. These temporary interventions must never become the norm, but rather should be seen as exceptions to the norm.

56. See Mary Stewart Van Leeuwen et al., *After Eden: Facing the Challenge of Gender Reconciliation* (Grand Rapids: Eerdmans, 1993), 389-415.

If the doctrine of vocation is to be rightly used, then it is crucial to discern the complex and dynamic nature of the interdependencies among social spheres. Though the directive "abide in your calling" sounds conservative, it can become reformist, or even revolutionary, when it is aimed at a totalitarian state. Mid-sixteenth century English preacher Robert Crowley used this directive to castigate "those who sought to increase their estates, enlarge, raise rents, buy more land, or in any way add to, rather than help overcome, the burdens of the poor."[57] He told them instead to "abide in your own calling."

The Roman Catholic notion of "subsidiarity" is helpful in providing a basic structure for how to relate social spheres. Pope John Paul II writes about the role of the state in providing economic welfare for its citizens:

> a community of a higher order should not interfere in the internal life of a community of a lower order, depriving the latter of its functions, but rather should support it in case of need and help to coordinate its activity with the activities of the rest of society, always with a view to the common good.[58]

This process of discernment is difficult in a complex and changing world, but it is also necessary for right use of vocation. Attentive consideration to the obligations and possibilities for justice in and through diverse callings, and mutual concern across callings, will ensure that diversity among spheres will not be abused so as to insulate victims from assistance or impose the will to power.

Affirmation of Hierarchical Order

As we saw in Chapter One, Calvin and Luther understood vocation within the context of a social hierarchy they believed to be grounded in God's creation and providence, and so expressive of the will of God. Superordinate persons (husbands, fathers, princes) are to rule subordinate persons (wives, children, subjects) with wisdom and love. Subordi-

---

57. Cited by Paul Marshall, *A Kind of Life,* 33.

58. Pope John Paul II, *Centesimus Annus,* sec. 48. The pope does allow for a "substitute" function of the state or community of a "higher order."

nate persons are to obey the will of superiors, even when harsh or unreasonable. Only when a superior requires subordinates to violate the will of God should they disobey authority. In their disobedience to authority, Christians are not to rebel but to be subordinate, enduring the sufferings caused by their refusals to obey superiors even as Christ endured the cross. Luther and Calvin thus confer *theological legitimacy* upon the authority of persons occupying positions of power within the social order. Parents, princes, employers, teachers, pastors, and judges represent in their offices not themselves, but God. Though relativized by the supreme authority of the Word of God, this structuring of obligations and freedoms in terms of one's place amid varied authorities is deeply bound up with the early reformers' idea of calling.

Many Reformed Christians, notably those in England, the United States, and the Netherlands, have challenged this hierarchical pattern. The challenge was generally restricted to political powers in developing the right to revolution. Hierarchical relations in the family and the workplace tended to follow the pattern traced above. This hierarchical structure leads easily to abuse of the doctrine of vocation, as many Christian feminists have argued.

Challenges to Hierarchy

Feminist critiques begin from painful realities of the subordination, oppression, and abuse of women.[59] The home is often a more dangerous place for women than crime-plagued slums of large cities. At Luther Northwestern Seminary's bookstore some time ago I saw a sign that read, "Wife battery, child abuse, and incest have been moved to the 'Marriage and Family' section of the bookstore." The lexicography of the bookstore attendants has more than a theoretical foundation. The realities, even within the economically prosperous United States, are grim.

For children ages six to twelve, between one in three and one in five girls, and one in eleven boys, are victims of child sexual abuse. Forty-

---

59. For an analysis of some of these issues with a view to forming a Reformed feminist theology, see Mary Stewart Van Leeuwen, *Gender and Grace: Love, Work and Parenting in a Changing World* (Downers Grove, Ill.: InterVarsity Press, 1990); Douglas J. Schuurman, "Humanity in Reformed and Feminist Perspectives: Collision or Correlation?" *Calvin Theological Journal* 27/1 (April 1992); and Van Leeuwen et al., *After Eden*, 117-83.

four percent of the women surveyed report either sexual assault, rape, or violent rape.[60] There is no statistical difference for children living in "Christian" homes.[61] Increasingly feminists are becoming more concerned about children and maternal/paternal functions. After divorce, on average, the living standard for ex-wives drops by thirty percent while that of ex-husbands improves by eight percent; two-thirds of African American babies were born to single mothers; one-fourth of children under age 18 have little or no contact with their fathers; forty-one percent of divorced men walk away from their families without a child support agreement.[62] Powers that cause and perpetuate dire struggles reflected in these statistics are organized in an intricate and complex pattern of attitudes, practices, and systems that are at least in some small part supported by theological justifications for the subordination of women.

Beverly W. Harrison claims that the Reformation failed to improve the condition of women:

> The truth is that nothing in the Reformation can be read as a genuine reversal of this negative antisexual, antifemale, antisensuality heritage. . . . Nor did the Reformation strengthen women's social role in society. The Reformers . . . closed down women's religious houses, destroying the one clear institutional base of women's culture in the late Middle Ages. The Reformers and their followers did nothing to change women's role in the church. . . .[63]

60. Joy M. K. Bussert, *Battered Women: From a Theology of Suffering to an Ethic of Empowerment* (Division for Mission in North America, Lutheran Church in America, 1986), 24-25.

61. Stewart Van Leeuwen, *Gender and Grace,* 119.

62. These and many other disturbing statistics are from economist Sylvia Ann Hewlett's book, *When the Bough Breaks: The Cost of Neglecting Our Children* (New York: Basic Books, 1991); see also Susan Moller Okin, *Justice, Gender, and the Family* (New York: Basic Books, 1989), and Mary Stewart Van Leeuwen, "Family Justice and Societal Nurturance: Reintegrating Public and Private Domains" in *After Eden,* 416-51.

63. Harrison, "Human Sexuality and Mutuality," in *Christian Feminism: Visions of a New Humanity,* ed. Judith L. Weidman (San Francisco: Harper & Row, 1984), 144-45. For a different assessment, see Steven Ozment, *When Fathers Ruled: Family Life in Reformation Europe* (Cambridge: Harvard University Press, 1983). Ozment argues that the "domestic legislation of the Reformation encouraged both spouses to be more sensitive to the other's personal needs and vocational responsibilities, thereby enhancing the status of both men and women" (p. 99). Ozment also points out that the Reformers' closing

Women's divinely ordained "place" was bearing and raising children, being subordinate to their husbands, and general administration of the household. Submission was not mutual, but one-sided so that weaker parties were advised to tolerate even severe physical and sexual abuse in the name of a vocational understanding of marriage and of social authority.[64] In a letter to an abused woman, Calvin expresses sympathy for "poor women who are evilly and roughly treated by their husbands, because of the cruel tyranny and captivity which is their lot." But he tells wives not to leave their husbands

> except by force of necessity; and we do not understand this force to be operative when a husband behaves roughly and uses threats to his wife, nor even when he beats her, but when there is imminent peril to her life, whether from persecution or some other source. . . . We exhort her . . . to bear with patience the cross which God has seen fit to place upon her; and meanwhile not to deviate from the duty which she has before God to please her husband. . . .[65]

Later, in the eighteenth and nineteenth centuries, when the democratizing impulses of the Reformation and Enlightenment were challenging and replacing the divine right of kings, economic, legal, and political powers combined to ensure women's subordinated status. Until the twentieth century, the common law "rule of thumb" principle governed legal decisions relating to wife abuse in the United States and England. This rule stipulated that a man had the right to "'whip

---

down of "religious houses" was often motivated by a desire to liberate women who had been assigned there by fathers who either would not or could not pay the dowry required for marriage.

64. For example, one case before the Consistory at Geneva in the seventeenth century involved spouse-beating where a woman, Martinaz, was beaten so severely by her husband, lumberjack Claude Soutiez, that one of her eyes was "put out." The council's penalty: They called him to promise not to "irritate" *(corroser)* his wife and ordered him to appear before the Small Council (who apparently did nothing of any consequence to him); they enjoined Martinaz to obey and live peacefully with her husband, and required her also to promise not to irritate her husband. (From a letter dated April 3, 1990, from Jeff Watt, History Department, University of Mississippi, to Dr. Richard Gamble, Director, Meeter Center for Calvin Studies).

65. Cited in Jane Dempsey Douglass, "Women and the Continental Reformation," in *Religion and Sexism: Images of Women in the Jewish and Christian Traditions,* ed. Rosemary Radford Ruether (New York: Simon & Schuster, 1974), 300-301.

his wife provided that he use a switch no thicker than his thumb.'"[66] Until the late nineteenth century, battered wives were prevented from obtaining court protection from abuse by the principle of "coverture," which saw husband and wife as legally one person. In many European countries, until recent times, women could not inherit property and other wealth from their parents. In countries where they could inherit property, they often lost their right to this property when they married, for then it became legally their husband's property. A wife who divorced or left her husband often was forced to live in poverty.

For many feminists, vocation's complicity in the sexism of culture and society is not an accidental abuse of an otherwise valid doctrine. They allege that the *basic understanding* of God, humanity, and world beneath it is flawed so that it inevitably contributes to the problem. From Calvin's emphasis upon Christ as "Lord of Lords" whose call is heard in the demand of a potentate, to the Puritan image of God as a general whose call is a "summons" to battle, to the Neo-Orthodox concept of God as "Wholly Other" whose call breaks into life from without to demand spontaneous, unquestioning obedience — mainline Protestant traditions seem extraordinarily preoccupied with power and conflict.

The central issues of life are divided into two poles: God and world, humanity and nature, men and women, soul and body, reason and emotion, culture and nature, sacred and secular, public and private.[67] The poles of these *binary* realms are then often seen to be *conflictual:* The first in each pair is active and the second is passive. Emotions impair reason, nature threatens humanity, and so forth. The conflict is resolved *hierarchically,* so that the first term in each pair rules the second. God rules the world, humans rule nature, men rule women, and so on. Beverly Harrison claims that "Almost all of the theological ethics formulated in Protestant Christianity from 1920 until the present bears the stigma of this envisagement of God as all-controlling agent. The watchword for the Christian life and faith in this . . . ethic remains 'obedience' — the giving over of self-control to another."[68] Dorothee Soelle argues that Christians should reject the "old terminology, in the mode

---

66. Bussert, *Battered Women,* 19.

67. See Dorothee Soelle, *To Work and to Love,* 13-14, 23-25, 77. See also R. R. Ruether, *Sexism and God-Talk: Toward a Feminist Theology* (Boston: Beacon Press, 1983), 72-82.

68. Beverly W. Harrison, *Making the Connections: Essays in Feminist Social Ethics,* ed. Carol S. Robb (Boston: Beacon Press, 1985), 36.

of 'Praise the Lord, the Almighty'" because it hinders moral agency. She also rejects the doctrine of creation *ex nihilo* because it suggests a God who is "wholly other," essentially independent of the world.[69]

This hierarchical pattern has also been abused to justify and perpetuate slavery. Allen Boesak tells a story that reveals the dangers of this hierarchical view of society. A Dutch pastor, M. C. Vos, who migrated to South Africa in the late eighteenth century, explained how he tried to persuade farmers to allow him to instruct his slaves in the gospel:

> "It is natural that your slaves will not become worse but, rather, better through education. . . . Put yourself in the place of one of them for a few minutes and think in the following way: I am a poor slave, but I was not born in this status. I was taken from my dear parents, my loving wife or husband, from my children, my brothers and sisters, by human thieves who kidnapped me and took me away from my own country. . . . Here I was sold as an animal. Now I am a slave. I must do everything which is commanded me even to the point of doing very undesirable work. . . ."
>
> "Suppose for a few minutes," the pastor continued . . . , "that this was the situation in which *you* found yourself. Tell me . . . would you have the desire to do your work? Would you not rather frequently be despondent, sorrowful, obstinate, and disobedient?"
>
> The man was moved. . . .
>
> "Well," he continued, "if you permit them to remain stupid and ignorant, upon occasion thoughts of this type will arise and, at times, come to expression in terribly extreme actions. If they are instructed correctly . . . that God rules all things; that nothing happens apart from his rule; that God is a God of order; that in the same way in which they must serve their master and mistress, their master and mistress must serve those who are in positions of authority over them; that those who do not serve obediently are punished. . . . You can make clear to them that which seems evil to us frequently turns out to our advantage. . . . When they begin to understand this a bit, the despondent and grieving thoughts will change. Then they will begin to think: if that is the way things are, then I shall be content with my lot and I shall attempt to do my work obediently and joyfully."
>
> The farmer cried out, "Why weren't we told these things before?

69. Soelle, *To Work and to Love,* 37-53.

. . . From now on I shall never dissuade anyone from educating his slaves. I, rather, shall persuade everyone to educate their slaves."[70]

Here the vision of society as ordered by God, constituted hierarchically, and offering a place to be provided by God's will — themes central to Protestant vocation in its earliest forms — serves the interests of the oppressor and harms the weak.

Responses to Challenges

Feminists and liberation theologians are right to challenge those who associate God and God's will with the more powerful person and position in asymmetric social relations. It is dangerous, both for those who hold social power and for those subject to it, to equate divine agency with official use of social power, whether in the home, workplace, or state. Though God's callings do come through those in authority, they come also and perhaps more clearly through weakness and need. Perceiving God's call in the need of the neighbor must be reemphasized in light of feminist and other liberationist perspectives.

Feminists who criticize the hierarchical nature of Protestantism, and Christianity, often fail to recognize the way vocation resists the "dualisms" that help sustain sexism. The very heart of vocation resists a "sacred/secular" dualism by infusing mundane life with religious meaning. The "public/private" split, and attendant vacillation between glorifying and demonizing women and the domestic realm, is also undercut by vocation's recognition that all of life is created good but fallen, that no part is intrinsically more valuable than the other. Though dualistic elements mark the thought of Luther and Calvin, their celebration of creation resists "mind/body" dualism and its denigration of the body and manual labor. By locating the fundamental religious issues in the heart, and by seeing thought, will, and emotions as flowing from there, a simple "reason/emotion" dualism is also undercut in principle. Because of these themes and others, the theological vision implied and presumed by Protestant vocation is finally not dualistic. Since the Sovereign Lord of the Universe is the fount of all

---

70. Allan Boesak, *Black and Reformed: Apartheid, Liberation and the Calvinist Tradition,* ed. Leonard Sweetman (Maryknoll, N.Y.: Orbis, 1984), 13-15.

good, champion of the poor and friend of the weak, singing praise to the "Almighty" gives rise to resistance to injustice and oppression — including sexist oppression — or it is idolatry.[71]

Luther's emphasis upon the incarnational theme is to the point. He wanted parents to see the infant Jesus in their babies' need for food, clothing, and care. It is finally the need of the neighbor that justifies use of coercive measures to protect innocent life from those who would destroy it. Calvin's idea of the "image of God" in the neighbor, and of nature as a "mirror" of God, reflect similar incarnational themes. Lewis Smedes notes that marital fidelity is a response to the vocation to make "the legal marriage a real marriage":

> The call does not come as a voice in the night; the call comes out of the matrix of every day's common demands and every day's potential for creating a better relationship out of an injured and gasping one. Where we hear the calling is in the breakdowns every marriage suffers. The call does not come merely as a law laid down in the Bible, but as a challenge hidden in the ingredients of marriage itself; it comes whenever failures of communication occur, whenever one partner is left weeping for understanding, or whenever the partnership groans under the load of guilt. Then it comes with a summons: heal the wounds and make the marriage real again.[72]

Or, as Frederick Buechner put it, "The place God calls you to is the place where your deep gladness and the world's deep hunger meet."[73]

Protestantism has neglected this important theme in its preoccupation with order, law, and authority. The emphasis must be corrected. God's call is often not heard in the form of a "summons" of a divine commander, or of a "dictate" of a demanding ruler. It is often heard as a still small voice beckoning us to love God and neighbor. God's will is that in all our callings we serve the least of these, for in serving them we serve Christ.[74] More so than Luther and Calvin, Christians today must

71. See Richard J. Mouw, *The God Who Commands* (Notre Dame: University of Notre Dame Press, 1990), 161-69, for an argument supporting the claim that an egalitarian intra-human relation depends upon a hierarchical divine-human relation.

72. Lewis Smedes, *Sex for Christians* (Grand Rapids: Eerdmans, 1976), 177-78.

73. Cited in Robert Benne, *Ordinary Saints: An Introduction to the Christian Life* (Minneapolis: Fortress Press, 1988), 106.

74. The difficulty here is in combining God's sovereign transcendence with God's

emphasize the need for continual transformation of societal institutions in light of God's will. We must work for justice, mutuality, and shalom in all our institutional life. In this respect, Luther and Calvin provide only a beginning.

Today we must lift up aspects of the doctrine of vocation that criticize hierarchies — whether based on gender, race, or class — and which point to mutuality between men and women, and among all people. At least three aspects merit retrieval from the writings of Luther and Calvin. The first is the ground vocation establishes for resisting and reforming authority. Resistance implies that institutions and orders, and officials working in them, though expressive of God the Creator, also express human corruption.[75] They can and must be changed, reformed, brought in line with God's creative and redemptive purposes.

Luther did not "submit" to papal authority or quietly endure the penalties imposed by the pope. He wrote and spoke in ways nothing short of revolutionary, and in ways that advanced far-reaching political and social change. When criticizing parents for forbidding their children to marry, Luther limited parental authority and advised children to disobey parents. The limits of parental authority are (a) it must accord with God's word and command, and (b) it must conform to the purpose of parental power; namely the child's nurturance and salvation. Since marriage is a divine ordinance, willed by God and structured into the very fabric of creation, it is contrary to God's will to forbid marriage. Parents contradicting these bounds "are to be regarded as if they were not parents at all, or were dead; their child is free to become engaged and to marry whomsoever he fancies."[76] Luther also limits parental authority by calling upon other authorities:

immanence. Richard Mouw in *The God Who Commands* tries to "make room" for feminist immanental themes within a basically hierarchical view of the God-human relation. He also stresses the Reformed teaching that the Spirit internalizes God's law, so that Christian obedience is spontaneous and joyful rather than grudging submission to the arbitrary will of a potentate. Calvin distinguished "servile" obedience — that given by a slave to a master — from "filial" obedience — that given by a loyal son to a loving father — and insisted that Christian obedience is the latter and not the former.

75. See Nicholas Wolterstorff, *Until Justice and Peace Embrace*, 16.

76. "That Parents Should Neither Compel Nor Hinder The Marriage of Their Children, and That Children Should Not Become Engaged Without Their Parents' Consent" in *Luther's Works*, 45:390. Earlier in this treatise, Luther advises children to submit obediently to parents who force them to marry a specific person, even against the child's

It is my advice, then, that if the father or father's deputy refuses to give a child in marriage, and if good friends, the pastor, or the authorities recognize that the marriage is honorable and advantageous for the child and that the child's parents or their deputies are seeking their own advantage or caprice, then the authorities shall adopt the child in the father's stead, as they do with abandoned children and orphans, and compel the father. And if he refuses to comply, they shall seize him by the neck and throw him into jail, and thus deprive him of all paternal power and, in addition, punish him as a public enemy, not only an enemy of his child and of God, but as an enemy of the discipline and honor of all. . . .[77]

This advice also undermines a "public-private" ideology that isolates victims of domestic abuse from communal and political help.

Calvin notes that we are to obey our parents only "in the Lord" and that therefore "the submission paid to them ought to be a step toward honoring that highest Father. Hence, if they spur us to transgress the law, we have a perfect right to regard them not as parents, but as strangers who are trying to lead us away from obedience to our true Father. So should we act toward princes, lords, and every kind of superior."[78] In politics the obedience subjects owe rulers is "never to lead us away from obedience to him, to whose will the desires of all kings ought to be subject. . . . And how absurd it would be that in satisfying men you should incur the displeasure of him for whose sake you obey men themselves!"[79] As Luther appeals to members of the community to prevent a tyrannical parent from imposing wicked demands upon a child, so too Calvin advises the "lesser magistrates" to resist a tyranni-

---

wishes, though Luther says it is wrong for parents to force such a choice. Luther directs children to Matthew 5 and the duty not to resist evil, to "let your cloak go with your coat, and turn the other cheek also. From this it would follow that a child should and must obey, and accept the injustice which such a tyrannical and unpaternal father forces upon him" (p. 388). It appears, then, that for Luther authorities ought not be disobeyed for any and all immoral demands, but only for those demands that force the subordinate party to disobey a clear command or ordinance of God.

77. "On Marriage Matters," *Luther's Works*, vol. 46: *The Christian in Society III*, ed. R. C. Shulz and H. T. Lehmann (Philadelphia: Fortress, 1967), 308-9.

78. Calvin, *Institutes*, 2.8.38.

79. Calvin, *Institutes*, 4.20.32.

cal king based on the divine ordinance giving them authority and the duty to serve those in their care.[80]

As the transformationists among the later reformers appealed to vocation to redefine political power relations and to resist and eventually reform them,[81] so too vocation, properly interpreted, can challenge the patriarchal status quo.[82] Luther challenged the totalitarian pretensions of the medieval church by appealing to vocation and creation ordinances; Puritans challenged the totalitarian impulses of the state by limiting its sphere of operations.[83] If it interfered with the church or family life, the state was stepping outside its legitimate vocation. When the state did overstep its calling, one's calling as parent or church member became the basis for resisting its demands.

There are, then, solid grounds for disobedience and even resistance to authority. What is unclear, especially in the writings of Luther and Calvin, is (a) how the mutuality brought about by baptism and expressed in the priesthood of all believers relates to the inequality implied by a subordinationist and hierarchical social structure, (b) how the basis of resistance relates to directives to obey or submit even to abusive authorities, and (c) how to determine when such demands do require or permit resistance rather than submission to authority.

A second aspect of Protestant vocation that can lead to criticism of hierarchy, especially its patriarchal forms, is its positive vision of domestic roles and general revaluation of mundane roles and relations. This positive vision can generate alternatives to sexist stereotypes and devaluation of women, children, and the home. Though Calvin and Luther did not work out the implications of the priesthood of all believers for restructuring gender relations, they established a trajectory. The fundamental calling of all Christians to be united in Christ's death and resurrection, to participate in God's mission and in the church, and to use

---

80. Calvin, *Institutes*, 4.20.31.

81. For a helpful discussion of "Imperialist" and a liberative "transformationist" Calvinism see John deGruchy, *Liberating Reformed Theology*.

82. See Van Leeuwen et al., *After Eden*, 1-18, 117-83.

83. See Michael Walzer, *The Revolution of the Saints: A Study in the Origins of Radical Politics* (Cambridge: Harvard University Press, 1965), and Gary S. De Krey, "Rethinking the Restoration: Dissenting Cases For Conscience, 1667-72," *The Historical Journal* 38, no. 1 (1995): 53-83. De Krey is especially concerned with the role of conscience as a basis for religious freedom and pluralism in England.

gifts to serve the neighbor — this call creates equality and mutuality between women and men. Christ no more defined men by their "careers" than he defined women by their "families"; rather he judged women and men based on whether they heard and believed his word. A wife whose husband refuses to recognize her calling to develop professionally would be on solid Protestant ground were she to appeal to her calling as a basis to resist, and hopefully to change, her husband's desires. By considering domestic roles vocations, the early reformers elevated the status of the activities of women — which, if not ecclesial, were almost exclusively domestic.[84] The effect of this elevated spiritual status is to incline asymmetric relations between husband and wife toward mutuality and symmetry.[85] Luther does not glorify the tedium and difficulty of domestic work; he infuses it with a religious and social value that dignifies it, thereby avoiding fitful vacillation between debasing and glorifying women and domestic life. Spiritual equality expressed in Protestant views of faith and the priesthood of all believers must permeate and transform gender relations in all significant social contexts.

A third aspect of Protestant vocation with much potential for transforming hierarchical relations is opposition to subordinationism and affirmation of authority as service. This theme overlaps with the first two stated above. The doctrines of vocation and the priesthood of all believers work to transform asymmetric relations. The social expression of equality and mutuality created by faith and baptism is loving service to the neighbor. Subordinationism is perpetual and influential discrepancies in social power based merely on race, class, or gender. Of course, Protestant vocation does recognize differences in power and authority within asymmetric relations: teachers have authority over students in matters relating to the discipline taught; parents have authority over children in matters parental; preachers over parishioners in pastoral affairs.

Vocation ought to transform asymmetric relations in at least four ways: (a) it should ground the authority of the more powerful party upon God's calling and gifts, not upon race, class, or gender; (b) it

---

84. We should keep in mind that the domestic sphere was much larger then than now. There was much less separation of "public" and "private" life, since most occupations (farming, artisans, etc.) had their "paid work" right in or near their own homes. Luther's wife, Katherine, even ran a brewery — with Luther's full approval.

85. On this point, see Ozment, *When Fathers Ruled*.

should require that the goal of authority be service to others, not being served; (c) it should demand that authorities respect the status of the one served as created and potentially redeemed by God; and (d) it should view the imbalance of power as temporary and dynamic, moving toward symmetry and mutuality. Parental authority, for example, is distorted when it falls into a stifling form of parenting that never lets children mature. Positively, authority is based on God's gift and calling to care for children, to serve them, and to bring the child to the status of equality with the parent. A teacher using authority to encourage students to depend too much or too little on the teacher likewise abuses authority. In a similar way all authority is tempered by the ideal of service to the neighbor and aims at symmetry.[86]

It is a pernicious evil when persons in positions of social power abuse that power to cause suffering, and then recommend that their victims turn to the cross as a remedy for their suffering. Unless a Christian is working to resist injustices and remove suffering, it is likewise a grave evil to tell victims, "Go to the cross and find solace there for all your sorrows." The cross is a source of solace, and carrying out one's calling amid one's vocations will bring suffering and self-sacrifice, even as Christ's calling led him to the cross. As Karl Barth says,

> We also think of the sacrifices which those of the so-called "higher" social classes would never think of applying to themselves but for many years demanded and expected as self-evident from the so-called "lower" classes (and this with more or less genuine moral zeal and often enough with the support of the Church). In these cases hypocrisy is obviously at work. And where those who resist these demands are driven to rebellion, and take measures to improve their position and attain equality, it is a two-fold hypocrisy to try to denounce this as revolt against a divine imposed renunciation. Where someone who is well fed himself tries to inflict hunger upon others, and makes out that it is their duty to suffer hunger, God takes the

---

86. The movement toward symmetry and equality is not always obvious or evident. The authority of a judge, for example, over a criminal about to be sentenced does not directly aim at making the sentenced criminal an equal with that judge. But, in aiming to lead the criminal to a respect for the law, which would in turn liberate the criminal from the punitive powers of the judge, it does indirectly aim at a kind of symmetry.

side of the hungry, and He and not they will be the first to see that they are satisfied.[87]

Considerations such as these should help ensure that the doctrine of vocation is not abused, but rather properly used so that life amid all one's ambiguous callings conforms to Christian love, and advances God's shalom. This requires humble honesty, a prayerful, listening spirit, and communal discussion. Only in this way can Christians heed Christ's call within all their vocations, and so bear witness to the good news of God's love for this fallen world in Jesus Christ.

87. Karl Barth, *Church Dogmatics*, 3/4, 346-47.

CHAPTER FIVE

Vocation, Decisions, and the Moral Life I

College students, when they see the topic of vocation on my course syllabus, immediately expect to find some guidance for their career choices. While it is understandable that vocational guidance is a central concern of college students, and of members of the working population who may be considering career moves, career choice was at best a peripheral concern in the early reformers' doctrine of vocation. With some exceptions they, and especially Luther, saw paid work and other significant relational settings as domains not freely chosen, but providentially assigned to each person. Sociologists refer to this earlier pattern as "ascriptivism," where significant social relations are not a matter of individual choice but are assigned based largely on class, parentage, and gender.[1] One does not so much choose one's callings as discover oneself within their network. Vocation is not mainly about guiding individual choice of spouse or paid work; it is about interpreting these, and other relational settings, in faith as divinely assigned places to serve God and neighbor.

A related modern assumption is that to have a calling is to experience self-fulfillment in that calling. A job is a way to get a paycheck, but a vocation is more than that; it is a realm for self-fulfillment. Central choices about marriage, paid work, and family are accordingly governed by their potential for optimal self-actualization. Luther and Cal-

---

1. Nicholas Wolterstorff, *Until Justice and Peace Embrace* (Grand Rapids: Eerdmans, 1983), 17.

vin, on the contrary, see callings as places for service and self-sacrifice. It is not fulfillment of the self but the glory of God and the welfare of the neighbor that ought to determine "vocational" choices, insofar as there is room for choice. In and through one's vocations one picks up one's cross, follows Christ, and participates in his self-sacrificial sufferings. Christians should not aim at self-fulfillment. The Bible has strong words on the subject: "For those who want to save their life will lose it, and those who lose their life for my sake will find it" (Luke 9:24). Before examining in greater detail how vocation should affect decisions and the moral life, we should examine further the relation of this classic notion of vocation to the modern emphasis upon expanded choice and self-fulfillment.

Vocation, Expanded Freedom, and Self-Fulfillment

Vocation and Expanded Choices

By far the dominant concern of Luther was how the idea of vocation should influence Christian interpretation of the roles and occupations they already occupied. Luther's words to those who lamented that they have no calling apply as well to those who are always seeking their callings:

> Are you a husband, and you think you have not enough to do in that sphere. . . . Again: Are you a son or daughter, and do you think you have not enough work with yourself, to continue chaste, pure, and temperate during your youth, obey your parents, and offend no one by word or deed? . . . See, as no one is without some commission and calling, so no one is without some kind of work. . . . [S]erve God and keep his commandments; then . . . all time will be too short, all places too cramped, all resources of help too weak.[2]

Luther assumed that both one's social locations and the obligations attending them are obvious. He had little concern for moral ambiguity or

2. Luther, *Church Postils,* Gospel for the Day of St. John the Evangelist, *Luther's Works,* vol. 22, as cited in Constance Gengenbach, "The Secularization of Vocation and the Worship of Work," *The Cresset* 51, no. 2 (December 1987): 8.

moral conflict; aside from pimping, thieving, or serving as a papal priest, all occupations glorify God and serve the neighbor. His main concern was the then-dominant value structure, reinforced by popular wisdom and the Roman Catholic Church, that demeaned marriage, family, and secular life while elevating celibacy and the "religious" life of priests, monks, and nuns. Luther insisted that all believers are priests, called to holy work in marriage, home, and society.

We need to recover the sense that our lives are in many ways "given" to us by forces beyond our control but ultimately in the loving hands of a provident God. We need also to be aware that the numerous and regular obligations that attend our varied routines and roles are expressions of what God wants us to do in our particular locations, always with a view to serving our neighbor and serving God through our neighbor. This is the heart of the Protestant idea of vocation. The secularized character of modern life may impede, but it need not prevent Christians from perceiving their social locations through the eyes of faith as callings.

To some extent, modern difficulties with vocation and decisions are due to the expanded freedom that is the hallmark of the modern era. Especially in the North American mythology, which holds that anyone can change his lot through discipline and hard work, the expansion and presumption of freedom are powerful. It is true that, for many, freedom has expanded. Parents no longer choose their children's spouses; spouses choose each other. Through education and training, a person can enter professions other than those of her parents. Women now are told they can "have it all," and more than a few do. They can marry and have children and they can develop a fulfilling career. No-fault divorce makes possible freedom from one's spouse and opportunity to find and marry another. Job mobility invites workers to choose whether or not to remain in a given profession, or in a given location in that profession. In an effort to help people facing a beleaguering array of choices, experts devise and administer career inventory tests to help people narrow the otherwise unlimited range of choices. Retirement and periods of financial independence provide opportunity for all manner of unpaid service activity and leisure activity. These features of modern American life pose new challenges for the doctrine of vocation and are only remotely of concern to Luther and Calvin.

Are, then, the views of Luther and Calvin relevant to these challenges? I believe they are. But initially we should consider two points about the modern increase of freedom. The first is that the kind of freedom described above applies mainly only to a select group of people: middle- to upper-class members of society. For the poor, life is more about survival than about self-actualization. In America, more black males of college age are in jail or prison than in college, and between one in four and one in five children of all races grow up below the poverty line.[3] A great many of them live in dangerous, drug-infested neighborhoods and can barely achieve literacy in under-funded public schools. Their fathers are often absent. How free are these children and their mothers? And when we examine the plight of the poor of other countries, the conditions we find are often even worse.

The second point to consider is a warning that the myth of modern freedom can conceal the fact that many crucial aspects of our lives do not depend upon our own choices, but are "given" to us in ways that limit our actual and potential choices. Some of them are obvious, but still not given the weight they merit. Not one of us has chosen our DNA structure, our parents, or the communities of our early nurture. Whether we were nurtured in a supportive, life-enriching context or an abusive, life-impoverishing one is determined by powers beyond our control. Other ways are less obvious. We internalize the values and priorities of our parents and surrounding communities in ways that are not often conscious, and these in turn shape our "free" decisions. Gender expectations, for example, both patriarchal and feminist, deeply influence the patterns of our choices. The vast majority of young women and men continue to believe that the most important characteristic in a prospective husband is success in a career, exerting strong pressures upon males to give career success top priority. Prospective wives are "free" to advance in a career or to spend more energy in domestic activity. Some use this freedom to actualize their potential in both home and workplace; others experience it as a burden too heavy to bear.

When I was teaching a class in Medical Ethics at Pritzker Medical School of the University of Chicago, I asked my class of a dozen or so students why they had chosen medicine as their profession. After several students identified having one or both parents in the medical pro-

---

3. See William C. Placher, "'You Were in Prison . . .'" in *The Christian Century,* September 26–October 3, 2001, 18.

fession as an important factor, I asked the class to raise their hands if they had at least one parent who was a medical doctor. Nine of the twelve had either one or both parents in the medical profession. Obviously the internalized example and influence of their parents and family shaped their "free" choices. At St. Olaf College, where I teach, a huge percentage of every entering class identifies "Pre-med" as their chosen program of concentration. The percentage is so great that one cannot help but wonder whether this is based on freedom or on a slavish dependence on prevailing values of American society, where wealth, science, technology, and medicine have high status. After taking a biology class or two, a great many Pre-med students discover the painful reality that they lack the aptitude in natural sciences that must be mastered to become medical doctors. They are forced to choose another concentration and professional direction.

My point is not that there has been no increase of freedom. There has. My point is that this increase has only been for some — a select few if looked at globally — and that even for them freedom often serves as a myth that masks the ways in which we are not free, but are being formed by powers beyond our control. Christian faith perceives these powers to be ultimately in the hands of a merciful, provident God. Perhaps we are not so far from Luther and Calvin as it first appears.

Luther and Calvin also qualified the ascriptivism of their day. They acknowledge God's freedom to call someone to a station in ways that run contrary to their society's expectation. Luther, for example, says,

> We ought to know that God is a wonderful lord. His trade is to take beggars and make them lords, just as He makes all things out of nothing. This trade of His no one will interfere with or hinder. He has the whole world sing of him, in Psalm 112, "Who is like the Lord, Who sitteth so high and beholdeth so deep? Who lifteth the small out of the dust and raiseth the poor out of the filth, that He may make them sit among the princes, even among the princes of His people." Look about you, at the courts of all the kings and princes, at the cities and the parishes; see whether this Psalm does not rule with many strong examples. There you will find jurists, doctors, counselors, writers, preachers, who were usually poor and have certainly been boys at school, and have mounted and flown up by their pens (feathers), until they are lords, as the Psalm says, and like

princes, help to rule lands and peoples. It is not God's will that born kings, princes, lords, and nobles should rule and be lords alone; He wills to have His beggars with them, so that they may not think that noble birth alone, and not God alone, makes lords and rulers.[4]

Vocation and Self-Fulfillment

In recent years, religious writers have associated vocation directly with self-fulfillment. Parker Palmer, for example, makes self-fulfillment the core of vocation:

> Vocation does not mean a goal that I pursue. It means a calling that I hear. Before I can tell my life what I want to do with it, I must listen to my life telling me who I am. I must listen for the truths and values at the heart of my own identity, not the standards by which I *must* live — but the standards by which I cannot help but live if I am living my own life.[5]

Later, he adds,

> Discovering vocation does not mean scrambling toward some prize just beyond my reach but accepting the treasure of true self I already possess. Vocation does not come from a voice "out there" calling me to become something I am not. It comes from a voice "in here" calling me to be the person I was born to be, to fulfill the original selfhood given me at birth by God.[6]

For Palmer, reflecting both his Quaker background and a central aspiration of the broader culture, the goal is to "live my own life," to be my own self by actualizing the potential God placed in me when God created me. Palmer is confident that if we find our authentic selves and actualize them, then others will be served as well. Speaking of Rosa Parks and others who have acted in ways that changed society, Palmer

---

4. Luther as cited by Donald R. Heiges, *The Christian Calling* (Philadelphia: Fortress Press, 1958), 58-59.

5. Parker Palmer, *Let Your Life Speak: Listening for the Voice of Vocation* (San Francisco: Jossey-Bass, 2000), 5.

6. Palmer, *Let Your Life Speak,* 10.

says, "[T]hey decide to claim authentic selfhood and act it out — and their decisions ripple out to transform the society in which they live, serving the selfhood of millions of others."[7] Others may be helped, but the primary intention is to discover the authentic self.

Luther and Calvin, along with the bulk of Christian tradition, are far less confident in the self and its aspirations. Because the self is a fallen self, even our deepest desires are tainted by sin. The primary consideration is not discovering the self; it is to serve the neighbor, even to the point of sacrificing the self and its interests. In Luther's words,

> A man is to live, speak, act, hear, suffer and die for the good of his wife and child, the wife for the husband, the children for the parents, the servants for their masters, the masters for their servants, the government for its subjects, the subjects for the government, each one for his fellowman, even for his enemies, so that one is the other's hand, mouth, eye, foot, even heart and mind.[8]

In a similar vein, Calvin writes,

> We are not our own: in so far as we can, let us therefore forget ourselves and all that is ours.
>
> Conversely, we are God's: let us therefore live for him and die for him. We are God's: let his wisdom and will therefore rule all our actions. We are God's: let all the parts of our life accordingly strive toward him as our only lawful goal. . . . For, as consulting our self-interest is the pestilence that most effectively leads to our destruction, so the sole haven of salvation is to be wise in nothing and to will nothing through ourselves but to follow the leading of the Lord alone.[9]

Vocation is first of all about serving God through serving the neighbor. The modern association of vocation and self-fulfillment runs against the main thrust of the Protestant tradition on this point. The point is not to seek one's self — even one's authentic self. The point is to love

---

7. Palmer, *Let Your Life Speak,* 32.

8. *Luther's Church Postil: Gospels: Advent, Christmas and Epiphany Sermons,* Vol. 1 in *The Precious and Sacred Writings of Martin Luther,* Vol. 10, ed. John Nicholas Lenker (Minneapolis: Lutherans in All Lands Co., 1905), 37.

9. Calvin, *Institutes of the Christian Religion,* ed. John T. McNeill, trans. Ford Lewis Battles (Philadelphia: Westminster, 1960), 3.7.1.

God and neighbor, and to take up the cross in the self-sacrificial paths defined by one's callings.

To the extent that being in Christ also involves receiving a new self, which lives in the fruit of the Spirit to the glory of God, there is a qualified sense in which Luther and Calvin might say that vocation involves self-fulfillment. But the focus does not reside there. The fulfillment of the self for them is a hope to be enjoyed mainly in the life to come. In this life, we have service, self-sacrifice, and much misery. Echoing the warning of Jesus, "Servants are not greater than their master. If they persecuted me, they will persecute you" (John 15:20), Calvin says,

> For whomever the Lord has adopted and deemed worthy of his fellowship ought to prepare themselves for a hard, toilsome, and unquiet life, crammed with very many and various kinds of evil. . . . Beginning with Christ, his first-born, he follows this plan with all his children.[10]

When Christ calls people to follow him, he invites them to take up his cross. Luther accused priests, monks, and nuns of being selfish in forsaking secular life. If anyone really wants to know self-sacrifice, says Luther, let him marry and have children! The cross is experienced in the sufferings endured within one's callings.

The way gifts relate to vocation in Calvin and subsequent Protestant tradition may imply self-fulfillment. God gives gifts for the common good of the body of Christ (Rom. 12, 1 Cor. 12), not primarily for the individual. But most people enjoy a sense of fulfillment when they actualize their gifts and abilities as they contribute to the common good. Though self-fulfillment may be inferred from the role of gifts and vocation, this theme is definitely muted in the Lutheran and Calvinist traditions. A Christian's deepest satisfaction comes from serving the neighbor, and serving God by serving the neighbor. It is this reality that gives meaning to one's acts — indeed, to one's life.

With these clarifications it is possible to apply and extend Protestant vocation's insights to major life decisions. The aim here is to remain true to the historic spirit of vocation in both challenging elements of our modern world and addressing areas of life neglected by the tradition, notably the relation of vocation to major life choices and

10. Calvin, *Institutes*, 3.8.1.

to the shaping of life within one's social locations. I will first explore ways in which the theology of vocation sketched in this book influences *pivotal* decisions, decisions to enter this or that form of paid work, to marry or remain unmarried, to have or not have children. I call these decisions "pivotal" because they determine the larger institutional and relational contexts of so many of our subsequent actions. Secondly, I will explore how Protestant vocation shapes decisions and character *within* our chosen spheres.

Vocation and Pivotal Decisions:
Gratitude, Freedom, and Love

Misconceptions

There are several misconceptions today's Christians have about calling and pivotal decisions. The first is that God has a rigid, highly detailed blueprint for each life. Within this blueprint, God calls individuals to a single specific place of work, and to no other. God also has a particular person in the blueprint for one's spouse, for those called to marriage. Christians who hold this view are highly anxious that they might miss their one and only chance to heed God's call. They fear they may choose the wrong profession, or accept the wrong job offer. They worry about whether or not the person they are now dating is God's one-and-only choice of spouse for them. Later, when things get tough, whether in a marriage or at the workplace, they worry that they may have missed God's call and made a huge mistake, losing an opportunity they can never recover.

Those who hold this view often ignore the elements of risk and uncertainty that apply to all major decisions, and so deceive themselves by failing to think honestly and accurately about themselves and their opportunities for service. This view easily leads to an evasion of responsibility. A student in his junior year once came to talk with me when I was teaching at Calvin College. He had been in a close, serious relationship with another student for over a year. She wanted a mutual commitment of the sort usually expressed in an engagement to be married. He instead decided to break off the relationship. When she asked him why, he said he had prayed to God about it and God told him he should break it off. God had called him to break away from the familiar and to embark on an unknown path to an unclear destination, and he assumed (perhaps wrongly) that this meant he should no longer stay with his girlfriend. The woman, heartbroken, truly believed their relationship had much potential for the long term. But she could hardly argue with the Almighty! I tried to help him acknowledge the possibility that the limits and dangers of long-term commitment frightened him, and accept responsibility for the injury he'd inflicted upon his former girlfriend. In my view there was a good chance that this student was using the idea of calling to evade his responsibility.

The view I've developed departs from the blueprint model of providence and vocation. Its main concern is not whether one has missed an irretrievable opportunity, but rather whether one's decisions are made out of gratitude to God, trust in God's word of grace, and desire to serve God and neighbors. If these are the ruling impulses behind choice of a career or spouse, it matters little whether one chooses to become a mechanic or an engineer, whether one chooses to marry one person or another. The New Testament pattern is much more relaxed about specifics than the blueprint view suggests. When needs arose, the community prayerfully decided who should use their gifts to meet those needs. They acted, trusting that the Spirit of God had been leading them throughout the process. "It seemed good to the Holy Spirit and to us" reflects this prevailing pattern (e.g., Acts 15:28). Vocation is in the realm of Christian freedom. God does not lay down any commandments to marry or remain single, to have children or not, to become a pastor or an entrepreneur. These are matters sometimes called *adiaphora,* "indifferent" matters in which Christians exercise discernment in Christian freedom. God does command that this freedom does not become a license for self-indulgence, but that it be used in faith to serve the neighbor (Gal. 5:13).

Luther was less concerned that we might miss God's call to a new job or social location than that we might fail to respond obediently to the many and constant callings reaching out to believers all the time: "Reflect on your condition, and you will find enough good works to do if you would lead a godly life. Every calling has its own duties, so that we need not inquire for others outside of our station."[11] Here is Lu-

---

11. *Luther's Church Postil,* 282.

ther's advice to someone who wonders if folly, or Satan, has led them to their lot:

> Therefore, where you are in a calling that is not sinful in itself, you are certainly placed there by God, and in the state that is pleasing to God; be only on your guard and do not sin in it. If you fall from a loft and break a bone the room or the bed therefore is not the worse or God more displeasing, into which the fall brought you and constrained you to remain, although another came there without such a fall.[12]

For Luther the main point is using every opportunity afforded by one's current social locations to serve God and neighbor. God's providence triumphs over even our folly and Satan. Therefore Christians can relax and not be anxious. So long as they seek first God's kingdom and its righteousness, it matters little whether they marry this person or that one or choose this profession or that one.

A second misconception is that God's call comes as a miraculous and unmistakable word of direction. Like Moses before the burning bush or Saul on the road to Damascus, some think that to have a calling they must hear God's voice and see tangible signs of God's presence. Lacking such an encounter with the Almighty, many Christians do not feel called by God to the places in which they live out their lives. But as I argued in Chapter Two, this is by far the exception to the broader biblical pattern. In numerous and quiet ways, God's callings are mediated by nature, family, community, friends, and more. Though some Christians have encounters of a miraculous nature, God's callings and leading are for the most part quietly and gently received, mediated by prayerful individual and communal discernment of gifts and needs. Though miracles can attend these processes, they usually do not.

A third misconception is that only clergy and members of religious orders have callings. Those who believe this also usually assume that pastors have an extraordinary sense of God's presence, both in receiving their call and in their work of ministry. They overestimate the possibilities for experiencing God's presence in the pastoral calling and

---

12. *Luther's Church Postil*, 248-49.

underestimate the possibilities for experiencing God's presence in "secular" callings. Thomas Merton approvingly cites St. Basil on prayer and manual labor:

> For prayer and psalmody every hour is suitable, that while one's hands are busy with their tasks we may praise God with the tongue, or, if not, with the heart. . . . Thus in the midst of our work we can fulfill the duty of prayer . . . and . . . we keep before our minds the aim of pleasing him.

Merton adds, "Obviously, Basil is talking of manual work, which can quite easily be united with any form of prayer. But how about more 'distracting' occupations, such as the apostolic ministry?"[13] In a similar vein, Benedictine Norvene Vest says,

> Based on our own situation and gifts, each of us is invited to lead a life illumined by these two factors: a desire to respond to God and a willingness to see daily life as the place where that response is formed. To be a Christian is to be called to a life of prayer and work, transformed interiorly by the indwelling of the Holy Spirit, and expressed exteriorly in the midst of the very brokenness and separation which Christ Jesus came to heal.[14]

Every Christian is called to such a life, not just a few.

Without denigrating the importance of church-related vocations, we must resist this misconception and the sacred/secular dichotomy that lies beneath it. Christ's lordship claims the entire life of every Christian, and the gracious presence of the Holy Spirit should permeate all of life. The priesthood of all believers means that the same basic religious and moral obligations of the clergy and members of religious orders apply to all Christians. Perhaps a good way to begin is to view "secular" callings as analogous to "religious" callings. Traditionally the call to pastoral ordination involved a personal sense that God was leading a person to become a pastor, having the gifts and abilities necessary for the tasks of ministry, and communal confirmation of both the per-

---

13. Thomas Merton, *Contemplative Prayer*, Foreword by Douglas V. Steere (New York: Image Books, 1971), 48-49.

14. Norvene Vest, *Friend of the Soul: A Benedictine Spirituality of Work* (Cambridge: Cowley Publications, 1997), 76.

sonal sense of call and the gifts necessary to it. Each of these elements can apply to many forms of paid work. An innovative church in the Washington, D.C., area has developed liturgies for ordaining church members to their work in society. A "Service of Ordination" includes the following:

> MINISTER TO PARTICIPANT: Your work and your worship are inti-
> mately interwoven. In fact, they are not separate at all: Your
> work grows out of your worship and your worship grows out of
> your work. (name), do you come today to acknowledge that the
> place where you work is as holy as the place where you wor-
> ship?
>
> PARTICIPANT: I do *(Kneels and speaks as follows, or in words of his own):*
> Enabled by Christ's love for me, I shall endeavor to make each
> day's work a sacrament. I pray that my work will be cleansed of
> all spiritual or material selfishness, of all impatience or criti-
> cism, of all secret desire for consolation, recognition or reward.
> Turn, O God, my seeing into loving, that I may witness to the
> redeeming love of Jesus Christ for all men. In His name I make
> my prayer. Amen.[15]

The priesthood of all believers and related view of vocation provide a stimulus and confirmation for this liturgical affirmation for paid work as vocation.

A fourth misconception is that God's callings follow a predictable direction away from one's current social locations. The synoptic gospels do emphasize the truth that God's call in Christ may sever existing social bonds. The disciples must leave their parents and drop their nets if they are to follow Christ. But God's callings do not always move away. Most of us, like the Gerasene demoniac, are commanded to return home, and to proclaim God's mighty acts there. When Paul contrasts his status as unmarried with the other apostles, he implies that the other apostles had wives. Priscilla and Aquila remained married, and supported each other in the Lord's work. Paul counsels the Corinthian Christians to remain in their positions as circumcised or

---

15. Elizabeth O'Connor, *Call to Commitment: The Story of the Church of the Savior,* Washington, D.C. (New York: Harper and Row, 1963), 105-6.

uncircumcised, slave or free (1 Cor. 7:17-24).[16] God's callings are free to direct us away from one or more of our present social locations, but they also direct us to remain in them "with God" as avenues of service (1 Cor. 7:24).

Vocation and Pivotal Decisions

All pivotal decisions should be shaped by a sense of calling, by our desire to express gratitude to God for the gift of salvation by using our gifts to serve others and glorify God. This includes career decisions, decisions relating to marriage and family, decisions to join this or that church community, and various other major commitments to voluntary organizations. All of these should be motivated by *gratitude* toward God and directed by *freedom* working in love to serve God and our neighbors. The call to be a Christian must govern all decisions about callings. The orienting norms set forth in Chapter Four apply here as well. Pivotal decisions, like decisions within one's callings, ought to be guided by love, shaped by shalom, and tested by discernment.

Pivotal Decisions about Paid Work

What This Moral Guideline Rules Out　　This general guideline rules out some motives and occupations. Other motives often supplant gratitude and love in decisions about paid work. High on the list of sinful motives are greed, grasping for power over others, slavish need to please one's parents, lust for prestige and status, and arrogant and unbeliev-

---

16. Dietrich Bonhoeffer sees a basic continuity between the synoptic gospels and Pauline teachings about vocation in 1 Corinthians 7: "How different it all sounds from the calling of the first disciples! *They* had to leave everything and follow Jesus. *Now* we are told: 'Let each man abide in the calling wherein he was called.' How are we to reconcile the contradiction? Only by recognizing the underlying motive both of the call of Jesus and of the exhortation of the apostle. In both cases it is the same — to bring their hearers into the fellowship of the Body of Christ. The only way the first disciples could enter that fellowship was by going with Jesus. But now through Word and Sacrament the Body of Christ is no longer confined to a single place. The risen and exalted Lord had returned to the earth to be nearer than ever before. The Body of Christ has penetrated into the heart of the world in the form of the Church." Bonhoeffer, *The Cost of Discipleship*, rev. ed., trans. R. H. Fuller (New York: Macmillan, 1963), 290.

ing desire to justify oneself by achieving significance in the larger scheme of things. The matter is subtle because each of these sinful motives is closely related to legitimate factors motivating a pivotal decision about paid work. Greed is a perverse form of a legitimate concern for life's necessities; grasping for dominance is a twisted form of a legitimate need for exercising agency; a slavish need to please parents is a distorted form of honoring them; lust for prestige and status is an idolatrous version of the need to belong and fill a place that contributes to the common good; the unbelieving effort to justify oneself is a sinful form of a proper need to feel one is loved and valued by God. Sin is a disordering of what should be rightly ordered; it is a parasite that depends upon the goodness of God's creation.[17] The central issue is one of priority. Is one's motivation in life governed finally by a free and grateful response to God's gracious word of acceptance? Or is it governed by one or another form of self-advantage?

It is difficult, if not impossible, for us to know our motives with certainty. Only God knows the heart. For sinners like us, self-deception is as remarkably resourceful as it is difficult to track. The banner of God's forgiveness hangs over all our vocational activity. Aware of these things, we should strive to discern what drives us in the major decisions of our lives. Is it gratitude to God for grace in Christ and a genuine desire to serve God by promoting the welfare of our neighbors? Or is it some desire, principality, or power other than Christ? Motives in reality may be mixed, but we should seek the ideal prayerfully and continually, especially when we are in the process of making pivotal decisions. Comfort and hope are present in the assurance of God's forgiveness and in the confidence that God's grace and providence will ultimately prevail in spite of our sin — and even use that sin to serve God's purpose in surprising ways.

This guideline also rules out some forms of paid work. It demands that our paid work contribute to the welfare of our neighbor and of God's good creation. Paid work creating products or services that harm the neighbor cannot be vocations. Devoting oneself to organized crime, for example, harms others and so is contrary to vocation. One reason Luther said that the papal priesthood of his day could not be a

---

17. See Cornelius Plantinga Jr., *Not the Way It's Supposed to Be: A Breviary of Sin* (Grand Rapids: Eerdmans, 1995), 78-95, for an illuminating discussion of sin as parasite.

calling was that he believed it to be harmful to people.[18] Some jobs create goods and services that contribute to the welfare of others, but require work processes and conditions that are dehumanizing and harmful. Labor as it was practiced for some time in sugarcane fields of the Dominican Republic, for example, is contrary to vocation. This labor produced a needed food, but it violated human dignity by using children who were kidnapped, trapped on large plantations, and forced to work fifteen-hour days without adequate diet or sanitary conditions. Some occupations fail on both counts. Child pornography, as an obvious example, creates products that harm the neighbor and involve processes that exploit and abuse children.

Most forms of paid work, like our motives, are ambiguous mixtures of good and evil. Working as a stockbroker, for example, implicates one in an economic system that in many ways exploits others and fails to meet genuine needs, but in other ways helps people by meeting real economic needs. The same ambiguity applies to being a Marine, a realtor, a teacher, or a pastor. The orders of our economic life express God's sustaining creative power, but they also express the fallen character of human activity and institutional life. A central strand of Protestant vocation, as we saw in Chapter Four, honestly acknowledges how fallen and corrupt are the institutions in which Christians are called to serve the neighbor. In spite of this fact, and because of it, love of neighbor propels Christians into the world as agents of God's redeeming grace.

But where do we draw the line? Can working in the promotions department of a company making yachts, or some other luxury item, be a calling? How about working for Philip Morris? When I was lecturing on vocation for a pastors conference at Union Seminary in Richmond some years ago, a pastor expressed his difficulty counseling parishioners who worked for a large tobacco company. Tobacco money helped build and continues to support his church. Tobacco money helped build and endow Union Seminary, where I was delivering lectures. All the best medical science indicates that smoking tobacco harms people. Unlike alcohol, which can be used moderately without harming health,

18. Luther thought the corruption was so deep and pervasive that it was unreformable. I think he would not condemn the Catholic priesthood, and numerous religious orders, as they are practiced in our day.

even a few cigarettes a day harm one's health. Perhaps a Christian employee could still experience some aspects of the job as vocational, such as using opportunities to help fellow workers and using the money gained to support family and others. But if a Christian wants unity of his or her faith and paid work in a sense of calling, then the work must not harm the neighbor, but should rather contribute to God's shalom. The church should provide temporary support for members who are working in harmful industries and help them find jobs that promote rather than hinder the common good.

At my high school, the physics and chemistry teacher, Mr. Adams, was a favorite among students. Before he came to our high school, Mr. Adams had been a researcher in a government-funded lab. The lab's goal was to invent a more efficient rocket fuel for the missiles that would carry nuclear warheads. Though the job paid well and utilized his gifts, and though he found comfort in the possibility that his lab's discoveries might have unforeseen uses that would help others, his Christian conscience and sense of calling troubled him so much that he quit. He was not a pacifist, but he could not endure the conflict between his Christian confession and engaging in activities so directly aimed at increasing the efficiency of nuclear weaponry. After quitting, he sought and found employment in another part of the country as a teacher at a Christian high school. He and his family had to move and adjust to a large pay cut. But he told us that it was one of the best decisions of his life.

The U.S. Catholic bishops, in their pastoral letter on the United States economy, propose this guideline:

> Personal decisions, policies of private and public bodies, and power relationships must all be evaluated by their effects on those who lack the minimum necessities of nutrition, housing, education, and health care. . . . Meeting fundamental human needs must come before the fulfillment of desires for luxury consumer goods, for profits not conducive to the common good and for unnecessary military hardware.[19]

---

19. National Council of Catholic Bishops, *Economic Justice for All* (United States Catholic Conference, 1986), as cited in Lee Hardy, *The Fabric of This World* (Grand Rapids: Eerdmans, 1990), 97.

This is a high standard. Because we often cannot know the effects of our actions, it is difficult to know how much influence our choice of one or another form of paid work will have. How does one determine which military hardware is unnecessary? In this interdependent society, how directly must our work be implicated in its production? Given what Jesus says about the rich and the poor, Christians should always have "the least of these" in view as they make major decisions. Even if they do not choose, say, social work for their profession, there are numerous ways in which carpentry, medicine, business, law, dentistry, and all legitimate callings can be creatively directed to serve the poor and oppressed of our world.

Does this view of vocation rule out the creative arts? Many students I've taught feel a deep tension between wanting to enter the creative arts as a profession and wanting to serve the poor and fight against injustice. The students who grapple with this tension are morally passionate. Many have encountered the poor through domestic and overseas programs offered by St. Olaf College or learned about their plight through their course work. They want to change the world. They are also extremely gifted and promising musicians, dancers, composers, and visual artists. Because they enjoy their art immensely, and because they must spend hours and hours alone practicing their art if they are to have any real chance at becoming paid professionals, they feel they are being selfish. They also feel guilty for desiring a profession that does not more directly serve their neighbor.

An essay by Dorothy Sayers entitled "Why Work?" may be helpful in this context.[20] Sayers argues that we do not "work to live, we live to work." Reacting against the instrumentalism of post–World War II capitalism and consumerism, Sayers focuses on the intrinsic value of work. Work for her is the medium by which people offer themselves to God. The worker's first duty is to "serve the work" rather than make the work a means to other ends — leisure or even the good of the community. Like a master sculptor absorbed in the creative process of chiseling out the form contained in a piece of marble, without thought about what will happen to it later, or like a playwright in the grip of a muse as she creates a play, mindless about whether the crowd will jeer or cheer,

20. Dorothy Sayers, "Why Work?" in *Creed or Chaos* (New York: Harcourt Brace, 1947).

so too Christians should seek first excellence in the work, and others might just benefit as well.

This view of work-as-art is unrealistic when applied to many forms of employment; even in Moore's Utopia, the mundane, dirty work must by done, and is done as a means to other ends rather than for its intrinsic value. But Sayers's view does point out a weakness in much Protestant thought about vocation: it can be so concerned about effectiveness and so exclusively focused on the neighbor that it neglects the importance of delight in God and joy in the Spirit that also should mark the Christian life. In his polemics, with the emphasis upon contemplation, relics, and religious activity that had no clear benefit to one's neighbors, Luther stressed effectiveness in helping the neighbor as a major criterion of good works. His powerful sense of Christian freedom and intensely incarnational view of the neighbor made this concern a deeply theological matter as well. His expansive view of the neighbor's needs, and of the many avenues in which they must be met, has ample room for the vocational status of the arts. He is famous for saying that after theology, music was God's greatest gift to humankind. But without these larger contexts, his statements can easily be misused to reduce vocation to a crass instrumentalism. Max Weber has traced the ways in which Calvin's rich notions of grace and calling were transformed, under modern capitalism, into economic activity dominated by instrumental reason.[21]

Though Calvin also stresses the importance of effective service to the neighbor, he emphasizes the glory of God more so than does Luther. Good works spring from the assurance of God's benevolence toward us, and they should aim at the honor and glory of God. The glory of God certainly includes serving the neighbor, but it is a broader tent than that. The Christian artist, inspired by the beauty and tragedy of this created-but-fallen world, seeks to glorify God in her art. Certainly she hopes that the work she offers to God will also contribute to the welfare of others. Art can be a powerful medium of the Word of God and an inspiring expression of worship. Humans reflect God's image by creating culture and growing in knowledge of this wonderful creation.

Accordingly, caring for animals, plants, soil, and ecosystems can be vocations, even where these activities have no noticeable benefit for hu-

---

21. Max Weber, *The Protestant Ethic and the Spirit of Capitalism*, trans. Talcott Parsons (New York: Charles Scribner's Sons, 1958).

man beings. God takes delight in all of creation, repeatedly calling it "good" in the first chapter of Genesis. Confident that God creates and loves the whole universe, Christians can devote themselves to its care and keeping. A former classmate of mine who left college to become a farmer once told me, with a playful grin on his wide face, that he considered himself to be "God's missionary to the soil." No doubt he also saw his calling in terms of supplying food for others, using his income to support and nurture his family, and contributing to the community in various ways. But he found special satisfaction in knowing that God loved the piece of land he was called to care for and tend.

What This Guideline Rules In   Vocation rules out some motives and some forms of paid work, but what does it rule *in?* It rules in the motives of gratitude for God's gracious gift of salvation and desire to express love for God by using particular gifts and opportunities to serve others and contribute to God's shalom. This does not mean that all other motives are excluded. As I said above, motives are mixed and hard to know for certain. It does mean that Christians should examine their hearts in light of this new reality: their lives belong not to themselves but to their faithful Lord and Savior, Jesus Christ.

So long as an occupation respects human dignity and contributes to the common good, the word of Protestant vocation for career choices is one of freedom. Unlike this world, which demeans some jobs and exalts others through differences in pay or prestige, Paul insists that even functions seemingly trivial are in fact crucial to the good of the whole (1 Cor. 12). The professor or pastor should not look down upon the custodian or landscaper, as though their jobs were of lesser value in God's scheme of things. Work in a career should not be exalted over work in the home and family, or vice versa. Both home and paid work must be offered in service to Christ and the kingdom.

There are value systems, Christian and non-Christian, that deny or hinder this freedom. The classical Greek view scorns manual labor, prizing the contemplative life above all others. The Marxian view glorifies the laborer, placing manual labor far above contemplation and other forms of work. Our culture, economic systems, and public policy decisions systematically devalue domestic work. Many Christians wrongly rank occupations in terms of spiritual value, so that there are "sacred" and "secular" occupations. God's call is here seen as "otherworldly" in that it calls people away from the mundane world. For these Christians, God calls people *out of* the mundane world of family, business, and friends; God calls people *into* the spiritual world of "full-time" service. Usually full-time service here means a "paid job" as pastor, evangelist, missionary, education director, or some other church-related work. Those who make a living in the secular world, marry, and raise a family, are seen as "second class" Christians. The spiritually serious Christians, those who *really* want to serve God with all their heart, soul, strength, and mind, will forsake the secular world.

I recall reading an evangelical periodical praising a missionary couple as an ideal Christian example. They had left their young children (four or five of them) at the home of a relative (I think it was grandparents) while they obeyed God's call to be missionaries in Africa. Others raised their children while they converted people to Christianity. Here was the heroic ideal, forsaking all to follow the call of Christ.

No one ever thundered as loudly against this "otherworldly" view of vocation as did Martin Luther. He preached that the Devil, not God, calls people to forsake God's divine ordinances of marriage and family to perform some great "religious" work. True calling is experienced *inside* the ordinary, mundane world, not *outside* of it. Commenting on those who might feel called to follow the example of the prophetess Anna, who "never left the temple but worshipped there with fasting and prayer night and day" (Luke 2:37), Luther says,

> God cannot bear to see anyone neglect the duties of his calling or station in life in order to imitate the works of the saints. If therefore a married woman were to follow Anna in this respect, leave her husband and children, her home and parents in order to go on a pilgrimage, to pray, fast and go to church, she would do nothing else but tempt God, confound the matrimonial estate with the state of widowhood, desert her own calling and do works belonging to others. This would be as much as walking on one's ears, putting a veil over one's feet and a boot on one's head, and turning all things upside down. Good works should be done, and you ought to pray and fast, but you must not thereby be kept from or neglect the duties of your calling and station.[22]

22. *Luther's Church Postil*, 281.

He also writes, "[I]t is the God of the world, the Devil, who so slanders the marital state and has made it shameful . . . that it would be fair to marry in order to spite him and his world and to accept his ignominy and bear it for God's sake."[23] In our own times — as the domestic, social, political, and other spheres of "ordinary" life become more and more secularized and consumerist — the pull of an "otherworldly" call becomes all the more strongly felt. But the impulse of vocation is to instead re-infuse the mundane world with religious and moral meaning.

Pivotal Decisions Mainly about Marriage and Family

Decisions to marry or remain single, to have children or not have them, are also shaped by vocation. These too must be motivated by gratitude and governed by love for God expressed in love for neighbors and advancing God's shalom. It is a divine calling to be a husband or wife or parent. The marriage form used by the Reformed denomination in which my wife and I were married stated three purposes for Christian marriage: enrichment of the lives of those entering the state of matrimony, procreation of the human race, and advancement of God's kingdom. Marriage is not a limited liability contract one enters to obtain individual fulfillment. It is a divine calling through which one serves — and is served by — one's spouse, contributes to the larger human community, and participates in God's kingdom.

Two main obstacles to freedom in vocation as it relates to decisions involving marriage stem from tendencies to ascribe greater value to either the married or to the celibate state. The medieval tradition of "counsels of perfection," and the symbolism of a celibate clergy, can easily suggest a spiritual superiority to being single and hide the vocational status of marriage. If one is really serious about serving God, the thinking goes, one must follow Christ's advice to those who would be perfect and give up marriage and possessions. The other danger is more common in Protestant churches, where the single life is often seen as a deviation from the "norm" of marriage, the preferred form of life. When I was a seminary student, two of my fellow seminarians were

---

23. As cited by Heiko A. Oberman, *Luther: Man Between God and the Devil*, trans. Eileen Walliser-Schwarzbart (New York: Image Books, 1992), 272-73.

called into a professor's office and admonished to find a wife if they wanted full opportunity as a pastor. The single life was of lesser status than the married life, and even drew suspicions that would impede their ministry.

To become married or to remain single should be a decision expressing one's sense of calling. Either condition can be one in which God and neighbor can be effectively served. The same holds for the decisions about raising children. Most couples have children. Parents shape children's basic affective responses to God, the world, and society. They represent God to their children in a most extraordinary way, and this is indeed a high calling. But some may be called to devote their marriage to other forms of service in the kingdom by deciding not to have children. It is true that some couples remain childless because they want a bigger home, a cottage by the lake, freedom to travel, or other self-centered luxuries. But others remain childless to increase their availability for forms of Christian service not as accessible to couples with children. Still others may face more complicated decisions.

A couple I've known for many years decided not to have children so that they could more single-mindedly devote themselves to specific forms of service. Their house was a refuge for estranged people needing a place to stay; they divided up their yard into plots of fertile soil so that people who lived in the city or in apartments could enjoy gardening, for which they also supplied the tools; they bought a second car, paying unusually high insurance, so that students and young professors could use it for trips; and they were very active in their local congregation. I mention this example not to lift up the childless marriage over one with children, but to illustrate how decisions can be influenced by vocation. Other childless couples adopt children, take in foster children, or use their greater relative freedom for some other distinctive form of service.

Gratitude, love of God and neighbor, shalom, and freedom ought to govern pivotal decisions. But, concretely, how do I decide what path to follow, to marry or to remain single, to plant corn or preach Christ,[24]

---

24. There is a story relating to vocation that is popular in the Midwest. A young man once saw a vision in the night sky. The letters, "P.C." were visible against the backdrop of the starry heavens. The young man thought God was calling him to "Preach Christ," but in fact God was calling him to "Plant Corn."

to remain in this job or move to another, or to move to another institution while remaining in the same career? In an ideal world, a person should find a partner with a high degree of mutual compatibility and mutual attraction. A person should also find a job that enables optimal development of gifts on the one hand, and produces the greatest good for the world on the other. In the real world, people marry each other aware of and in spite of each other's warts and limitations. It means that a person accepts the one job offered, hoping that this job allows for some intrinsically meaningful activity and some contribution to the common good. There are so many specific considerations that must be taken into account to answer these questions that I hesitate even to make the attempt. God's callings are free, person-specific, and in many ways unpredictable, so generalizations can be dangerous. Uncertainty and anxiety cause people to want to avoid the struggles involved in discerning God's will by latching onto a "five steps" method for making pivotal decisions. Without falling into the five-step, self-help method so popular in America, there are directions that can be drawn from the general principles laid out in this book.

Some Practical Guidelines

Need

Because vocation is directed in service to the care and redemption of all that God has made, attentiveness to the needs of the world guides pivotal decisions. These needs are diverse. The non-human world needs tending, healing, and stewarding. Agriculture, forestry, care of local, state, and national parks, and veterinary services, for example, include a wide variety of needs. People need the gospel of Jesus Christ and the power of the Holy Spirit in the Christian community. They need food, physical and emotional health, recreation, clothing and shelter, education, music, scientific knowledge, the arts, just political order, and more. Because God's shalom includes human flourishing in all its fullness, human needs go beyond what is necessary for survival.

Some needs are objectively more pressing than others. Luther rightly ranked faithful preaching and teaching of the gospel as of paramount importance in meeting a profound human need. Acute awareness of this need causes some to choose paid work as a Christian preacher or teacher, or in an office directly contributing to the ministries of Christian churches. They become pastors, teachers, church musicians, and church office assistants. Others are acutely aware that so many people in the world lack even the basic necessities of life, and feel the weight of biblical teaching about how important these needs are to Christ, so they choose forms of paid work that directly serve the poor and engage the injustices of society. They become social workers, activists, and employees of the Salvation Army.

Because the needs of the human and non-human communities are diverse, God does not call everyone into forms of paid work whose specific focus is preaching or advocacy. God calls some to be carpenters, engineers, lawyers, or investment bankers. To the extent that these people are to express God's call in all their callings, they should struggle to bend their occupations and skills in ways that spread the good news of the gospel and to help feed the poor and clothe the naked. Since their callings include more than their paid work, they can express this part of their calling by contributing to the life of churches and to other voluntary societies that meet the needs of the poor.

One Christian businessman I know built, owns, and operates a company that paints the interior and exterior of homes. He hires a crew of about a dozen employees. He sees this business as an important part of his vocation as a Christian. He pays a living wage and provides an attractive benefit package. He developed a structure for advancement in responsibilities and pay to enable employees to augment their services and rewards. He meets a genuine need in enhancing and preserving homes. He does honest work and stands behind his promises. All of this he sees as his vocation. But in addition to all this, he formed a weekly Bible study for his employees, having made it absolutely clear that attendance was optional. He also hires several members of racial minority groups who have potential but whose histories point to risks that might lead other employers not to hire them. His aim is to make his business a kind of microcosm of the kingdom of God, where reconciliation and mutual understanding rule.

Some needs can be objectively more pressing at a particular time. If there is a glut of medical and law students, for example, but a shortage of elementary education or seminary students, the need for pastors and teachers is more pressing than the need for lawyers and doctors. A person whose gifts could equip him for either field may be led by the more pressing nature of the need in the direction of becoming a pastor. It is not that pastoring is a more important vocation than lawyering; rather, given the social realities of this community at this time, pastors are more needed than lawyers.

Need is not the only factor. There are some individuals who would make great surgeons but poor pastors. There are some who might be able to do both, but who have no interest whatsoever in becoming a pastor. But if there is the ability for and interest in all three professions, then need might be a deciding factor. Sometimes God's calling is discerned in the unique ways in which an individual may be fitted to meet needs at a specific institutional setting. Her religious, ethnic, personal, and institutional background come to fit her and no others (or very few others) for a particular job. Such factors are relevant to the process of discerning God's calling.

There is also an important subjective factor relevant to need and pivotal decisions. Though it does not apply to all vocations, Frederick Buechner's widely cited definition of vocation as the place where the world's greatest need meets the heart's deepest gladness does note the importance of perceived need in vocational choice.[25] God has so shaped us that we are attentive to different needs. Some evangelical communities use the language of having a "burden" for this or that need. For some, the burden is the need for health; for others it is need for education. Some see needs for beauty and music; others see needs for buildings and houses. Some Christians feel so strongly about such needs that they devalue the needs others see. Those who stress the need of the lost to hear the gospel, for example, sometimes fail to see the importance of food, shelter, clothing, and the arts. The multiplicity of needs, and the Pauline teaching that what seems trivial is often very important, ought to lead to humility. Develop passionately your vocation to address the needs you believe most pressing, but do not judge another who is passionate about a different set of needs.

---

25. Though this idea of vocation is true for some cases, it is not true for all. The calls of Jeremiah or Hosea, for example, hardly seem to fit this pattern. Many callings meet human needs but are in themselves unpleasant, and whatever satisfaction is found in them is found in extrinsic factors, such as knowing one is supplying a needful service or using the income for beneficial purposes, rather than in the work itself.

Gifts

God has given each person a particular constellation of gifts to be identified and exercised for the good of the whole. As we saw in Chapter
Two, the New Testament very closely associates gifts with callings
(Rom. 12, 1 Cor. 12, Eph. 4). In sovereign freedom, the Holy Spirit distributes gifts, which are in turn to be used to build up the body of
Christ. These gifts differ strikingly. They are intellectual, artistic, ad-
ministrative, mechanical, emotional, biological, and social, just to mention a few. Within each of these there are numerous subdivisions.
God's call takes account of these aptitudes. Discovering and developing our aptitudes are important for discerning what God is calling us
to do.

It is unlikely that God is calling someone to become a philosopher
if that person has little aptitude for ideas and contemplative wonder.
Tone-deaf people are unlikely candidates for musical callings. People
without particular motor skills are not usually called to become mechanics or surgeons. People who cannot feel the rhythms of God's
grace amid the hopes and fears, the wonder and the agony of life, are
not likely candidates for the preaching or pastoral calling. There are exceptions, of course. In many of the "call" stories of the Old Testament,
such as those of Moses, Isaiah, and David, the inadequacy of the one
called is highlighted. Some have concluded from this that God calls
people to positions they do not enjoy and for which they have little or
no aptitude. There is an element of duty and a sense of inadequacy in
the way the vast majority experience God's callings, but God usually
works with, not against, our abilities and aptitudes. The biblical stories
that seem to suggest otherwise only prove the rule by their exceptional
character. They finally underscore the basic truths that all gifts and
callings depend upon God's grace and good will, and that God delights
to take what is weak in the eyes of the world to shame the strong.

I once had a conversation with a student who was planning to go
to seminary after his senior year. His grades at the time placed him in
the bottom tenth of his class; he was not very interested in theology, lit-
erature, or philosophy; and he had little insight, even for someone his
age, into human spiritual and personal struggles or joys. He told me
that his friends couldn't believe it when he told them his plans to become a pastor. I asked him why he thought he should pursue the pasto-

ral calling. He said that whenever he sang the liturgy, family members would say, "You should be a minister — you sing like an angel." His mother and father had marked him for a pastor since his youth, and now he pressed on in that direction even though he felt very uncomfortable with his prospects as a pastor. He viewed his discomfort and resistance as further confirmation of God's call; after all, were not Jeremiah and Moses resistant at first? The Pietist movement at one time had a rule: "What we take ill, will be God's will." And since God is free, it is possible that God was calling this student to become a pastor — but it seemed unlikely.[26]

Some people have so much aptitude that they find it almost impossible to know which direction to pursue. Albert Schweitzer, by the ripe age of thirty, had already firmly established himself as one of Europe's leading organists, had written a definitive study of Bach that transformed the way musicians performed Bach all over the world and was soon translated from French into German and English (844 pages in the German), was Principal of the Theological College of St. Thomas, lectured regularly on New Testament studies, had written all but the final chapter of *Quest for the Historical Jesus,* a book that redirected the course of New Testament scholarship, and he had also mapped out the rough lines of Pauline theology, later published as *The Mysticism of Paul.*[27] In his early twenties, Schweitzer felt the need for a "more direct" form of service, and resolved to make a "career move" when he turned thirty. True to his earlier resolve, after achieving the sort of acclaim in three fields that most only hope to achieve in one field in an entire lifetime, at the age of thirty Schweitzer began his seven years of medical studies in order to become a medical doctor in Africa. Schweitzer was, of course, extraordinary in aptitude and in the opportunities he found to express this aptitude.

A person's gifts form one important indicator of directions in which God may be calling that person. Although the rapid pace of

26. The student did in fact become a very effective pastor. Karl Barth, *Church Dogmatics* 3/4, ed. and trans. G. W. Bromiley (Edinburgh: T&T Clark, 1961), 635. Barth does affirm that one's choice should be in response to something that has something of the character of a command to it, and so gives partial approval of the Pietist saying. But Barth finally says it should not be "stated as a general rule."

27. See Albert Schweitzer, *Out of My Life and Thought: An Autobiography,* trans. C. T. Campion (New York: Henry Holt and Co., 1949).

change in today's society creates stress, it also provides new opportunities for aptitudes to shape one's callings. Only a generation ago, for example, the mother stayed at home with the children and the father went out to a paid job — even if in this particular marriage, the father had much greater parental aptitude than the mother, and the mother had much greater aptitude for paid work. Today there is more freedom than ever for parents to take on the particular tasks suited to their abilities and interests. There is also increasingly more freedom for women to follow their gifts into their callings, rather than be arbitrarily kept out of occupations where their gifts might otherwise be developed and expressed for the common good.

Opportunity and Limit

Karl Barth offers some useful guidelines to help people discern the special spheres of responsibility to which God calls them.[28] He advises Christians to consider three aspects of their lives, each of which he identifies as a "limit of obedience" that shapes what I have called pivotal choices. Each of these three aspects is relatively given by divine decree; we do not choose them so much as discover ourselves within them. As such they both open and close possibilities for God's callings. One is aptitude, or gifts, which I have already treated above. The other two are our place in the life cycle and our place in history.

God calls us to different possibilities and tendencies depending on our stage in life. As Barth sees it, *youth* is the time of stepping into freedom from the past for new opportunity; it is the time of preparation, hope, and planning. The young are called to explore new possibilities and to be diligent in hope of a full harvest. *Middle age* is the time for maturity of obedience. Now we are called to harvest what we have sown. It is no longer too early for many activities, and it is not yet too late for others. We are no longer inexperienced, but we are not yet exhausted. We are young enough to be open, and to shape our future in definite ways. *Old age* is the special time to see life in the light of all eternity, to see the future as gift more than as task. God calls us, then, to basic directions depending on our time in the life cycle. The time of each stage has its own special opportunities and limits.

---

28. My discussion of these guidelines follows Barth, *Church Dogmatics* 3/4, 607-647.

Barth's specific interpretations of life's stages are debatable. Many studies show that people in their middle ages are much less open to possibilities and to change than they are in old age. Today's heightened sensitivity to the processes of aging and to stages of spiritual and moral development would refine Barth's insight. The protracted time now spent in retirement must also be taken into account more seriously than Barth takes it. But his basic insight is helpful: there are limits and possibilities constituting the range of what God might be calling us to at a given time in our lives. It is highly unlikely, for example, that God is calling a sixty-year-old woman to start a family; the time for that is usually in youth or early middle age. For the most part, professions and occupations requiring a great deal of preparation must be entered earlier in life rather than later. Again, there are exceptions — Abraham was one hundred years old and Sarah was ninety-one when Sarah bore Isaac. But the rule is that God's callings are coordinated with the ways in which one's life cycle opens and closes possibilities for service.

Barth also calls attention to our "place in history." Here he has in mind our citizenship, the century in which we live, our family history, the political structures that govern us, our economic class, the church community in which we find ourselves. Barth's first word to us about our place in history is to accept and keep our place. If I have been raised as a Presbyterian, am married, and feel called to ordained ministry, then it is unlikely that God wants me to become a Catholic priest. Barth says that God's providence controls the general and particular sway of historical forces that constitute our historical location. According to Barth, in God's eyes each historical situation is equally good and promising; none is absolutely bad or hopeless. Thus we must first accept the contexts that both open up and close off possibilities for us.

Dietrich Bonhoeffer's decision to return to Germany from Union Theological Seminary offers a dramatic example of Barth's general guideline. Reinhold Niebuhr and Paul Tillich tried to persuade Bonhoeffer to remain at Union, but their efforts were unsuccessful. His family had been a very wealthy and influential one before the war; during the war they were active in the resistance, and eventually spearheaded an attempt to assassinate Adolf Hitler. Bonhoeffer returned to his country, his family, and his church. God's call now was not "otherworldly" but very "this-worldly." Dietrich's embeddedness in a particular "history" directed him to hear God's call not in the advice of Niebuhr and Tillich, but in the need of his family and country. The plot failed, Dietrich was imprisoned for many months, and — only hours before the allies liberated his prison camp — he was hanged. Accepting our historical situation can be very costly.

When I was in South Africa giving lectures in August 1998, many people I spoke to were either leaving or advising their children or grandchildren to leave South Africa. Some of them were creative, enterprising people capable of making substantial contributions to the new South Africa. Their concern for themselves and their children caused them to fear for their safety and future. And many had reason to fear. High crime rates, affirmative action policies that seriously disadvantaged whites in job opportunities, and the many adjustments that were necessary as a new constitution and government came to power caused many white, wealthy, accomplished people to leave. But there were other people, Christians who helped to dismantle Apartheid, who now felt deeply called to remain in South Africa to contribute to its life and future. Perhaps they too had thought of leaving. But they felt Christ calling them, as he called the Gerasene Demoniac, to "return home and declare what God has done" for them. The challenge is great. It might have been easier for them to leave. But after counting the cost, they chose to obey Christ and remain home.

Barth also challenges Christians to "grapple" with their historical situation, to bring it into obedience to God's will. Our country, century, family, class, race — and the particular institutions mediating these to us — are not only expressive of God's sustaining providence; they also express human sin, and so must be transformed. The historical situation, he says, is "one's cradle, not one's grave." For Barth the presence of God's providence means that we should not flee or absolutely oppose our situation. We cannot assume that the demands of our contexts are expressions of God's command; we must determine anew, in each context, what God is requiring. We must bring each situation into line with God's will as much as is in our power.

Barth's point about "grappling" with our situation needs expansion and greater emphasis today. Barth was well aware of the ways in which the political situation of his day failed to conform to God's will. He did not "accept" Nazism; he grappled with it, tooth and nail. In his first parish he publicly opposed the rich factory owners, demanding better wages and working conditions for the workers. These owners tried to oust him, but Barth prevailed against them.[29] Barth's first counsel to *accept* must be complemented by this example of his second word: *grapple*. If at least one school of economic analysis is right, the abject poverty in the world is due in large measure to the policies and neglect of the wealthy — both the local wealthy and the wealthy in other parts of the world. Racism compounds the problem. Black males are much more likely to end up in prison than in college; racial minorities are more often exposed to dangerous chemical waste and hazardous living areas than are whites. Sexism is deeply ingrained in the cultural and social fabric of our lives. Discrepancies in pay, failure to ensure that divorced husbands pay child support, and governmental neglect of children and women combine to trap millions of women in poverty, even in the United States. Because of the deeply flawed nature of culture and society, we cannot merely "accept" our social-historical contexts. These contexts do not measure up to the standards of God's will and Word; they must be grappled with and transformed. Vocation leads to participation in our various defining contexts, but with a view to transforming them to express God's justice and peace.

In addition to the general limits of place in the life cycle and in history, there must be a concrete opportunity. The job must be offered; the other person must say, "I will marry you." You may have identified the need of higher education and gained the necessary credentials for teaching college, but being a professor is not your calling until and unless you get a concrete offer to teach at this or that college, university, or seminary. You may feel called to serve as a senator, but that is not your calling until and unless you get elected. You may think Mary is the one God is calling you to marry, but if she does not concur, then God is not calling you to marry Mary. There may very well be other concrete opportunities for paid work and marriage. The Ph.D. without an offer from a school in this country may lead to an offer in some other country, or to a staff of a church with an ambitious adult education program, or to a publisher of books in one's field of expertise. A new relationship may develop with potential for a life-long, exclusive mutual commitment.

It is often difficult to know how long to persist, whether in seeking

---

29. See Eberhard Busch, *Karl Barth: His Life from Letters and Autobiographical Texts*, trans. John Bowden (Philadelphia: Fortress Press, 1976), 68-71.

a job offer in the area of one's choice or in pursuing a prospective but reluctant potential spouse. The oxymoronic "creative destruction" of capitalist economies plunges people into unemployment and requires re-tooling for new jobs. A sense of vocation can be a bulwark for such anxious times. The Christian call is far broader than one's marriage or one's paid work. We are freer to be patient during adversity if we believe that our life belongs to God in Christ, who gave his life for us. If the point of our whole existence is to serve Christ in and through all our lives, then our existence will find its ultimate meaning and worth elsewhere than in our particular vocations. It will find avenues of concrete expression, even if not in the ways we anticipated. Adversity often becomes a spur for creative change and discovery of new places where God is calling us to serve.

What if there are multiple jobs, or even multiple marriage opportunities? If this is the case, the general rule is that one should choose the option that will best enable one to be faithful to God's call. Perhaps the offer from a church-related college should be taken over the offer from the university because of the importance and endangered nature of Christian higher education. Or perhaps the research possibilities of the university will enable larger contributions to the common good than the limited possibilities in a small, under-funded church-related college. Perhaps the location of one of the companies making the offer will bring you closer to extended family and friends whom God has called you to support in special ways. Perhaps one of the prospective spouses will lead to a union more fruitful for God's kingdom than another.

Communal Discernment

There are profoundly personal and individual dimensions to making pivotal decisions. Often it is in the dark nights of the soul, or in the brightness of an experience of God's presence, that we perceive God's callings. Prayer, honest self-examination, and clarifying one's motives and intentions are all very difficult personal work that should accompany pivotal decisions. As in the case of responding to God's call to be a Christian, responding to God's particular callings requires individual decision in the sanctuary of God's presence.

But there are also important communal elements in the process of discerning God's callings. Traditionally, those who felt called to the ministry of Word and sacrament must have their internal sense of call confirmed by the external confirmation of the Christian community. This represents the role community plays in the process of discerning one's callings. Christians should consult with those who know them well when they are deliberating about employment and marriage. Often God's direction comes through parents, coaches, friends, pastors, teachers, spiritual directors, or other authorities in our lives.

Though God's calling often comes through the community, it does not always do so. Communities, like individuals, are plagued by sin. Women and minorities, for example, have always been more than welcomed to menial and low-paid forms of work. But institutionalized sexism and racism have for centuries been unjust, barring women and racial minorities from holding public offices and from the more prestigious and lucrative forms of paid work. In the late nineteenth century, the Supreme Court of the United States ruled that it was "unnatural" for a woman to become a lawyer, upholding an American Bar Association ban on women lawyers. Pervasive injustices like these should remind us that the Spirit distributes gifts and callings "as the Spirit chooses" (1 Cor. 12:11) and not along lines defined by race and gender. God's call to Amos and Jeremiah came freely, cutting against the grain of the established leaders of ancient Israel. An incredibly strong sense of calling is required to swim against the stream. But, by God's power and grace, it is at times necessary and possible to do so. With this important qualification, the community can be a very important source of guidance for discerning God's callings.

CHAPTER SIX

Vocation, Decisions, and the Moral Life II

We have focused so far on vocation's influences on "pivotal" decisions. Though these decisions are obviously very important, we do not spend most of our time and energy trying to decide whether to enter this or that profession, whether to marry or remain single; we spend them actually working in a particular job, or living as married or single. My own present "spheres of operation" include being a professor at St. Olaf College, a husband, a father to three daughters, a member of Bethel Lutheran Church, a member of a particular neighborhood, and a friend to certain persons. God's providence has placed me in these spheres. How does vocation shape our actions, decision, and attitudes as they are expressed *within* our particular spheres?

A very general answer to this question is this: Vocation encourages Christians to see themselves as created and redeemed by God's grace, so that they will express their love for God and God's world through each and all of these spheres. In all of them Christians should exhibit the fruit of the Spirit. Specific answers depend much upon the specifics of the person and his or her contexts. There is much room for Christian freedom and discernment in these matters. Based on the view of vocation I have developed, however, I can offer a few principles, which I hope will be helpful to Christian discernment necessary for action within one's several callings.

Decisions and Character within Our Callings

Vocation and Idolatry

Ethicist Eric Mount Jr. warns against institutional idolatry. We are tempted to devote total loyalty to an institution, especially when that institution stands for noble ideals and defines our identity in a significant way. When this happens, says Mount,

> The institution is vested with the god-like prerogative to define what is good and right. The institutional role consumes us. We lose our selves in our work. When we become so committed to one institution, either voluntarily or involuntarily, that it becomes the total definer of our personhood, we have become "institutionalized."[1]

All of us are aware of "workaholics," people who devote so much time and energy to their paid work that they neglect spouse, children, church, and friends. Men are especially tempted in our society to equate our identity with our paid work, though in recent years many women have experienced similar temptation. When I am introduced, whether informally in small gatherings or formally in large ones, I am "Douglas Schuurman, Professor at St. Olaf." Gustafson notes that in Sweden's telephone directory, men's occupations are listed along with their names. This feature of our culture is made more striking when contrasted with Native American values. When they are introduced, it is "Wendy Helgemo, Lakota," or "Richard Grounds, Sioux," or "Running Deer, Ojibwe." Tribal heritage, not occupational standing, is significant.

But idolatry need not be of one's occupation and its institutions. Many people make an idol of the nuclear family: "I can't come to church today; Sunday is family time." Many are tempted to make an idol of the family when it comes to what gives meaning to their existence. Everything is turned into the focus upon family; identity is gained exclusively from our place in the family. One's racial identity can also become an idol, as can one's national identity, or one's particular church denomination or congregation. Whenever any one of these

---

1. Eric Mount Jr., *Professional Ethics in Context: Institutions, Images and Empathy* (Louisville: Westminster/John Knox Press, 1990), 32-33.

spheres persistently dominates the others in the demands it makes upon our time, attention, and care, then it is an idol.

Vocation reminds us of the call that defines our identity: the call of the gospel to union with Christ. When a woman in the crowd blurted out to Jesus, "Blessed is the womb that bore you and the breasts that nursed you!" Jesus replied, "No, rather blessed is the one who hears and obeys my words." Responding to Christ, not place in the family or paid work, determines worth and meaning. Vocation invites us to give absolute loyalty to God in Jesus Christ, and in so doing liberates us from the tyranny of idolatry. People who are mindful that God's creating and redeeming grace is the source and goal of their entire existence will be more likely to be free from the subtle and not so subtle temptations toward idolatry of paid work, family, or any other relational field.

Vocation, Limits, and False Guilt

This second principle is closely related to the first. Much of the conflict with which we struggle is not the Great Conflict that demands "either" Christ as Lord "or" the lordship of some idol. Instead it is often confusion and anxiety over the many ways in which our finitude leads to conflict. My stated duties as professor include scholarship, teaching, and community service. To excel in any one of them is to pilfer time and energy from the others. Pastors are especially vulnerable here; they are to write elegant, short, life-changing sermons, teach everyone brilliantly regardless of the ages and abilities of their pupils, provide insightful counsel to people in times of great distress, administer churches containing power groups accustomed to control, and be everyone's good friend. To make matters even worse, members of the church rank each of these differently, so that what may be top priority for one may be at the bottom of the list for another.

Beside conflicts within a given sphere, there are conflicts between one sphere and another. Besides being carpenter, businessperson, or teacher, we are spouse, parent, child, sibling, friend, board member, citizen, member of the human race, etc. Should I spend more time with my family and less with my colleagues? Should I go out tonight with my spouse or with my friend? Should I attend the local caucus in order to elect a representative most likely to pursue justice, or should I attend the church board meeting? Should I try to save up money so that my daughters will be able to attend a church-related college when they are older, or should I give the money to Amnesty International or my church relief agency? What is God calling me to do?

Many of these decisions are made spontaneously, out of habit, and so are not always before our minds or consciences. This is natural. But when we do feel some tension here, and try to resolve it, a robust doctrine of vocation can at least remove some obstacles that often get in the way of responsible decision-making. Vocation frees us from some of the guilt that might otherwise plague us by helping us to recognize that we are limited. Some people refuse to recognize the limits of their callings, believing themselves to be responsible in the same way for needs outside and inside their divinely assigned spheres. Vocation helps us avoid "false guilt" arising from an overly extended sense of what is possible to accomplish.

For example, although I may feel pain for the many children who need parental love because they have no fathers, or have abusive ones, I am first of all father to my three children. I should not neglect them for the sake of others; God has specially assigned me to represent God's grace to my own children. This does not mean that I should do nothing at all for other children. Through my teaching I emphasize God's care for all children, and the demands of justice and love, especially for the weak. As citizen I try to vote, and encourage others to vote, for candidates who will promote wholesome marriages and families, and who see care of orphans and the fatherless as an important issue. As a member of a church I donate money and support efforts to see that justice and compassion improve the lives of the weak and vulnerable. I aspire to instill in my own children resources they need to become good parents themselves, and to become the kind of people who will contribute to God's mission on earth.

Of course, all this assumes that there is a legitimate conflict. If one feels guilt because one is amassing a fortune, or squandering one, instead of helping the poor, then the guilt is not false, but real. And the appropriate response is repentance, not honest acknowledgment of limits.

Vocation and Priorities

Flexibility and Reassessment of Priorities

Vocation encourages periodic revision of priorities. The positive side of avoiding the danger of idolatry of a given sphere is the freedom to reassess one's manner of life. The goal of this reassessment is to discern which needs should be emphasized at a given time, or for a given period of time.

In my own case, my preparation for paid work took a strategic priority over family and church participation for a time. We moved to places where this preparation could occur; we denied ourselves the financial foundations other middle-class people in America normally build for their families during their twenties and early thirties; we stitched together numerous part-time jobs to survive financially. After four years of college, three years of seminary, and four years of Ph.D. studies, I left the University of Chicago to accept a one-year terminal faculty position at Calvin College. My wife and I then had three children (ages one month, 20 months, and four years), an aborted dissertation, and exhaustion.

At this time, my wife and I took inventory, and decided that for a while I would spend less time on the dissertation and more time with the family. So for a year I set it aside in order to teach and be more engaged with my children. Because my position was terminal, this involved substantial risk. It was rare for an unfinished Ph.D. candidate to get good job offers in the 1980s. The dissertation waited till summers, and even then did not dominate my attention. After several years of this emphasis, I managed to teach on terminal contracts for two years at Calvin College and two years at St. Olaf College, applying for jobs along the way. During my fourth year I realized that if I were to continue teaching religion at a college, I had to finish the dissertation. In addition, my dissertation advisor was moving, and he sent me a letter saying it had to be done by May of 1988 if he were to be my dissertation advisor. So I shifted emphasis back to the dissertation, spending less time on teaching preparation and family matters. It consumed much of my summer. During the academic year I worked on it before my teaching day began, from 3:30 to 6:30 a.m. on weekdays, and then for several hours on Saturdays and holidays. It all came together for me in February 1988, when on the same day I received two tenure-track job offers and a letter from my advisor telling me the dissertation draft I sent him would be accepted. Finishing the dissertation was exhausting, and I was forced to reorder my priorities for a time, but for the sake of persevering in my calling as a professor, I had to devote more of my finite time and energy to my dissertation.

Most people go through similar processes of revision of priorities. By devoting one's ultimate loyalty to Christ, trusting in God's good providence finally to prevail — whether or not we get what we presently want and think we need — and by viewing all significant spheres as divine callings, we can be free from an overly rigid, inflexible set of priorities. We become open to new emphases, suggestions, and priorities.

Special Relations and General Relations

Vocation makes a person's duties to love concrete. A parent is not to love the neighbor in general, but the neighbor who is that parent's child. Because a parent has a special, divinely assigned, obligation to see to the nurturance and faith of that parent's children, he or she is justified in giving priority to the needs of his or her children when they conflict with the needs of others. As Luther says, the general imperative of Jesus' Sermon on the Mount to "give to those who ask," is limited. A father who gives away necessities to beggars is actually stealing from his dependents and disobeying God. This way of thinking about duties and obligations extends to other special relations.

Following the pattern developed in this book, the duties of any particular calling must never override the call to be a Christian and to take up its attendant duties. If and when the two are in conflict, it is always the call to Christ that has priority. When the kingdom of God is at stake, all Christians must sing with Luther,

> Let goods and kindred go,
> This mortal life also;
> The body they may kill,
> God's truth abideth still,
> His kingdom is forever.

It is best to view vocation in terms of two dangerous extremes. One extreme is to neglect obligations to particular persons to which one is related as child, friend, spouse, parent, or teacher in order to fulfill obligations to people with whom one is not so related. The other extreme is to neglect obligations to strangers in order to meet obligations to persons to whom one is specially related. Because of their anti-monastic concerns, Luther and Calvin saw neglect of special relations as the more dangerous extreme. As we saw in Chapter Four, others see neglect of strangers to be the more dangerous sin. The way most Christians praise as moral heroes those who are not engaged in family life or other "mundane" daily obligations supplies a good reason to side with Luther and Calvin here, though not in a way that omits Yoder's concerns.[2]

Yet in addition to insisting that obligations of special relations be met, vocation always widens the circle to include strangers and enemies, and even non-human communities of being in its embrace. Calvin puts the point well:

> Now, since Christ has shown in the parable of the Samaritan that the term "neighbor" includes even the most remote person [Luke 10:36], we are not expected to limit the precept of love to those in close relationships. I do not deny that the more closely a man is linked to us, the more intimate obligation we have to assist him. It is the common habit of mankind that the more close men are bound together by the ties of kinship, of acquaintanceship, or of neighborhood, the more responsibilities for one another they share. This does not offend God; for his providence, as it were, leads us to it. But I say: we ought to embrace the whole human race without exception in a single feeling of love; here there is no distinction between barbarian and Greek, worthy and unworthy, friend and enemy, since all should be contemplated in God, not in themselves.[3]

Vocation and Style

Vocation generates a *style* of interaction, whether the interaction is among friends, between spouses, or among colleagues. Anxiety and

2. For an interesting discussion relating to this issue, see Robert M. Adams, "Vocation," *Faith and Philosophy* 4/4 (October 1987): 448-62, and his more recent discussion in *Finite and Infinite Goods: A Framework for Ethics* (New York: Oxford University Press, 1999), 292-317.

3. John Calvin, *Institutes of the Christian Religion,* ed. John T. McNeill, trans. Ford Lewis Battles (Philadelphia: Westminster, 1960), 2.8.55.

pride, both of which are exacerbated by economic uncertainty and the competitive spirit of our culture, often infect interactions with others. The symptom of this infection is seeing colleagues or friends not as image bearers of God whom we serve and in whom we delight, but as threats to our own welfare, as competitors whom we best and perhaps even destroy. We envy and resent others. Anxiety and pride incline us to use others, ranking others either "above" or "beneath" ourselves, so that we can scorn the inferiors and flatter the superiors. All of this makes genuine friendship impossible. Vocation resists this by instilling mutual respect and genuine appreciation for the well-being of others. It reminds Christians that this world is God's beloved creation, the people in it are image-bearers of God, and that Christ is incarnate in the people one is serving through one's callings.

A story told by a Christian cashier illumines my point about vocation and style. She thanks God for her small part in supplying life's basic necessities. Before each shift she prays that God will open her eyes to opportunities for service that the coming shift may provide. During one shift, she noticed that a customer coming through her line seemed particularly hurried and irritated. She said a prayer for her in her heart, and moved the items along as rapidly as she could, her words to the customer as brief and polite as possible. The next customer was a regular, a man in his late seventies whom she had seen many times before. His face looked drawn and very sad. He moved more slowly than usual. She took her time moving the items across her register, asking the elderly man how he was doing today. Almost in tears, the man said that a few days ago his wife of fifty-five years had died and he did not know how he could live without her. The cashier expressed her heartfelt condolences, as she placed her hand upon his. After a few additional words of consolation, she promised the man that she would pray for him in the days to come. At the end of her shift, the cashier thanked God for enabling her to represent God's care and grace to the people she served, asking God to cause her small acts of concern and kindness to bear fruit.

Often the small things — the kind word, supportive gesture, and thoughtful deed — become avenues of God's grace. When a person's identity is defined not by success as a professional or as a parent or by any other role, but by the call to Christ, then one is free to be attentive to others and to serve them in love. One's interpersonal style will express care, respect, and even delight for others and their gifts.

Vocation and Career Moves

Some estimate that on average young people today will have four to five different careers throughout their lives. Some careers require willingness to advance by moving from location to location. In the mobile society of America, moving from place to place in the same occupation, or in a new one, is common. How does vocation relate to this increased job mobility?

Barth says that answering this question involves an *external* and an *internal* dimension. Externally one must be clear that she or he has a service to perform. It must not merely be enticing; it must objectively be an opportunity to meet needs. If you feel called to become President of Union Theological Seminary, CEO at General Motors, or pastor of Riverside Church in New York, but objectively there is no need for your services, then Barth says, you're not called to those places. A concrete invitation would meet Barth's "external" aspect leading to confidence that one has chosen the right sphere. On the subjective side, one must feel inwardly compelled — by desire and by a sense of demand — to take up that sphere. The "inner voice" must correspond to an "external confirmation." Usually this involves a combination of factors: attractiveness of the new possibility, dissatisfaction with one's current occupation, and a sense of duty drawing one to a different place.

Barth warns that other possibilities must never distract a person from the tasks at hand. If disobedience to God's command in the present sphere is the source of one's desire to go elsewhere, then one ought not to make the move. It is interesting that Albert Schweitzer usually discouraged people from following his example of doing something unusual. He felt that in most cases a "restless spirit" drove people who came for his advice:

> Such persons wanted to dedicate themselves to larger tasks because those that lay nearest did not satisfy them. . . . Only a person who can find a value in every sort of activity and devote himself to each one with full consciousness of duty, has the inward right to take as his object some extraordinary activity instead of that which falls naturally to his lot. Only someone who feels his preference to be a matter of course, not something out of the ordinary, and who has no thought of heroism, but just recognizes a duty undertaken with so-

ber enthusiasm, is capable of becoming a spiritual adventurer such as the world needs. There are no heroes of action: only heroes of renunciation and suffering. Of such there are plenty. But few of them are known, and even these not to the crowd, but to the few.[4]

Restless discontent with one's present sphere, then, may not be a valid indicator of God's call to a new sphere. It may indicate the need for renewed prayer and obedience within the existing sphere.

One must also beware the blindness of coveting when considering a new post. Restlessness born of coveting was a major concern for Luther and Calvin. In Luther's words,

> Moreover it is a common plague that no one can be satisfied with his own lot, so that the heathen say: How does it happen that there is always better fruit in another's field, and that the neighbor's cow gives more milk than my own? Whoever is a merchant praises the lot of a mechanic, that he sets home and rests, while he must wander around in the country as if going astray. On the other hand, the mechanic praises the lot of the merchant, because he is rich and is out among the people, and so on. Every person is tired of his own lot and sighs for a change.[5]

Luther advises such a person not to "think of changing his lot, but of changing his spirit of discontent. Cast aside and change your restless spirit, then the lot of one would be like that of another, and all would be prized alike, as you have experienced that you neither needed nor wished a change." He also says, perhaps with more confidence than most Christians today, "God governs all alike, places each one in the lot, that is the most useful and suitable for him, and that it could not be better arranged, even if he did it himself. This faith brings rest, contentment, peace and banishes the tired spirit."[6]

4. Albert Schweitzer, *Out of My Life and Thought: An Autobiography,* trans. C. T. Campion (New York: Henry Holt and Co., 1949), 91.

5. *Luther's Church Postil: Gospels: Advent, Christmas and Epiphany Sermons,* Vol. 1 in *The Precious and Sacred Writings of Martin Luther,* Vol. 10, ed. John Nicholas Lenker (Minneapolis: Lutherans in All Lands Co., 1905), 246.

6. *Luther's Church Postil,* 248. Though Luther and Calvin recognize that God is free to call a person elsewhere, they seem to think that envy and restlessness are usually behind discontent. Calvin says, ". . . the Lord bids each one of us in all life's actions to look

Barth noted that things often look different from within a particular sphere than they look from outside. His vivid description reminds me of long-distance phone conversations I've had with seminary friends about their first parish. His senses of wonder and anxiety are to the point:

> [N]othing is more astonishing than the daily routine of a sphere of operation. The contours displayed, the factors involved, the true features of its goals and tasks and requirements, emerge only when we have chosen it as our daily routine. . . . So this is its real nature! What have I done? Could I really have had this in view? Would I want it if I could begin again at the beginning? But it is now too late; I have begun. I was asked once; I am not asked again.[7]

When one becomes intimately acquainted with the ambiguities, limitations, pains, and possibilities of an existing sphere, other spheres can look better than they really are. The freedom of the single life often looks better than the obligations of marriage, at least to the married. The intimacy and constancy of marriage often looks superior to the freedom of the single life, at least to those who are single. It is a temptation to covet what other people have, and to demean one's own spheres. My wife modified a famous proverb in a way that I have found helpful: "The grass is always greener on the other side of the fence. But there's manure over there, too." Coveting is often doubly blind: blind to the difficulties involved in the new condition, and blind to the opportunities for meaningful growth and service in the current post.

Although one must take care not to switch spheres out of disobedience or coveting, one must also take care not to remain in one's post because of sloth or pride. The comforts of a known routine can deaden one to new challenges. Thinking that one's present institution is the

---

to his calling. For he knows with what great restlessness human nature flames, with what fickleness it is borne hither and thither, how its ambition longs to embrace various things at once. . . . And that no one may thoughtlessly transgress his limits, he has named these various kinds of living 'callings.' Therefore each individual has his own kind of living assigned to him by the Lord as a sort of sentry post so that he may not heedlessly wander throughout life" (*Institutes* 3.10.6). This rules out meddling in others' affairs as well as restlessly shifting around one's posts.

7. Karl Barth, *Church Dogmatics*, 3/4, ed. and trans. G. W. Bromiley (Edinburgh: T&T Clark, 1961), 637.

best one on earth can be a form of pride that gets in the way of God's call. We must always be open to the possibility that God will call us to other forms of paid work, to new social relations, to a different marital status, to different roles in our churches and communities.

Vocation and Paid Work — Meaning and Transformation

The task of developing a concrete doctrine of vocation for paid work requires participation from Christians actually engaged in that work. As Emil Brunner said over half a century ago,

> The Christian community has a specific task in just this field, namely, to work out a concrete doctrine of vocation through its lay members who know the jobs and their threat to working morale, and to demand and to create such technical and psychological conditions as are necessary to regain the lost sense of work as a divine calling.[8]

Those who are closest to your work are in the best position to determine what vocation means for their work. As they do so, the following general principles help guide their efforts.

To view one's work in terms of divine calling transforms work in two ways, each of which is crucial in modern times: (1) It infuses work with religious meaning, leading to integration of one's life, and (2) it requires constant ethical assessment of the products and processes of work. Like Christ, Christians are called to be participants in God's name in this world. But as we participate in the world, we must discern good from evil, and promote what is good while resisting what is evil. Thus we follow Paul's injunction, "Do not be conformed to this world, but be transformed by the renewing of your minds so that you may discern what is the will of God — what is good and acceptable and perfect" (Rom. 12:2).

8. Emil Brunner, *Christianity and Civilization,* 2 vols. (New York: Charles Scribner's Sons, 1948), 2:69.

Work Itself

Vocation Creates Meaning

To view one's work as divinely given vocation makes it meaningful work. Workers find meaning in their work in several ways. One source of meaning is the work itself. The deepest meaning of one's work comes from faith: to believe that God has placed you in this particular place for this particular time, to use your gifts and opportunities to express gratitude for God's great gift of salvation by serving God and your neighbor through your work — that is true meaning, the source of real satisfaction and joy. One works finally not for one's boss, not for one's spouse and family, not for the sake of the country, but for the Lord. The eyes of faith make work holy. And when work is holy it is meaningful, and even full of joy.

Vocation can infuse even dull and distasteful work with religious meaning. When Luther advised Christian fathers to imagine they were holding the infant Jesus in their hands as they changed their baby's dirty diapers, he said it was angel's work. Faith makes all jobs, even the ones seemingly the most trivial or distasteful, equally holy. The apostle Paul reminds the church at Corinth that even the part of the body that seems the most trivial is as important as all the other parts. When industrial workers do their work "as to the Lord," it becomes meaningful. Christians should seek work in which their gifts can be most effectively utilized for the welfare of others, but even work that fails to make use of their gifts can still be meaningful as a calling if it serves others.

Vocation Calls for Transformation

Vocation also calls for continuous transformations of work so that in and through work a person's gifts are best utilized for the common good. Studies have shown that nothing destroys motivation and productivity in the workplace more than deadening routines.[9] If there is room for exercising responsibility, developing one's gifts, and expressing one's agency in one's work, then that work creates satisfaction and fulfillment, adding meaning to one's life. It also makes employees more productive.

9. See Lee Hardy, *The Fabric of This World* (Grand Rapids: Eerdmans, 1990), 138-40.

The "Hawthorne Experiment" reveals how important it is for employees to feel they are participating in the design of their own work.[10] The experiment took place at the Hawthorne Works of Western Electric, on Chicago's west side, between 1927 and 1932. Five female relay assemblers were put in a special room, set off from the main assembly room by partitions. Unlike the rest of the workers, the women were subjected to changes in their work routine — number of breaks, changes in schedule, and payment scheme. Practically every change brought a boost in productivity, and the highest boost came when the workers returned to their original conditions. Elton Mayo, Professor of Industrial Research at Harvard University, was brought in to help interpret and explain the test results. Over two years, Mayo interviewed 21,000 employees at Hawthorne Works. He found that the secret to productivity was not in the changed conditions, but in the human relations between management and workers. In the test situation, workers had a greater sense that they were participating in determining their own working conditions. They were consulted before every experimental change, and their comments were discussed and accepted. Increases in productivity through this kind of participation became known as the "Hawthorne Effect."[11]

A fully developed sense of vocation should lead managers and CEOs to allow for as much agency, responsibility, and employee participation as possible in job design. The central idea of vocation is to use one's God-given gifts to be of use to the broader community. Those responsible for job design should do all they can to make this possible. It also places an obligation on workers to think creatively about more effective ways to organize their work. As Peter Drucker, leading authority on business organization for the past thirty years, puts it,

> Workers must be made responsible for their own work. And that means, among other things, that they must be involved in designing their own jobs. Not because such involvement will satisfy their ego need for control, making them happier and thus more productive — although it might — but because the workers possess a significant pool of knowledge and expertise in matters pertaining to their own

10. I am depending here on Hardy, *The Fabric of This World*, 143-44.
11. Hardy, *The Fabric of This World*, 144.

jobs. . . . It is a matter . . . of making "use of the worker's knowledge and experience in the one area where he *is* the expert."[12]

Though managers must balance workers' development and job satisfaction with the productivity and profitability of the company, their calling is to facilitate the exercise of vocation of the workers.

For work to be a vocation, it must not be alienating, dehumanizing work. Every job has its tedious, unpleasant, distasteful parts. Vocation invites us to do even these "for the Lord," and see them as holy. But it also challenges us to think creatively about job design and employee participation so that gifts are used as effectively as possible for the common good.

The Context of Work

Vocation Creates Meaning

Another source of meaning is the *context* of the work. For some jobs, and for some people, the work itself may not be the primary source of meaning. Instead what makes work meaningful is the context of one's work. Jobs provide opportunities for solitude and reflection. As we saw earlier, Thomas Merton has written that manual labor is more conducive to prayer and reflection than is the work of priests and bishops. The spirit of worship and prayer can permeate one's work, adding meaning and joy.

Work also provides community. Friendships and other relationships develop in the workplace. There is room for humor, for sharing of ideas and concerns, and the sense of satisfaction that comes from engaging in a common project with others. Even if a job is tedious and demanding, meaning and satisfaction can be obtained through interaction with co-workers.

Vocation affects the context of work, for our fellow workers, and the various people our jobs bring us into contact with, are our neighbors. And as we express love for our neighbors we express our love for

---

12. Peter F. Drucker, *Management: Tasks, Responsibilities, Practices* (New York: Harper & Row, 1974), 267-73, as summarized by Hardy, *The Fabric of This World*, 164.

Christ. As Luther saw Christ in the needy infant, so we can see Christ in the needs of our neighbors. In this way vocation infuses the context of our work with new meaning.

Another contextual feature of work that makes it meaningful is the interdependence of business with other forms of community. Marriage and family cannot survive without an economic basis; education, culture, and the arts require financial and institutional support; whole towns and small cities can be destroyed if industry shuts its doors and moves on; the nation as a whole needs an economic foundation; people in other countries throughout the world are influenced by what happens here, for good or ill. In contributing to the success of a valid business enterprise, one is indirectly contributing to these other communities as well.

Vocation Calls for Transformation

Sin also infects the context of work. Relations among workers, and between workers and managers, can be marked by suspicion rather than trust, by antagonism rather than mutual support, by servile conformity rather than mutual respect. Racial and sexual discrimination often infect the workplace, dictating who gets hired, who gets promoted, and who is intimidated. Especially in times of high unemployment, historic injustices continue in veiled form, and affirmative action policies are at best an imperfect response to discrimination. Resentment and envy bear the fruit of hatred.

Working conditions must be humane and conducive to the work being done. Pope John Paul II calls upon the state to ensure safe, humane working conditions as a basic human right because he is aware of the powerful temptation to exploit workers and neglect working conditions within a competitive capitalist global economy.

In our interdependent global economy, Christians are called to do all they can to avoid harmful effects of industry upon other human beings and upon the natural environment. The power of some of the larger companies is startling. Christian ethicist Larry Rasmussen describes large corporations this way:

> As of the 1990s the whole world has become a kind of "non-union hiring hall" for these giants as they create the effective working ma-

166

trix for what they casually combine as "human" and "natural" "capi-
tal" and "resources." And their economic clout is enormous. In the
1990s the one hundred largest corporations in the world had more
economic power than 80 percent of the world's people. In 1991 the
aggregate sales of the world's ten largest corporations totaled more
than the aggregate GNP of the one hundred smallest countries of
the world. . . . The 1992 sales revenue of General Motors alone ($133
billion) was about the same as the combined GNP of eight countries
whose combined population is one-tenth of the world's — Tanzania,
Ethiopia, Bangladesh, Zaire, Nigeria, Kenya, Nepal, and Pakistan.[13]

Rasmussen points out that while nation-states used to control corporations, in a "spectacular turnabout, nation-states now vie to be included in the wealth generated by corporations in the global economy.
'When it comes to global markets these days,' a *New York Times* article
reports, 'the motto of governments is: There they go, I must catch up,
for I am their leader.'"[14]

Many say at the rate we are currently using industrial materials, we
will soon have used up natural resources and be no longer "sustainable" environmentally. The United States, for example, used 100 million metric tons of industrial materials in 1900, 500 million in 1950,
and 4.5 billion in 1993.[15] As Rasmussen puts it, "[E]very day the world-
wide economy burns an amount of energy the planet required 10,000
years to create. Or, put another way, 27 years worth of stored solar energy is burned and released by utilities, cars, houses, factories, and
farms every 24 hours."[16]

Because vocation links our daily work with other communities,
and with the community of nature, and finally with God, Christians
must be concerned about such issues. Rasmussen reminds us that justice in society and in the workplace does not conflict with sustainability of the natural environment:

---

13. Larry Rasmussen, *Earth Community, Earth Ethics* (Maryknoll, N.Y.: Orbis Books,
1996), 64. Rasmussen is citing David C. Korten, *When Corporations Rule the World* (San
Francisco: Berret-Koehler, 1996), 220-21.

14. Rasmussen, *Earth Community*, 64.

15. Rasmussen, *Earth Community*, 66.

16. Rasmussen, *Earth Community*, 59. Here Rasmussen is citing Paul Hawken, *The
Ecology of Commerce: A Declaration of Sustainability* (New York: HarperCollins), 21-22.

"the lesson to be learned for our own quest for sustainable development" is that "justice and equality are important factors in assuring
sustainability". . . . [H]ighly stratified societies controlled by a relatively small elite generate institutions that aim to keep social arrangements intact when the cost is obvious and there is progressive
environmental deterioration. . . . [W]here maldistributed power and
inequality reign, powerful forces usually continue to benefit from
the depletion of both peoples and land — until it is too late. . . .
[S]ustainability and unsustainability correlate roughly with just and
unjust social arrangements.[17]

In such a complex interdependent world, it is easy to become either
cynical or slothful about our responsibilities. But vocation calls Christians to be concerned about them, and to struggle with others to find
policies, practices, and perspectives that do not worsen matters, but
improve them. This is part of our unique vocation, as members of the
world community during this time and this place.

The Product of Work

Vocation Creates Meaning

The *product* of one's work is another source of meaning. Knowing
that fruit of one's labor is meeting the genuine needs of others creates
meaning and adds joy to work. Knowing that what one produces will
harm the neighbor removes this meaning.

By meeting the needs of others through their work, workers participate in God's providence, as agents through which God's care and love
are expressed to the world. Luther believed that God milked cows
through those called to do that work. The needs of peoples are numerous and varied: they need food and shelter, clothing and transporta-
tion, medical care and education, tools and utensils of many kinds,
sources of energy for heat and protection, music and art, leisure and
entertainment, justice and peace. Through various callings, God's

17. Rasmussen, *Earth Community*, 42. Rasmussen is citing Gowdy, "Place, Equity,
and Environmental Impact: Lessons from the Past," *Ecojustice Quarterly* 14, no. 2 (Spring
1994).

provident care for the world is expressed. Insofar as work meets genuine human needs, then, it is religiously meaningful as cooperation in God's provident care for the world.

Sometimes it is easy to see how the products of our work meet human needs. The cobbler in Luther's day could feel satisfaction during the week, seeing that the members of his village were comfortably using the shoes he'd made or repaired for them. Sometimes the importance of the product at a given time will infuse even tedious work with profound meaning. Christian philosopher and playwright Dorothy Sayers described working on the assembly line in England during WWII as some of the most meaningful work she'd experienced. It was boring — attaching nuts to bolts for war machinery. And the noise made communication with colleagues difficult if not impossible. But with every turn of the nut she knew she was contributing to the demise of Hitler and his demonic Third Reich.

Yet in our modern, global economy it is often difficult to gain meaning from the products of our work. Many industries make only small parts of a larger product, and are shipped off from one side of the world to another. So too, the completed products are transported far and near, and workers cannot often see that what they are making is in fact meeting the needs of their neighbors.

Because of this, Christians require more hope and faith to gain meaning from the products of their work. They also need at least a small measure of confidence that the market system — which largely but not exclusively determines distribution of goods — is effective. According to Pope John Paul II's encyclical, *Centissimus Annus*, "It would appear that, on the level of individual nations and of international relations, *the free market* is the most effective instrument for utilizing resources and effectively responding to needs."[18] Vocation adds meaning to work by evoking hope and trust that needs are met, and therefore workers are agents of God's provident care.

---

18. Pope John Paul II, *Centissimus Annus*, sec. 34. The pope immediately adds that not all goods are marketable and not all needs "solvent." He says, "It is a strict duty of justice and truth not to allow fundamental human needs to remain unsatisfied, and not to allow those burdened by such needs to perish." A large part of the duty of the state is to provide a safety net, and other incentives within the largely capitalistic economy, to ensure that basic needs are met.

Vocation Calls for Transformation

Though there is much room for many kinds of goods and services, that room is not unlimited. Vocation condemns jobs and industries that harm the neighbor, and commends those devoted to meeting the needs of "the least of these" in society. Child pornography, for example, is an industry. But being, say, a photographer for such an industry cannot be a vocation because it exploits and harms one's neighbors.

Because leisure and recreation are important needs, producing products to serve those needs can be a vocation. But the deepest integration of faith and life occurs when essential needs are met through one's products, and when they are met for the most vulnerable and needy of the world. The United States Catholic Bishops wrote in their 1986 pastoral letter on the economy, "Personal decisions, policies of private and public bodies, and power relationships must all be evaluated by their effects on those who lack the minimum necessities of nutrition, housing, education, and health care." And "Meeting fundamental human needs must come before the fulfillment of desires for luxury consumer goods, for profits not conducive to the common good and for unnecessary military hardware."[18]

Because of limited employment opportunities it may be unrealistic to apply this ideal instantly. But insofar as one is able, one should seek occupations that meet the needs of others. Again, there is much room here for Christian freedom and discernment, depending also upon opportunity and ability.

The Income from Work

Vocation and Meaning

Another source of meaning is the *paycheck* one receives for one's work. This enables one to avoid poverty, to support spouse and children, to contribute to churches and other worthy causes, and even pay for hobbies and recreational activities. Though income is an instrumental

---

19. National Council of Catholic Bishops, *Economic Justice for All* (United States Catholic Conference, 1986), as cited by Hardy, *The Fabric of This World*, 97.

value, it can be used well. And when it is well used, it contributes to the meaning one experiences in one's work.

Vocation and Transformation

Vocation calls for fair compensation. What is fair will depend upon the financial basis necessary to become a participating member of one's community. Pope John Paul II, in harmony with the past century of Catholic moral teaching, defines a "just wage" as income needed to support oneself and one's family, and to put a little aside for retirement. This is the minimum standard that all profitable companies should respect.

Fair compensation will also depend upon the profitability of the company. Companies must make a profit over time to survive in a competitive economy. If they become very profitable, the profits should return to the employees, whether in the form of higher wages or stock options. Workers, managers, CEOs, and stockholders should all benefit from the profitability of the company. Huge gaps between salaries of CEOs and average employees are inexcusable from the perspective of vocation. In 1990, CEOs at major American corporations made 85 times the pay of the average factory worker. In the decade of the 1980s, CEO pay has risen 212 percent, while worker pay has risen only 54 percent. According to Lutheran ethicist James Childs, "such disparities create a trust gap that threatens to undermine morale."[20]

Fair compensation will also depend upon the contribution one has made to the product and its distribution. Though it is sometimes very difficult to determine whose role is most important to the overall success of a company, it is possible to give equal pay for equal work, and have a fair scale to reflect length of service to the company. Pay discrepancies based on gender or race violate justice, and so are contrary to Christian vocation. It is important that Christians who receive less pay for the same work simply because they are women or members of groups historically discriminated against pressure their employers for fair compensation. They should do so not only because they deserve it, but also because failure to press such interests promotes continued dis-

---

20. James M. Childs, *Ethics in Business: Faith at Work* (Minneapolis: Fortress Press, 1995), 75.

crimination and injustice. And this is good neither for the workers, nor for the employers, nor for the larger society.

Admittedly, these principles are general in nature. They cannot be understood or applied without a determination to discern God's call as it meets us in the details of our lives. And they rely ultimately on the art of prayerful understanding of the will of God.

CHAPTER SEVEN

Vocation in the Wider World

Reemphasizing Christian Identity

The question of what basic stance Christians should take as they engage the world through their callings still remains. That stance should be guided by two central tasks. First, because Christian belief and practice are so pervasively and seriously threatened by American culture, there is a pressing need to reemphasize Christian identity. Churches must focus anew on their nature and calling as communities of witness to the gospel in light of the increasingly corrosive effects of the broader culture upon Christian beliefs and practices. The media either fail to say anything about religion or depict it in the most bizarre forms imaginable. Public education in our pluralistic society cultivates legitimate values of tolerance, mutual respect, honesty, and self-respect, but the worldview it conveys systematically excludes attention to religion, thereby directly implying the irrelevance of religion to all of life. Without religious narratives and practices to frame them, moral values easily become distorted. Tolerance slides into moral relativism; self-respect becomes unbridled individualism; mutual respect turns into negative freedom shorn of any notion of the common good.

Many of the students I have taught have been raised in mainline Protestant denominations, but when they come to college they know almost nothing about their faith — its biblical roots, historical development, ethical implications, or theological articulation. There are of course exceptions. But for the most part, when students arrive on campus, their moral views are shaped more by public education and the media than by the church. Many of them are relativists who believe that whatever others' moral or religious beliefs and practices are, they are fine for them, so long as individuals hold them sincerely. Intolerance is the most grievous moral fault possible. Sexual intercourse is fine, so long as the persons having sex "love each other" and freely agree to it. They want to succeed in the larger world, to become wealthy and prestigious, and enjoy the fruits of their success. Their religious life, if active at all, is sequestered off from their larger aims and practices.

Christian formation must be more comprehensive, intentional, and sustained. In such challenging times, it is crucial to attract the brightest and best to become church pastors, educators, and administrators. The education of all members, but especially of youth and new converts, needs emphasis. Churches must explore new forms of community, forms that exhibit integrity, compassion, and solidarity with those in need. Churches must work harder to form their members into a way of life that faithfully reflects the gospel. An hour or so of worship on Sunday simply is not enough. The teachings of Christianity must be socially embodied in a community. One learns to play the violin by practicing under the guidance of an accomplished violinist; one learns what it is to be in the woodwind section of an orchestra by playing in that section. So too one learns to be a Christian by engaging in Christian practices, guided by the wisdom and example of more experienced believers. These practices include entering into the historic liturgies of the church, giving an account of Christian hope when demanded by those who are punishing Christians for doing what is right (1 Pet. 3:15), listening attentively to the teachings of the faith, participating in the sacraments of baptism and the Eucharist, prayer, singing, forgiveness and reconciliation, and engaging in actions of compassion and justice in the world.[1]

1. John Howard Yoder and Stanley Hauerwas have been emphasizing this need, and related view of practices, for many years. For other recent works that expand upon many of the practices I identify, see *Practicing our Faith: A Way of Life for a Searching People,* ed. Dorothy C. Bass (San Francisco: Jossey-Bass, 1997), and Duane K. Friesen, "The Church as an Alternative Community," in *Artists, Citizens, Philosphers Seeking the Peace of the City: An Anabaptist Theology of Culture,* fwd. Glen Stassen (Scottdale, Penn.: Herald Press, 2000), 126-66.

Christians must reexamine other institutions as well, for churches alone cannot accomplish this task. No religious community will survive for long without family-based practices to sustain its beliefs. It is not surprising that a great deal of the religious life of Hinduism and Judaism centers on family. These groups show an amazing ability to survive, and flourish, even in societies and cultures that are hostile to many of their core beliefs. Christian families must follow their example. Parents must learn to be "apostles to their children," as Luther recommends. From their parents' example, children must learn to study, reflect upon, and discuss their faith and its meaning for life. They must read the Bible to their children, and explain its teachings as best they are able. Many of the practices identified above can readily be expressed in family life. Parents should meet with other parents to discuss how they can become better apostles to their children.

Christian schools can play a crucial role. The ones that exist should be strengthened, and new schools should be founded. Although it is possible for church and family to accomplish faithfully the Christian nurture of youth without the help of Christian schools, there is more need than ever for Christian school teachers to help parents and churches to form a Christian worldview and way of life that can withstand the corrosive effects of the broader culture. There is also need for parachurch groups formed on the basis of various types of paid work. Christian clerical workers should meet together to discuss what their faith means for their work. Christian lawyers, business people, medical doctors, and others should form associations aimed at helping each other discern what their callings mean. These could be small, informal groups, or larger organized societies, or some combination of both.

Christians should not use coercive powers to impose their identity-forming beliefs and practices on the broader society. They should not, for example, try to pass laws forcing public school teachers to begin class and meals with Christian prayers. They should not punish people for failing to attend church worship or partake of the Lord's Supper.[2]

---

2. Witold Rybczynski, in *Waiting for the Weekend* (New York: Viking Press, 1991), notes, "The first Sunday law enacted by the Colony of Virginia, in 1610, enjoined all men and women to attend divine services in the morning and catechism in the afternoon. The penalty for a first offense was losing a week's provisions; for the second offense, whipping; and, for the third, death" (pp. 73-74). As late as 1985, thirty-nine states still

The constitutional separation of powers expresses legally the deeper moral demand to love one's neighbors as oneself. As Christians do not want others to use political powers to force them to engage in, say, Muslim practices, so too they should not want to use these powers to impose Christian beliefs and practices upon those who disagree with them. The kingdom Christ comes, not by the sword of worldly rulers, but by the power of the Word and Spirit.

Christians should demand that government provide the space necessary to develop the religious life of their communities. And to the extent that religious communities provide services that are available to all and advance the common good — such as food, clothing, housing for the poor, health, and education — government ought to provide non-discriminatory forms of support, such as tax relief and financial support. College students in America, for example, can use state and federal financial assistance to attend any college or university that is academically accredited, whatever its religious mission and affiliation may be. Vouchers for parents of children in grades K-12 would extend this support to primary and secondary schools. The "faith-based initiatives" of Presidents Clinton and Bush likewise encourage government funding of groups providing basic social services, not discriminating against groups simply because they also have a religious purpose. Though holding dangers of entanglement of church and state, and of de-emphasizing the role of religion in the activities and mission of these groups, the basic approach is sound.[3] Yet although the government has an important role in providing for religious freedom and encouraging religiously based humanitarian activity, it should not use its powers to impose any one religion upon the rest of the population.

---

had "blue laws" restricting activity, either by complete ban on commerce or by limiting specific kinds of activities: "Every Sunday, somewhere in the United States, it is illegal to barber; bowl; play billiards, bingo, polo, or cards; gamble; race horses; hunt; go to the movies; sell cars, fresh meat or alcohol; organize boxing or wrestling matches; hold public dances or sporting events; or dig oysters" (pp. 74-75).

3. See Stephen L. Carter, *God's Name in Vain: The Wrongs and Rights of Religion in Politics* (New York: Basic Books, 2000), for an insightful analysis of the dangers of state "neutrality" and "accommodation" in regard to religion.

Engaging Broader Publics Intentionally

Although the churches need to reemphasize their own identity, they must also engage intentionally the broader publics in which they reside.[4] Though there are dangers and temptations involved, love compels Christians to it. Much Christian influence upon the broader world will be unpredictable and so have unintended effects. Who could have predicted the social impact of the early religious training given to Desmund Tutu or Martin Luther King Jr.? Who could have foreseen the political implications of Luther's proclamation of the priesthood of all believers and of democratically structured Protestant congregations? Who could have anticipated the social impact of St. Anthony's decision to enter the desert for a life of prayer? John Howard Yoder and Stanley Hauerwas are right to call attention to the fact that by "being the church" and attending to her life, Christians influence the broader world. Paul's ministry at Ephesus turned so many citizens away from idolatry that it disrupted the city's economy, causing the merchants who sold idols to foment a riot (Acts 19:21-41). Paul's aim was not to alter the economy at Ephesus; it was to preach the gospel. Much of the church's impact on the wider society is unintentional.

But Christians should also aim intentionally to engage the other publics in which they live. To the degree that they are able to influence them, Christians are indeed responsible for the larger shape and direction of political, economic, and cultural life. To love one's neighbors is to care about their welfare. To care about their welfare is to take seriously the political, economic, and cultural forces that so influence their lives. The general aim should be to promote the common good and the neighbor's welfare in any way made possible by one's callings. As Pope John Paul II recently wrote, "the Church's *social teaching* is itself a valid *instrument of evangelization.*" It

> proclaims God and his mystery of salvation in Christ to every human being. . . . In this light, and only in this light, does it concern itself with everything else: the human rights of the individual, and in particular of the "working class," the family and education, the du-

4. Robert Benne, *The Paradoxical Vision: A Public Theology for the Twenty-first Century* (Minneapolis: Fortress Press, 1995), usefully distinguishes between "direct" and "indirect" connections where Christians influence society (184-224).

ties of the State, the ordering of national and international society, economic life, culture, war and peace, and respect for life from the moment of conception until death.[5]

At the center of the pope's engagement of the broader society is justice for the poor and the "witness of actions" against material, cultural, and spiritual poverty. The pope calls for cooperation of Christians with members of other religious groups, together using all the knowledge represented in the academic disciplines, to incarnate the truth of human dignity and vocation. Those who affirm Protestant vocation can only say "Amen!"

Like the Jewish exiles in Babylon, Christians in America should "seek the welfare [*shalom*] of the city where I have sent you . . . , and pray to the Lord on its behalf, for in its welfare you will find your welfare" (Jer. 29:7). If, like Daniel, Christians rise to positions of great political and social influence, they should use that influence wisely to promote justice and the common good. After courageously interpreting King Nebuchadnezzar's dream, predicting that the king would go insane for seven years as God's judgment upon the king's arrogance, Daniel advised, "Therefore, O king . . . atone for your sins with righteousness, and your iniquities with mercy to the oppressed, so that your prosperity may be prolonged" (Dan. 4:27). Also, like Daniel, we must never bend the knee to the idols of the empire, resisting even to the point of being thrown into a lion's den.

Christians should strive to form and maintain political institutions that create and enforce laws that are merciful and just, and that are conducive to the flourishing of human life in other spheres. Whatever the dangers of the Constantinian reformation of church and society, it should not be forgotten that Constantine's "Christendom" included divesting the emperor of his title to divinity, making it legally permissible to be a Christian, banning crucifixion as a cruel and inhumane form of punishment, making it illegal to commit infanticide and to bequeath wealth to mistresses, repealing laws penalizing celibates, making the first day of the week a holiday, and granting a degree of tax exemption for the sake of the church's welfare for the poor.[6]

---

5. John Paul II, *On the Hundredth Anniversary of Rerum Novarum (Centesimus Annus)* (Washington, D.C.: United States Catholic Conference, 1991), par. 54.

6. Roland H. Bainton, *Christendom: A Short History of Christianity and Its Impact on*

In a similar spirit, Christians should engage in economic life to ensure that needed goods and services are produced humanely and distributed fairly. They should be agents and examples of reconciliation and healing. They should participate in the projects of technology and culture, advancing knowledge, cultivating the arts, utilizing every resource to relieve human suffering and promote flourishing. Whether one has a large or small role to play in promoting the welfare of the city, one must serve faithfully as one is able. Knowing that their citizenship is in heaven, Christians should offer their earthly service as their worship to God.

Christians should seek the welfare of the city by bearing witness to the gospel of Jesus Christ and building communities that are icons of life shaped by that gospel. They should do so by word and deed, trying to persuade others to join them in their faith and life. They should also seek its welfare by participating in public debates about policy matters and other pressing problems of our time. The Roman Catholic encyclical tradition and the pastoral letters of the American Catholic bishops offer many fine examples that give guidance to Christians of all traditions. In them the church tries to bring the wisdom of its teaching and tradition to matters of war and peace, sexual and reproductive ethics, poverty and economic responsibility, and the nature and limits of political power in relation to other social communities. Many Protestant organizations have attempted similar social statements, but with less coherence and impact.[7]

In addition to the intentional efforts of institutionalized churches to influence the broader society, individual Christians should do what they can to seek the welfare of the city. The prodigious efforts of Richard John Neuhaus and Max Stackhouse to shape the minds and dy-

---

Western Civilization, Vol. 1: From the Birth of Christ to the Reformation (New York: Harper Torchbooks, 1966), 93-94.

7. In *The Paradoxical Vision*, Robert Benne argues that the efforts of mainstream Protestantism to influence the broader society have failed, largely because of a Calvinist doctrine of sanctification in which "expectations for human history were too expansive" (p. 42). Benne praises the pastoral letters of the American Catholic Bishops on nuclear deterrence and the American economy as "excellent illustrations of theology becoming public" (p. 202). Though I share his regard for Catholic social teaching, I think his analysis of recent efforts of churches from Calvinist traditions to influence the broader society is overly negative.

namics of the wider society are good examples. There is an "overlapping consensus" of core moral norms and values central to American society, even if it is difficult to identify them. These have deep roots in Jewish and Christian tradition. It is no accident that the widely accepted notion that individuals have fundamental dignity and human rights emerged in the West.[8] It is a Christian calling to make use of resources in the broader culture to oppose injustice, work for justice, and enable human life to flourish.

Conclusion

It is against this background that we need to think about vocation in the tradition of Luther and Calvin, for I believe it is imperative for Christians to regain key elements of their view. Those elements have, as we have seen, deep roots in the Bible. They are not exclusively Protestant, but have many resonances with the Roman Catholic and Orthodox traditions. My intention has not been to take on the modern challenge point by point, but rather to trace central aspects of vocation anew in light of the modern milieu to see if there are ways to review and reexperience life as vocation. Yet it is important to bear in mind that, in the process of rearticulation of vocation, some aspects of the early reformers' view of vocation have to be critiqued and revised.

What I have attempted here is a small beginning for the larger task of renewing a contemporary Christian doctrine of vocation. Before one can return to a tradition, one must know something about that tradition. So I have tried to make programmatic claims about how the early reformers and a few later strands of mainline Protestant traditions understand vocation, about vocation's critics, and about how to defend the tradition against and to reshape it in light of important criticisms.

It is my hope that Christians trying to relate their faith to the rest of life will be helped by these reflections on vocation. To those who have forgotten this language or exchanged it for the Babel of modern

8. See Max L. Stackhouse, *Creeds, Society, and Human Rights: A Study in Three Cultures* (Grand Rapids: Eerdmans, 1984), and David Novak, *Covenantal Rights: A Study in Jewish Political Theory* (Princeton: Princeton University Press, 2000), for two discerning studies of how Western notions of human rights are grounded in Jewish and Christian traditions.

times, much vocation talk may sound odd. But who knows — maybe some of the claims, insights, and images presented here will move them to seek their own Origin and Ending, and discover in their quest the Christ who is our Alpha and Omega, our Path and our Goal.

Bibliography

Adams, Robert M. *Finite and Infinite Goods: A Framework for Ethics.* New York: Oxford University Press, 1999.

———. "Vocation" in *Faith and Philosophy* 4/4 (October 1987): 448-462.

Allen, Joseph. *Love and Conflict: A Covenantal Model of Christian Ethics.* Nashville: Abingdon, 1984.

Augustine. *Confessions.* Trans. and intro. R. S. Pine-Coffin. London: Penguin Books, 1961.

Badcock, Gary D. *The Way of Life: A Theology of Christian Vocation.* Grand Rapids: Eerdmans, 1998.

Baillie, John. *What is Christian Civilization?* New York: Charles Scribner's Sons, 1945.

Bainton, Roland H. *Christendom: A Short History of Christianity and Its Impact on Western Civilization,* Vol. I: *From the Birth of Christ to the Reformation.* New York: Harper Torchbooks, 1966.

Barth, Karl. *Church Dogmatics 3/4: The Doctrine of Creation.* Ed. G. W. Bromiley and T. F. Torrance, trans. G. W. Bromiley. Edinburgh: T&T Clark, 1961.

Bellah, Robert N., et al. *The Good Society.* New York: Knopf, 1991.

———. *Habits of the Heart: Individualism and Commitment in American Life.* New York: Harper and Row, 1985.

Benne, Robert. *Ordinary Saints: An Introduction to the Christian Life.* Minneapolis: Fortress Press, 1988.

———. *The Paradoxical Vision: A Public Theology for the Twenty-first Century.* Minneapolis: Fortress Press, 1995.

The New Oxford Annotated Bible, 3rd edition (with Apocryphal/Deutero-canonical Books). Ed. Michael D. Coogan. New York: Oxford University Press, 2001.

Billing, Einar. *Our Calling.* Trans Conrad Bergendoff. Philadelphia: Fortress Press, 1964.

Boesak, Allan. *Black and Reformed: Apartheid, Liberation and the Calvinist Tradition.* Ed. Leonard Sweetman. Maryknoll, N.Y.: Orbis, 1984.

Bonhoeffer, Dietrich. *The Cost of Discipleship,* rev. ed. Trans. R. H. Fuller. New York: Macmillan, 1963.

———. *Ethics.* Trans. Neville H. Smith, ed. Eberhard Bethge. London: Collins, 1964.

Brunner, Emil. *The Divine Imperative.* Trans. Olive Wyon. Philadelphia: Westminster, 1937.

———. *Christianity and Civilization,* 2 vols. New York: Charles Scribner's Sons, 1948.

Busch, Eberhard. *Karl Barth: His Life from Letters and Autobiographical Texts.* Trans. John Bowden. Philadelphia: Fortress Press, 1976.

Bussert, Joy M. K. *Battered Women: From a Theology of Suffering to an Ethic of Empowerment.* New York: Division for Mission in North America, Lutheran Church in America, 1986.

Calvin, John. *Institutes of the Christian Religion.* Trans. F. L. Battles, vols. 20 and 21 in *The Library of Christian Classics.* Ed. J. T. McNeill. Philadelphia: Westminster Press, 1960.

———. *John Calvin: Treatises Against the Anabaptists and Against the Libertines.* Ed. and trans. B. W. Farley. Grand Rapids: Baker Books, 1988.

Carter, Stephen L. *God's Name in Vain: The Wrongs and Rights of Religion in Politics.* New York: Basic Books, 2000.

Catechism of the Catholic Church, 2d ed (www.scborromeo.org/ccc/p123a9p4 .htm#11)

Catholic Encyclopedia (www.newadvent.org/cathen/15498a.htm)

Childs, James M. *Ethics in Business: Faith at Work.* Minneapolis: Fortress Press, 1995.

Co-Creation and Capitalism: John Paul II's Laborem Exercens. Ed. John W. Houck and Oliver F. Williams. Washington D.C.: University Press of America, 1983.

The Compact Oxford English Dictionary, 2d Edition. Oxford: Oxford University Press, 1991.

Cotton, John. "Christian Calling" in *The American Puritans: Their Prose and Poetry.* Ed. Perry Miller. Garden City, N.Y.: Doubleday Anchor, 1956.

Davies, Paul. "Physics and the Mind of God" (Templeton Prize Address, 1995). *First Things: A Monthly Journal of Religion and Public Life* 55 (August/September 1995).

De Gruchy, John W. *Liberating Reformed Theology: A South African Contribution to an Ecumenical Debate.* Grand Rapids: Eerdmans, 1991.

De Krey, Gary S. "Rethinking the Restoration: Dissenting Cases For Conscience, 1667-72" in *The Historical Journal* 38/1 (1995): 53-83.

Dempsey-Douglass, Jane. "Women and the Continental Reformation," in *Religion and Sexism: Images of Women in the Jewish and Christian Traditions.* Ed. Rosemary Radford Ruether. New York: Simon & Schuster, 1974.

Diehl, William E. *In Search of Faithfulness: Lessons from the Christian Community.* Philadelphia: Fortress Press, 1982.

Droge, A. J. "Call Stories," *The Anchor Bible Dictionary,* Volume 1. New York: Doubleday, 1992.

Edwards, Jonathan. *The Works:* 2 vols. Rev. Edward Hickman, with an essay by Henry Rogers, a memoir by Sereno E. Dwight. London: Ball, Arnold, and Co., 1840.

Ellul, Jacques. "Work and Calling," in *Katallagete* 4/2-3 (Fall-Winter 1972).

Emmet, Dorothee. *Function, Purpose, and Powers,* 2d ed. Fwd. Victor Turner. London: Macmillan 1972.

Forrester, W. R. *Christian Vocation: Studies in Faith and Work.* New York: Charles Scribner's Sons, 1953.

Friesen, Duane K. *Artists, Citizens, Philosphers Seeking the Peace of the City: An Anabaptist Theology of Culture.* Fwd. Glen Stassen. Scottdale, Penn.: Herald Press, 2000.

Gengenbach, Constance. "The Secularization of Vocation and the Worship of Work," *The Cresset* 51/2 (December, 1987): 5-13.

Gerrish, Brian A. *Grace and Gratitude: The Eucharistic Theology of John Calvin.* Minneapolis: Fortress Press, 1993.

Goodin, Robert E. *Protecting the Vulnerable: A Reanalysis of Our Social Responsibilities.* Chicago: University of Chicago Press, 1985.

Graham, Fred W. *The Constructive Revolutionary.* Atlanta: John Knox Press, 1971.

Guroian, Vigen. *Ethics after Christendom: Toward an Ecclesial Christian Ethic.* Grand Rapids: Eerdmans, 1994.

Gustafson, James M. *Can Ethics be Christian?* Chicago: University of Chicago Press, 1975.

———. *Ethics From a Theocentric Perspective,* 2 vols. Chicago: University of Chicago Press, 1981, 1984.

———. "Professions as 'Callings,'" *The Social Service Review* 56/4 (December 1982).

———. *Varieties of Moral Discourse: Prophetic, Narrative, Ethical, and Policy.* Grand Rapids: Calvin College, 1988.

Hardy, Lee. *The Fabric of This World: Inquiries into Calling, Career Choice, and the Design of Human Work.* Grand Rapids: Eerdmans, 1990.

Harrison, Beverly W. "Human Sexuality and Mutuality," in *Christian Feminism:*

Visions of a New Humanity. Ed. Judith L. Weidman. San Francisco: Harper & Row, 1984.

————. *Making the Connections: Essays in Feminist Social Ethics.* Ed. Carol S. Robb. Boston: Beacon Press, 1985.

Hart, Julian N. "Encounter and Inference in Our Awareness of God," in *The God Experience.* Ed. Joseph P. Whalen, S.J. New York: Newman Press, 1971.

Hauerwas, Stanley. *After Christendom: How The Church Is To Behave If Freedom, Justice and a Christian Nation Are Bad Ideas.* Nashville: Abingdon Press, 1991.

————, with James Foder. "Remaining in Babylon: Oliver O'Donovan's Defense of Christendom" in *Wilderness Wanderings: Probing Twentieth-Century Theology and Philosophy.* Boulder, Colo.: Westview Press, 1997, 199-224.

————. "Work as Co-Creation: A Critique of a Remarkably Bad Idea" in *Co-Creation and Capitalism: John Paul II's Laborem Exercens.* Ed. J. W. Houck and O. F. Williams. Lanham, Md.: University Press of America, 1983.

Heiges, Donald R. *The Christian Calling.* Philadelphia: Fortress Press, 1958.

Hewlett, Sylvia Ann. *When the Bough Breaks: The Cost of Neglecting Our Children.* New York: Basic Books, 1991.

Hilkert-Andolsen, Barbara. "Agape in Feminist Ethics" in *Journal of Religious Ethics* 9 (Spring 1981): 69-83.

Lindbeck, George. *The Nature of Doctrine.* Philadelphia: Westminster Press, 1984.

Luther, Martin. *Luther's Works: Vol 21: The Sermon on the Mount and the Magnificat.* Ed. J. Pelikan. St. Louis: Concordia Publishing House, 1956.

————. *Luther's Works:* Vol. 44: *The Christian in Society I.* Ed. J. Atkinson, gen. ed. H. T. Lehmann. Philadelphia: Fortress Press, 1966.

————. *Luther's Works:* Vol. 45: *The Christian in Society II.* Ed. W. I. Brandt and H. T. Lehmann. Philadelphia: Fortress Press, 1962.

————. *Luther's Works:* Vol. 46: *The Christian in Society III.* Ed. R. C. Schultz and H. T. Lehmann. Philadelphia: Fortress Press, 1967.

————. *Luther's Church Postil: Gospels: Advent, Christmas and Epiphany Sermons,* Vol. 1 in *The Precious and Sacred Writings of Martin Luther,* Vol. X. Ed. John Nicholas Lenker. Minneapolis: Lutherans in All Lands Co., 1905.

MacIntyre, Alasdair. *After Virtue: A Study in Moral Theory.* Notre Dame: University of Notre Dame Press, 1981.

Marshall, Paul. *A Kind of Life Imposed on Man: Vocation and Social Order from Tyndale to Locke.* Toronto: University of Toronto Press, 1996.

Meilaender, Gilbert. *Friendship.* Notre Dame: University of Notre Dame Press, 1981.

Merton, Thomas. *Contemplative Prayer.* Fwd. Douglas V. Steere. New York: Image Books, 1971.

Minear, Paul S. "Work and Vocation in Scripture," in *Work and Vocation: A Chris-*

tian Discussion. Ed. and intro. John O. Nelson. New York: Harper & Brothers Publishers, 1954.

Moltmann, Jürgen. *Theology of Hope: On the Ground and the Implications of a Christian Eschatology*. Trans. James W. Leitch. New York: Harper & Row, 1967.

Mount, Jr., Eric. *Professional Ethics in Context: Institutions, Images and Empathy*. Louisville: Westminster/John Knox Press, 1990.

Mouw, Richard J. *The God Who Commands: A Study in Divine Command Ethics*. Notre Dame: University of Notre Dame Press, 1990.

Neuer, Werner. *Man and Woman in Christian Perspective*. Trans. Gordon J. Wenham. London: Hodder & Stoughton, 1990.

Novak, David. *Covenantal Rights: A Study in Jewish Political Theory*. Princeton: Princeton University Press, 2000.

Oberman, Heiko A. *Luther: Man Between God and the Devil*. Trans. Eileen Walliser-Schwarzbart. New York: Image Books, 1992.

O'Connor, Elizabeth. *Call to Commitment: The Story of the Church of the Savior, Washington, D.C.* New York: Harper and Row, 1963.

O'Donovan, Oliver. *The Desire of Nations: Rediscovering the Roots of Political Theology*. Cambridge: Cambridge University Press, 1996.

Okin, Susan Moller. *Justice, Gender, and the Family*. New York: Basic Books, 1989.

Ottati, Douglas. "The Spirit of Reforming Protestantism," *The Christian Century,* Dec. 16, 1992.

―――. *Reforming Protestantism: Christian Commitment in Today's World*. Louisville: Westminster/John Knox, 1995.

Outka, Gene. *Agape: An Ethical Analysis*. New Haven and London: Yale University Press, 1972.

Ozment, Steven. *When Fathers Ruled: Family Life in Reformation Europe*. Cambridge: Harvard University Press, 1983.

Palmer, Parker J. *Let Your Life Speak: Listening for the Voice of Vocation*. San Francisco: Jossey Bass, Inc., 2000.

Paul II, John. *On the Hundredth Anniversary of Rerum Novarum (Centesimus Annus)*. Washington, D.C.: United States Catholic Conference, 1991.

Perkins, William. *The Works of William Perkins*. Ed. Ian Breward. Abingdon, Berks.: Courtneny Press, 1970.

Pieper, Joseph. *Leisure: The Basis of Culture*. Intro. T. S. Eliot. New York: Random House, 1963.

Placher, William C. "'You Were in Prison . . .'" *The Christian Century,* September 26–October 3, 2001.

Plantinga, Cornelius. "Fashions in Folly: Sin and Character in the 90s." January Series lecture, Calvin College, 1/15/93.

―――. *Not The Way It's Supposed to Be: A Breviary of Sin*. Grand Rapids: Eerdmans, 1995.

Pope, Stephen J. *The Evolution of Altruism and the Ordering of Love*. Washington, D.C.: Georgetown University Press, 1994.

————. "Proper and Improper Partiality and the Preferential Option for the Poor," *Theological Studies* 54/2 (June 1993): 242-71.

Post, Stephen G. *A Theory of Agape: On the Meaning of Christian Love*. Lewisburg, Pa.: Bucknell University Press, 1990.

Practicing our Faith: A Way of Life for a Searching People. Ed. Dorothy C. Bass. San Francisco: Jossey-Bass Publishers, 1997.

Ramsey, Paul. *Basic Christian Ethics*. Chicago: University of Chicago Press, 1978.

Rasmussen, Larry. *Earth Community, Earth Ethics*. Maryknoll, N.Y.: Orbis Books, 1996.

Ross, W. D. *The Right and the Good*. Oxford: Clarendon Press, 1930.

Ruether, R. R. *Sexism and God-Talk: Toward a Feminist Theology*. Boston: Beacon Press, 1983.

Rybczynski, Witold. *Waiting for the Weekend*. New York: Viking Press, 1991.

Saving-Goldstein, Valerie. "The Human Situation: A Feminine View" in *Womanspirit Rising: A Feminist Reader in Religion*. Ed. Carol Christ and Judith Plaskow. San Francisco: Harper & Row, 24-42.

Sayers, Dorothy L. "Why Work?" in *Creed or Chaos*. New York: Harcourt, Brace & Co., 1947.

Schuurman, Douglas J. *Creation, Eschaton, and Ethics: The Ethical Significance of the Creation-Eschaton Relation in the Thought of Emil Brunner and Jürgen Moltmann*. New York: Peter Lang Press, 1991.

————. "Creation, Eschaton, and Social Ethics: A Response to Volf," *Calvin Theological Journal* 30/1 (April 1995): 144-58.

————. "Humanity in Reformed and Feminist Perspectives: Collision or Correlation?" *Calvin Theological Journal* 27/1 (Spring 1992): 68-90.

Schweitzer, Albert. *Out of My Life and Thought: An Autobiography*. Trans. C. T. Campion, with postscript by Everett Skillings. New York: Henry Holt and Co., 1949.

Smedes, Lewis. *Sex for Christians*. Grand Rapids: Eerdmans, 1976.

Smit, D. J. "What Does *Status Confessionis* Mean?" in *A Moment of Truth: The Confession of the Dutch Reformed Mission Church*. Ed. G. D. Cloete and D. J. Smit. Grand Rapids: Eerdmans, 1984.

Soelle, Dorothee. *To Work and to Love: A Theology of Creation*. Philadelphia: Fortress Press, 1984.

Stackhouse, Max L. *Creeds, Society, and Human Rights: A Study in Three Cultures*. Grand Rapids: Eerdmans, 1984.

————. "The Vocation of Christian Ethics," *Princeton Seminary Bulletin* 16/3 (November 1995).

Tawney, R. H. *Religion and the Rise of Capitalism*. New York: Mentor Books, 1926.

Theological Dictionary of the New Testament, Vol. 3. Ed. G. Kittel, trans. and ed. G. W. Bromiley. Grand Rapids: Eerdmans, 1965.

Troeltsch, Ernst. *The Social Teaching of the Christian Churches,* 2 vols. Trans. O. Wyon, intro. H. Richard Niebuhr. New York: Harper Torchbooks, 1960.

Van Leeuwen, Mary Stewart, et al. *After Eden: Facing the Challenge of Gender Reconciliation.* Grand Rapids: Eerdmans, 1993.

Van Leeuwen, Mary Stewart. *Gender and Grace: Love, Work and Parenting in a Changing World.* Downers Grove, Ill.: InterVarsity Press, 1990.

Vest, Norvene. *Friend of the Soul: A Benedictine Spirituality of Work.* Cambridge: Cowley Publications, 1997.

Volf, Miroslav. *Work in the Spirit: Toward a Theology of Work.* New York: Oxford University Press, 1991.

———. "Eschaton, Creation, and Social Ethics," *Calvin Theological Journal* 30/1 (April 1995): 130-43.

Walzer, Michael. *The Revolution of the Saints: A Study in the Origins of Radical Politics.* Cambridge: Harvard University Press, 1965.

Weber, Max. *The Protestant Ethic and the Spirit of Capitalism.* Trans. Talcott Parsons, fwd. R. H. Tawney. New York: Charles Scribner's Sons, 1958.

Werpehowski, William. "'Agape' and Special Relations," in *The Love Commandments: Essays in Christian Ethics and Moral Philosophy.* Ed. Edmund N. Santurri and William Werpehowski. Washington, D.C.: Georgetown University Press, 1992.

Wingren, Gustaf. *Luther on Vocation.* Trans. C. C. Rasmussen. Philadelphia: Muhlenberg Press, 1957.

Wolterstorff, Nicholas. *Until Justice and Peace Embrace.* Grand Rapids: Eerdmans, 1983.

———. "More on Vocation," *The Reformed Journal* 29 (May 1979).

Wuthnow, Robert. *Christianity in the Twenty-first Century: Reflections on the Challenges Ahead.* New York: Oxford University Press, 1993.

———. *The Struggle for America's Soul: Evangelicals, Liberals, and Secularism.* Grand Rapids: Eerdmans, 1989.

Yoder, John H. *The Politics of Jesus.* Grand Rapids: Eerdmans, 1972.

———. *The Priestly Kingdom: Social Ethics as Gospel.* Notre Dame: University of Notre Dame Press, 1984.

———, et al. *What Would You Do? A Serious Answer to a Standard Question.* Scottdale, Penn.: Herald Press, 1983.

Index